Early Chinese Civilizations Series

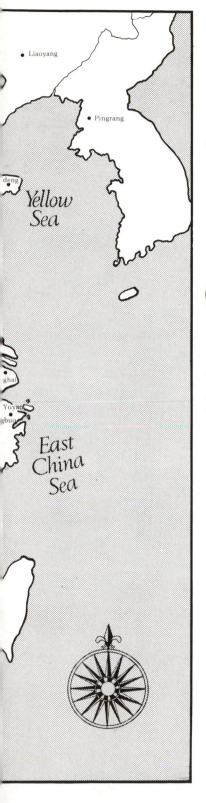

WANG ZHONGSHU

Han
Civilization

Translated by
K. C. Chang and Collaborators

NEW HAVEN AND LONDON
YALE UNIVERSITY PRESS

Published with assistance from the foundation established
in memory of Philip Hamilton McMillan of the Class of
1894, Yale College.

Set in Monophoto Apollo type by
Asco Trade Typesetting Ltd., Hong Kong.
Printed in the United States of America by
Vail-Ballou Press, Binghamton, N.Y.

Library of Congress Cataloging in Publication Data
Wang, Zhongshu, 1925–
    Han civilization.
    (Early Chinese civilizations series)
    "... a series of nine lectures on Han Dynasty
archaeology ... given in Chinese ..."—Foreword.
    Bibliography: p.
    Includes index.
    1. China—History—Han dynasty, 202 B.C. – 220 A.D.—
Addresses, essays, lectures. 2. China—Civilization—
221 B.C. – 960 A.D.—Addresses, essays, lectures.
3. China—Antiquities—Addresses, essays, lectures.
I. Chang, Kwang-chih. II. Title. III. Series.
DS748.W37   951'.01   81-11697
ISBN 0-300-02723-0   AACR2

10   9   8   7   6   5   4   3   2   1

Contents

v

Figures

Following page 91:

Following page 107:

Foreword

Of all the historical dynasties of imperial China, the Han is without question the most archaeologically dependent. On the one hand, because of the Han custom of richly furnishing the brick- and stone-constructed graves, archaeologists have been particularly amply rewarded with Han remains, including many written documents. On the other, because of Han's antiquity, its traditional literary documentation is glaringly incomplete. Therefore, a book on Han archaeology has long been awaited by not only Han scholars but also all students interested in Chinese history, art, and archaeology.

The present volume, in which Wang Zhongshu masterfully summarizes the important archaeological data pertaining to the Han civilization, is that long-awaited book. In it the latest data are carefully synthesized and presented by one of China's principal archaeologists of the Han civilization. Wang Zhongshu, research fellow and deputy director of the Institute of Archaeology, Chinese Academy of Social Sciences, has not only participated in many excavations at Han sites, he was the director of the excavations of the site of Changan in the 1950s and early 1960s.

In October 1979 Wang Zhongshu gave a series of nine lectures on Han dynasty archaeology at Harvard University. He came under the auspices of a senior lectureship program arranged between the Committee on Scholarly Communication with the People's Republic of China (Washington, D.C.) and the Chinese Scientific and Technological Association (Beijing). After speaking at Harvard, Wang delivered some of the same lectures at the University of Washington (Seattle) and the University of California (Berkeley) before returning to China. At Harvard, Wang's visit was sponsored by the American School of Prehistoric Research at the Peabody Museum of Archaeology and Ethnology, and his lectures were delivered at the departments of Anthropology, East Asian Languages and Civilization, and Fine Arts.

Soon after their arrival in Cambridge, Wang and his assistant, Xu Pingfang, who is a senior archaeologist best known for his work at Yuan Dadu, raised with me the possibility of publishing his lectures in this country. Having received the Chinese texts of his forthcoming lectures beforehand, I was familiar with their rich content and superb quality, and I reacted enthusiastically to the idea. Soon they decided to entrust me with the task that has resulted in the volume that appears before you.

The book could not have been prepared without two sources of generous support. The first is the National Endowment for the Humanities, which awarded me a grant to help prepare the manuscript for publication. I am grateful to the Endowment, which, of course, will not be held responsible for any of the views expressed herein.

The other source of support comes from my Harvard colleagues who served as interpreters during Wang's lectures, given in Chinese, and generously placed at my disposal the English translations of the various chapters they had prepared. They are Professor Ronald Egan of the Department of East Asian Languages and Civilization, who translated chapters 2 and 3; Dr. Loh Wai-fong, of the same department, chapters 5 and 6; Mr. Robert Mowry, of the Fogg Museum (now curator of the Asia House Gallery in New York), chapter 7; and Ms. Jenny So, of the Department of Fine Arts, chapter 4. (Chapters 1, 8, and 9 were translated by me.) Mr. Thatcher Deane of the University of Washington provided me with his own translation of chapter 6, a particularly difficult chapter to translate, and I frequently consulted it in preparing the final manuscript. I thank all of them for their excellent work and herein acknowledge their respective contributions. As editor, however, I alone am responsible for any errors of translation. Most of the illustrations in this volume appeared previously either in publications of the Chinese Academy of Social Sciences or in the journal *Wenwu*. In each case, the appearance is noted in the endnotes. The author and editor acknowledge their gratitude to the Academy and *Wenwu* for allowing them to be published here. The footnotes and the captions for illustrations were translated by me, and I prepared the appendix.

Figures 2, 28, 29, 30, 37, and 42, and the frontispiece have been redrawn by Mrs. Nancy Lambert Brown.

Harvard University   K. C. Chang
September 1, 1980

Han Civilization

1 Changan: The Capital City of Western Han

The ruins of Changan 长安, the capital city of Western Han 汉, are located about 10 km northwest of the present Xi'an 西安 city, Shaanxi Province, and 2 km south of the Weishui River. Seeing the remnants of its city walls (fig. 1) and the scattered tiles there, one can hardly imagine the magnificent scale and the prosperity of Changan in the past. The Qin capital city of Xianyang 咸阳 is north of the Weishui River. Probably the Han dynasty capital was built south of the river because the land here was more level and wider and because the south-of-the-river region had better access to the vast areas east of the Hangu 函谷 Gate.

The building of the city of Changan was accomplished in three stages during the Han dynasty. (1) Under Emperor Gao Zu 高祖, Changlegong 长乐宫 Palace was an expansion of the Xinglegong 兴乐宫, a Qin dynasty resort palace. In addition, Weiyanggong 未央宫 Palace was constructed to the west of Changlegong, and an armory was built between the two palaces. (2) Under Emperor Hui Di 惠帝, the city wall was constructed. The building of the wall probably began at the northwestern corner: the west wall was the first to be erected, next the south wall, then the east wall, and finally the north wall. (3) Under Emperor Wu Di 武帝, Mingguanggong 明光宫 Palace was built north of Changlegong; Guigong 桂宫 and Beigong 北宫 palaces were built north of Weiyanggong; and Jianzhang-gong 建章宫 Palace was constructed to the west, outside the city. In addition, Shanglinyuan 上林苑 Park was expanded and the artificial lake called Kunming-chi 昆明池 was opened. At that point, the capital city was basically complete.

CITY WALL

The plan of the city is basically square, with the city oriented according to the cardinal directions. However, the city wall was constructed after completion of

Editor's note: It might be useful to note here that in the Han system of measurement a *chi* 尺 is divided into 10 *cun* 寸, 6 *chi* make a *bu* 步, and 300 *bu* make a *li* 里. Most scholars agree that a Han *chi* is approximately 0.23 m.

the Changlegong and Weiyanggong palaces and adjusting its course to the locations of these two palaces caused the south wall to zigzag. The north wall also zigzagged, due to topography and the course of the river. The book *San fu huang tu* 三辅黄图 (*A Guide to the Three Military Districts of the Capital*) claims that the southern part of the city was shaped like the Southern Dipper and the northern part, like the Big Dipper. It appears that these so-called dipper shapes are a later speculation and were not represented in the original design. Neither Ban Gu 班固 nor Zhang Heng 张衡, in their famous poems about Changan, *Xi du fu* 西都赋 and *Xi jing fu* 西京赋, used the dipper analogy.

When archaeologists investigated the Changan ruins, they found that most of the wall was still exposed above ground. Many wall sections had collapsed, but underground the foundations still remained. According to the two surveys of 1957 and 1962, the east wall was 6,000 m long, the south wall 7,600 m, the west wall 4,900 m, and the north wall 7,200 m. The total length of the four walls was 25,700 m, which corresponds to a little over 62 *li* 里 according to the Han system of measurement. This basically conforms to the recorded 62 li in *Han jiu yi* 汉旧仪. The total area was about 36 square km (fig. 2).[1]

The city wall was built of rammed yellow earth. Its height was over 12 m, and the width at base was 12 to 16 m. The description of the wall's dimensions in *San fu huang tu* (3.5 zhang tall, 1.5 zhang wide at base, and 9 chi at top) is not accurate. Despite its construction of earth, without bricks or stones, the wall has proved to be unexpectedly strong (figs. 3, 4). According to the *Hanshu* 汉书 ("Hui Di ji" 惠帝纪), the wall was built by conscript labor provided by farmers who lived within a 600-li radius of Changan and by prisoners sent in by the feudal lords and princes. One wall section required a whole month of work by 145,000 or 146,000 laborers. The completion of all four city walls probably took five years. Outside the city wall was a moat, but 8 m wide and 3 m deep. The excavations in 1962 of the area outside the Zhangchengmen 章城门 Gate clarified the shape of the moat outside the city gate and also proved that wooden bridges were built over the moat (fig. 5).[2]

CITY GATES

There were twelve city gates, three to each wall. The gates along the east wall, from north to south, were known as Xuanpingment 宣平门, Qingmingmen 清明门, and Bachengmen 霸城门; the south wall gates, from east to west, were called Fuyangmen 覆盎门, Anmen 安门, and Xi'anmen 西安门; the west wall gates, from south to north, were the Zhangchengmen 章城门, the Zhichengmen 直城门, and the Yongmen 雍门; along the north wall, the gates, from west to east, were the Hengmen 横门, the Chuchengmen 厨城门 and the Luochengmen 洛城门. Of these, the Xuanpingmen, Bachengmen, Xi'anmen, and Zhichengmen were excavated in 1957.

The city gates followed strict designs. Each gate had three gateways, and each gateway was 6 m wide. The width of the gateway corresponded exacty to four times the width of a carriage (figs. 6, 7). This fact had been clearly stated in *San fu jue Lu* 三辅决录, *Xi jing fu* 西京赋, and the commentary on *Xi jing fu* 西京赋 by Xue Zong 薛综.[3] The distance between each two gateways was 4 m for Xuanping-men Gate and Zhichengmen Gate, but it was 14 m for Bachengmen Gate and Xi'anmen Gate. The greater the distance between gateways, the wider the whole city gate, of course, and the more majestic it looked. This greater distance in the latter case was possibly because Bachengmen Gate lay directly opposite the east entrance to Changlegong Palace and Xi'anmen Gate lay across the southern entrance to Weiyanggong.[4]

STREET GRID

The street system within Changan was made clear through surveys and excavations in 1961–62. No large avenues were built inside the four gates that were close to Changlegong and Weiyanggong (i.e., Bachengmen, Fuyangmen, Xi'anmen, and Zhangchengmen). All the other eight gates led into long avenues extending into the city. Therefore, although there were twelve city gates in Changan, the city had only eight major avenues within its walls, just as described in *Han jiu yi* and *San fu jiu shi* 三辅旧事. These avenues were straight, running north-south or east-west, forming many T-intersections and cross-sections. The longest was the Anmen Gate Avenue, 5,500 m long, followed by the Xuanpingmen Gate Avenue, 3,800 m long. The shortest was Luochengmen Gate Avenue, 850 m long. The length of each of the other avenues was about 3,000 m, and each had its own name. For example, Anmen Gate Avenue was probably called Zhangtai Jie 章台街; Zhichengmen Gate Avenue was probably Gao Jie 藁街; Qingmingmen Gate Avenue was probably Xiangshi Jie 香室街; and Hengmen Gate Avenue probably Huayang Jie 华阳街.[5]

Although their lengths varied, the eight avenues were of equal width; that is, about 45 m. Their width was obviously the result of uniform planning. It is noteworthy that each avenue was divided into three parallel lanes, which were separated by two drainage ditches, each about 90 cm wide and 45 cm deep. The ditches were semicircular in cross-section. The central lane was the widest, about 20 m, and the two on the outside were each about 12 m wide (fig. 8). According to textual records, the central lane was called "Chi dao" 驰道 and was meant exclusively for the emperor. Even imperial princes were not permitted to us it, let alone mere commoners and officials. These three-lane avenues are referred to in *Xi du fu* in th following line: "[It is] covered with wide avenues with three lanes." The layout of the avenues also explains why each gate had three gateways. The central one was for use of the emperor, and the two lateral gateways, for commoners' use.[6]

DRAINAGE

A drainage system is of obvious importance for a city surrounded by gigantic walls. At Changan water was drained mainly through large drainholes buried under the city gates. Finds from beneath the Zhichengmen and Xi'anmen gates indicate that the drainholes were 1.2 and 1.6 m wide, respectively, and 1.4 m deep, built with bricks and rocks, with the top part constructed of brick and forming an arc (fig. 9). Water that accumulated inside the city was carried away through the ditches alongside the avenues and then let out into the moat through the drainholes underneath the gates. *Hanshu* (the "Biography of Liu Qumao") describes a battle in which several tens of thousands were killed and blood flowed into the ditches. These must have been the ditches built alongside the roads. In addition, at some locations, when the wall was built, pottery waterpipes, pentagonal or round in cross-section, were buried under the foundation, to drain water away (fig. 10).[7]

PALACES, ARMORY, AND MARKET

Research was undertaken in the areas of the Changlegong and Weiyanggong palaces in 1961–62. Changlegong was located in the southeastern portion of Changan, surrounded itself by an enclosure. Changlegong and Weiyanggong were built before the city wall was constructed, and they themselves were enclosed by ramparts over 20 m wide at the base, for defense. Changlegong was an expansion of a resort palace of the Qin dynasty, not according to a separate plan, and therefore it was of irregular shape. From the foundation remains, it can be seen that the enclosure of Changlegong was in toto 10,000 m long, or over 20 li according to the Han system of measurement. The total area of Changlegong was about 6 square km, which is about one-sixth of the total area of the city.[8] According to historical texts, the Changlegong had four doors on four sides, the eastern and the western doors being the main ones. Outside the door on the east was a towering monument called *dong que* 东阙, and on the west, one called *xi que* 西阙. *Xi que* (West Que) was at the end of the Anmen Gate Avenue.

Located in the southwestern portion of Changan, the Weiyanggong was not quite in symmetry with the Changlegong to its east. Built entirely during the Han dynasty, it had a regular, square shape. The lengths of the encosures are: 2,150 m for both east wall and west wall, and 2,250 m for south and north walls, with a perimeter of 8,800 m (or 21 li according to the Han measurement system) and an area of 5 square km, about one-seventh the size of Changan. The walls are mostly gone, with only the foundations left, but a small section of the west wall 11 m high still stands. The famous *Qian Dian* 前殿, or Anterior Hall (the Audience Hall), is in fact located at the center of the Weiyanggong, its foundation still standing. Its length north-south is 350 m, its width east-west 200 m, and the highest northern end, located on a natural hill, is about 15 m above ground (fig. 11). The palace was indeed grandiose. No wonder Emperor Gao Zu accusingly questioned Xiao He 萧何, who built the palace: "All under heaven is chaotic, and battles are still raging on after several years, their results uncertain. Why are palaces constructed so much beyond their proper limits?" According to *San fu huang tu* the palace had doors on all four sides. The main ones were apparently the east and the north doors, according to *Hanshu* ("Gao Di ji" 高帝纪). Two gate towers (*que*) were built outside these two doors: the East Que and the North Que. When feudal lords came in for an audience, they would use the East Que, but the people would use the North Que for petitions. On the west and south sides, no gate towers were built outside the doors. Actually, the south and west walls of the Weiyanggong Palace were so close to the ramparts of Changan that in fact no room was left for *que* to be built.[9]

Hanshu ("Gao Di ji") says, "Xiao He build the Weiyanggong, erected the East Que, the North Que, the Anterior Hall, the Armory, and the Grand Storehouse." *San fu huang tu* places the Armory ("Wu ku" 武库) at the Weiyanggong, but according to *Shiji* 史记 ("Hulizi zhuan" 樗里子传) and other records, the Armory was in fact located between the Weiyanggong and the Changlegong. The *Zizhitongjian* 资治通鉴 commentary quoted *Yuanhe junxian zhi* 元和郡县志 as saying that the two palaces were one li apart. This information has proved through actual surveying at the site to be incorrect. The western wall of Changlegong and the eastern wall of Weiyanggong were separated by a distance of 950 m, which corresponds to over 2 li in the Han system. The Armory was located in this area.

Extensive excavations since 1975 have disclosed the areal scope, form, and structure of the Armory. Walls enclosed a rectangular area, 320 m on the east and west and 800 m on the north and south sides. A partition wall separates the Armory into two courtyards. The eastern courtyard had in it four houses and the western courtyard had three houses. Some of these houses provided shelters for the officials, but most served as warehouses for the storage of weapons (fig. 12). The largest of the warehouses was 230 m long, 46 m wide, and incorporated four storage areas, each about 1,500 square m in area (fig. 13). Within the storage area, weapons racks were densely arranged. The wooden racks have long been rotted, but their stone bases still remain, fully testfying to the description of such weapons racks in the *Xi jing fu* (fig. 14). According to the excavated remains, the Armory, like the other structures within Changan, was destroyed during the war at the end of the Wang Mang 王莽 period. Although most of the weapons that were stored here had been removed, a few remained, including iron armor, *ji*-halberds 戟, spears, swords, knives, and arrowheads as well as bronze arrowheads and *ge*-halberds 戈 (figs. 15–18).[10]

According to historical records, the Guigong was north of the Weiyanggong, and near the Jianzhanggong on the other side (to the west) of the city wall. Accordingly, its location should be north of Zhichengmen Gate Avenue, west of the Hengmen Gate Avenue, and south of the Yongmen Gate Avenue. Test diggings in 1962 in this area indeed disclose the enclosure of the Guigong, which was 1,800 m long on the east and west, 880 m long on the north and south, with a total perimeter of 5,300 m, or about thirteen li in the Han system. The plan of the palace was rectangular, and its area was 1.6 square km. As for Beigong and Mingguanggong, we are told by historical records that the former was north of the Weiyanggong and east of the Guigong and that the latter was north of the Changlegong, but these palaces have not yet been located on the ground. Finally, the Jianzhanggong outside the western ramparts was identified through test diggings in 1962, but only further excavations will disclose additional details.[11] North of the Jianzhanggong was Taiyechi, or Lake Taiye; its remains are vaguely recognizable. In 1973, a massive fish-shaped stone sculpture, almost five m long, was found to the north of the lake site (fig. 19), substantiating various records about stone fishes on the north shore of Lake Taiye at the time.[12]

According to historical records, there were nine markets within Changan, three of them "to the east of the avenue" and six "to the west." These were collectively referred to as Dong Shi 东市 (the Eastern Markets) and the Xi Shi 西市 (the Western Markets). Because the southern and the central portions of Changan were all palace areas, the nine markets could only be located in the northern part of the city area. According to *San fu jiu shi* the nine markets were located near the Tumen Gate 突门 (also called the Yongmen Gate) and on both sides of the Heng Bridge Avenue (also called the Hengmen Gate Avenue), and we can further narrow the location of the markets down to the northwestern portion of the city. On the surface in this area archaeologists have collected many pottery figurines and molds for coins, suggesting that this northwestern area had handicraft workshops, which may be regarded as a corroboration of the above judgment.[13] According to *Hanshu* ("Hui Di ji" 惠帝纪), "the Western Markets of Changan were built in the sixth year [or 189 B.C.]," suggesting that the location of the market was chosen even prior to the building of the city wall.

Zhouli kaogongji 周礼考工记 describes the ideal city plan of the Zhou dynasty as follows: "Its area is 9 li square; it has three gates on each side; within the city are nine longitudinal lines and nine latitudinal lines; the longitudinal avenues each are nine carriage tracks wide; the ancestral temple is located on the left and the earth altar on the right; the Audience Hall faces south; and the market is in the north." In actuality, practical considerations have to enter into the planning of a city; and, as the imperial capital, Changan was of a scope far greater than the prototype of the *Kaogongji*. But it is evident that Changan's planning does conform with the *Kaogongji* ideal. The enclosure was basically square; there were twelve gates, three to each side; each gate had three openings, which were measured according to carriage tracks; all avenues leading from the gates were each divided into three lanes; the principal palaces were located in the south; the markets were in the north. In short, the city of Changan built at the beginning of Western Han, like other early Western Han institutions, still retained the supposed Zhou tradition.

The palace probably occupied more than half the area of the southern and central parts of the city. A few mansions of the nobility were located near the North Que of the Weiyangong, referred to as the "Bei Que Jia Di" 北阙甲第. Otherwise, the ordinary people, including most officials, resided in the northern part of the city, especially in the northeastern part, the area near the Xuanpingmen Gate. Yu Xin's 庾信 *Ai Jiang Nan fu* 哀江南赋 has the following lines: "Perform rituals at the Changle, in the sight of the noble residences at Xuanping." These lines suggest that the Xuanpingmen Gate area was indeed a residential district. In the central and southern parts of the city, because of their extensive occupation by palaces, most of the gates were used exclusively for access to the palaces, and consequently the Hengmen Gate in the northwest and the Xuanpingmen Gate in the northeast were the gates that were used the most often. Hengmen Gate in fact controlled the communication in the northwestern direction. Not far outside the gate was the famous bridge Zhong Wei Qiao 中渭桥, also called Heng Qiao 横桥 or Hengmen Qiao 横门桥, which spanned the Weishui River, with Xianyang on the other bank of the river. Xuanpingmen Gate, on the other hand, controlled the communication in the southeastern direction. Coming out of this gateway, one traveled along the southern bank of the Weishui River to Hanguguan. Therefore, Xuanpingmen Gate (also known as Dongdumen 东都门 Gate or Dumen 都门 Gate) was the most important of the Changan gateways and the one most mentioned in *Hanshu* and *Hou Hanshu*.

HISTORY OF THE XUANPINGMEN GATE

Archaeological excavations have shown that many structures in Changgan—including Bachengmen Gate, Xi'anmen Gate, and Zhichengmen Gate—were destroyed during the warfare at the end of the Wang Mang period (fig. 20). The Xuanpingmen Gate suffered the same fate. The two walls of the gateways had been burned to a red color, and parts had collapsed. From the debris under the gateways were found coins of the Western Han dynasty and the Wang Mang period, especially the *huo bu* 货布 and the *huo quan* 货泉 of the latter period, which accurately date the burning of the gateway.[14] Evidence at Bachengmen Gate and Xi'anmen Gate shows that after they were destroyed the debris was never cleared away, indicating that these gateways were no longer in use during the Eastern Han, Wei, Jin, and the Six Dynasties periods (fig. 21). At a few other gates, such as the Zhichengmen, we find that one of the openings was cleared of debris for reuse on a reduced scale. On the other hand, although the Xuanpingmen Gate was destroyed at the same time, it was subsequently cleared of debris and repaired.

There have been at least two repairs of the Xuanpingmen Gate since the Eastern Han. The first took place during the early part of the Eastern Han, involving rebuilding of new walls of rammed earth at the northern and the southern openings (fig. 22). *Hou Hanshu* ("Du Du zhuan" 杜笃传) states that in the nineteenth year of Jian Wu 建武 (A.D. 43) the Dongduchengmen (the Eastern capital city gate) was repaired in Changan. This historical evidence not only confirms judgments formed in the course of archaeological excavations, it also precisely dates the repair. Thenceforth, the Xuanpingmen Gate continued to be used until the end of the Eastern Han. From the later years of the dynasty we have many records pertaining to this gate.[15] They indicate that the gate was still in use when Emperor Xian Di 献帝 was at Changan at the end of the dynasty and that it was complete with a gate tower. In the debris under the gateways we have found Eastern Han *wu shu* 五铢 coins and some small and poorly manufactured coins possibly of the Dong Zhuo 董卓 period.[16]

The second repair of the Xuanpingmen Gate consisted of the construction of new wall surfaces in the central and the southern openings, using fired and sun-dried bricks (fig. 23). Some of the bricks bear the inscription *Shi an* 石安 (figs. 24, 25). According to *Weishu* 魏书, ("Dixingzhi" 地形志), Shi an was the name of a prefecture under the Xian Yang Prefecture, established by Shi Le 石勒 of the Later Zhao 后赵. This evidence suggests that the new repair took place in the middle of the fourth century. Several texts mention that during the Later Zhao reign of Shi Hu 石虎, the city of Changan was rebuilt on a rather large scale, and the repair of Xuanpingmen Gate was probably part of the rebuilding.[17]

As shown from the excavated remains, no major rebuilding occurred after the Later Zhao, but throughout the Five Hu and Sixteen States period and the Northern Dynasties (fourth through sixth centuries), it continued to be used as a principal gateway. Its name however, had been changed to Qingmen 青门, as we see in the text *Han gong dian ming* 汉宫殿名. When Liu Yu 刘裕 of Eastern Jin was attacking Changan, Yao Hong 姚泓 of the late Qin had planned to come out of the Qingmen to surrender himself. During the Northern Zhou dynasty, the Qingmen was still an important gate; the *wu xing da bu* 五行大布 coins of the Northern Zhou have been found in later debris under the gateway. The gateway continued into the Sui; wheel tracks have been found under it, and *wu shu* coins of the Sui dynasty suggest that the gateway was in use then.[18] During the Tang dynasty, the three gateways were finally blocked forever.

In short, although Changan was badly damaged by war during the final years of the Wang Mang period, it continued to be an important city throughout the Eastern Han, Wei, Jin, Five Hu and Sixteen States, Western Wei, Northern Zhou, and early Sui dynasties, and many of these dynasties even used it as their capital. The Xuanpingmen Gate excavations have, thus, disclosed a cross-section of the whole history of Changan.

ROYAL PARKS

The Shanglinyuan royal parks were built by the Qin dynasty within its capital city in Xianyang, and they were abandoned at the beginning of the Han dynasty.

Emperor Wu Di incorporated the Shanglinyuan into the palace parks and expanded them. The vast area southeast to southwest of Changan, more than 200 li in perimeter, was roped in as a result. In the parks were placed birds and animals for the imperial hunt, and several dozen resort palaces were built. A great number of eaves tiles impressed with the name Shanglin 上林 are the most conspicuous remains of these palaces. In 1961, at Gaoyaocun 高窑村 in Sanqiaozhen 三桥镇 about 2 km southwest of Changan, an architectural site was found consisting of several house floors, the largest being about 340 m long by 65 m wide, probably the remains of an important palatial building within the Shanglinyuan parks.[19] A storage pit was discovered near the house floor, containing more than twenty bronze vessels such as basins, *ding*-tripods, *fang*-jars, and cooking pots. Inscriptions incised on the vessels (fig. 26) indicate that these were used within the Shanglinyuan parks; likely they were intentionally buried during the fighting at the end of the Wang Mang period.[20]

In the third year of Emperor Wu Di's reign period Yuan Shou 元狩 (120 B.C.), the artificial lake called Kunmingchi was excavated between the rivers Feng and Yu to the southwest of Changan, for the purpose of training a water-bound fighting force (in preparation for war with the state of Kunming) and to help alleviate the water shortage in the capital. After two thousand years the remains of the lake are still vaguely recognizable. The lake site now is a depression more than 10 square km in area. An elevated ground in the northern part appears to have been an island within the lake, possibly the site of the Yuzhang Hall 豫章馆 described in the *Xi jing fu*. In describing Kunming Lake, both *Xi du fu and Xi jing fu* refer to "the Niu Lang 牛郎 [or Cow Boy] on the left and the Zhi Nü 织女 [or Weaving Lady] on the right". A pair of sculptured stone human figures still stand today near Doumenzhen 斗门镇; their style is highly archaistic, apparently dating from Western Han period.[21] The stone sculpture on the eastern side of the lake is that of a male, presumably the Cow Boy (fig. 27, left), and the one on the western side that of a female, presumably the Weaving Lady (fig. 27, right), completely conforming with their descriptions in the two poems by Ban Gu and Zhang Heng.[22] The floors of many houses were brought to light around the ancient lake site, yielding a few stone foundations and a large number of tiles. These could be the remains that are described in ancient texts of the Xuanqugong 宣曲宫, Baiyanggong 白杨宫, and Xiliugong 细柳宫 palaces within the Shanglinyuan parks (fig. 28).[23]

RITUAL STRUCTURES

Emperor Wu Di paid great attention to Confucian rituals, and some of his Confucian officials had proposed to him that a new Ming Tang 明堂 (a ritual hall where the emperor pronounced the new year, officiated at festivities, performed rituals, and received the feudal lords) be built. However, it was not. (It should be

mentioned that there was a Ming Tang at that time, located on Tai Shan 泰山).
Under the reign of Emperor Cheng Di, officials suggested that a "Pi Yong" 辟雍
(a place where the emperor performed rituals and music and promulgated virtuous
principles) be built in the south of Changan, but again it was not done at that time.
At the end of Western Han, when Wang Mang became regent, he had Ming Tang,
Pi Yong, Ling Tai 灵台 (the spiritual terrace), and Tai Xue 太学 (the imperial
academy) built in Changan. After he enthroned himself, Wang Mang went even
further, building his Jiu Miao 九庙, or "Nine Temples." These "mysterious"
buildings, full of religious color, were designed in accordance with both traditional Confucian regulations and Taoist *yin yang* and *wu xing* (Five Elements)
阴阳五行 principles; they were of large scale and quite complex. The sites of these
buildings, which the archaeologists refer to as ritual structures, were first excavated in 1956, and since then more than ten such structures have come to light[24]
(fig. 29).

A ritual structure excavated in 1956, located south-southeast of the Anmen
Gate, consisted of a square building surrounded by a square composed of four
walls, each 235 m long. Through each of the four walls was a door. At each corner,
within the enclosure and close to the wall, were built elbow-shaped houses (fig.
30). At the center of the courtyard was a square hall (with side rooms on four sides)
built on a round platform 60 m across (fig. 31). Outside the courtyard was a large
circle 360 m long, formed by a ditch 2 m wide. In short, a peculiar architectural
plan characterized this building: a square was placed within a circle, and within
the square was another circle. These principles are consistent with the textual
characterizations of Ming Tang and Pi Yong, such as "circular above and square
below," or "circular outside and square inside." What is more, the records all
characterize the Pi Yong as a structure surrounded by water on all sides, and as
circular as a jade ring. It looks as if the excavated structure was indeed the Pi
Yong[25] (fig. 32).

All the other ritual structures are clustered in the area south-southwest of the
Anmen Gate. Their shapes are similar to the Pi Yong above, but they were not
surrounded by ditches, and their central halls were not built on round platforms.
Thus, they were probably neither the Ming Tang nor the Pi Yong. Artifactual
remains found here date from the Wang Mang period, and consequently most
archaeologists believe them to be the Nine Temples. It is noteworthy that the
eaves tiles used above the four doors of the temple were decorated with designs
representing the Four Deities: eaves tiles with Green Dragon designs, over the east
gate; White Tiger eaves tiles, over the west gate; Red Bird tiles, over the south gate;
and Black Turtle tiles, over the north gate. This usage is consistent with the
principle that "the Four Deities were in charge of the Four Directions"[26] (figs.
33–36). All of these ritual structures were destroyed at the end of the Wang Mang
period, too, and they were never rebuilt.

1. Remains of city wall of Changan of Han dynasty (southeastern corner)

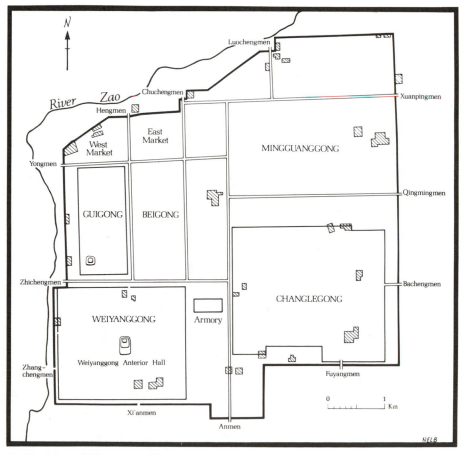

2. City plan of Changan of Han dynasty

3. Remains of city wall of Han Changan (stamped earth layers seen on collapsed section)

4. Han Changan city wall near Bachengmen Gate

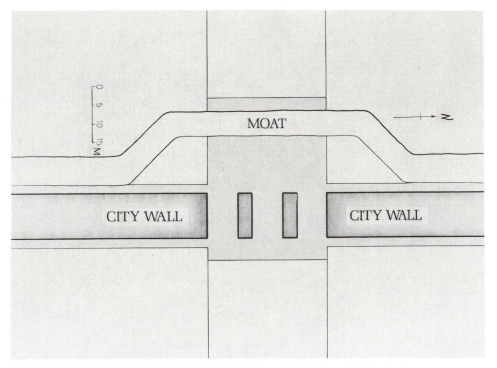

5. Plan of Han Changan's Zhangchengmen Gate and a section of moat outside the gate

6. Remains of Xuanpingmen Gate

7. The southern gateway and remains of carriage tracks at Bachengmen Gate

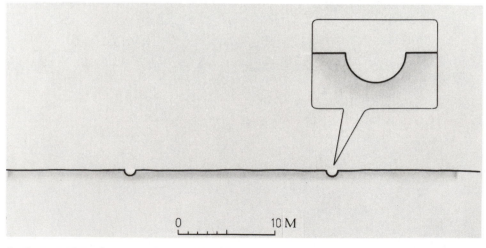

0 ⌊_ _ _ _ _⌋ 10 M

8. Cross section of street at Anmen Gate Avenue

9. Brick drainhole buried under Xi'anmen Gate

10. Ceramic water main pipes buried under city wall

11. Remains of the Anterior Hall of Weiyanggong Palace (aerial photo)

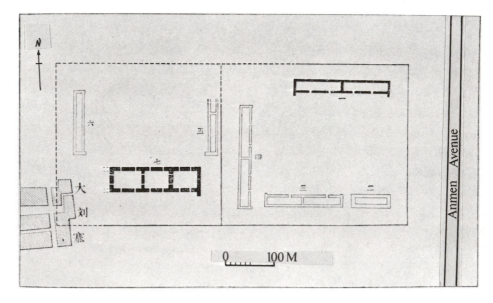

12. Plan of the Armory site

13. Remains of house number 7 of Armory

14. Remains of house number 1 of Armory and foundation stones of weapons rack

15. Iron armor plates unearthed at Armory

16. Iron ji-halberds unearthed at Armory

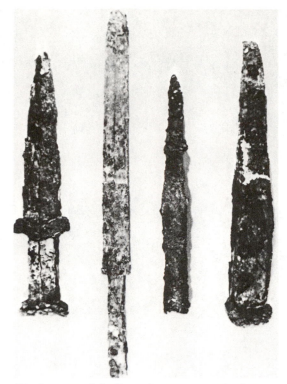

17. Iron sword, knife, and spears unearthed at Armory

18. Iron and bronze arrowheads unearthed at Armory

19. Fish-shaped stone sculpture found at site of Lake Taiye

20. Burned timber posts at the southern gateway of Bachengmen Gate

21. Ashes and other deposits at the southern gateway of Bachengmen Gate

22. Stamped earthen wall rebuilt during the Eastern Han period at the northern gateway of Xuanpingmen Gate. (The carriage tracks were left during the Sui dynasty.)

23. Brick wall built during the Sixteen States period at the central gateway of Xuanpingmen Gate

24. Brick (inscribed with "Cao Chu of Shi An") used for rebuilding during the Sixteen States period at Xuanpingmen Gate

25. Brick (inscribed with "Song Li of Shi An") used for rebuilding during the Sixteen States period at Xuanpingmen Gate

26. Inscriptions on bronze vessels in use at the Shanglinyuan royal park unearthed at Sanqiaozhen in Xi'an

27. Stone statues of the Cow Boy (left) and the Weaving Lady (right) at the site of Kunming Lake

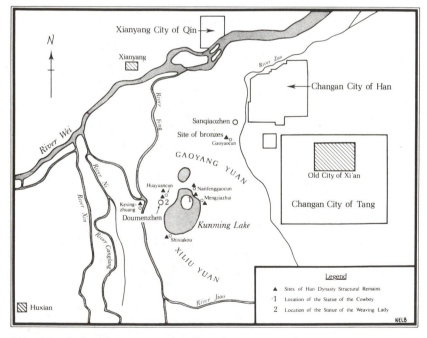

28. Map of Shanglinyuan royal park and Kunming Lake

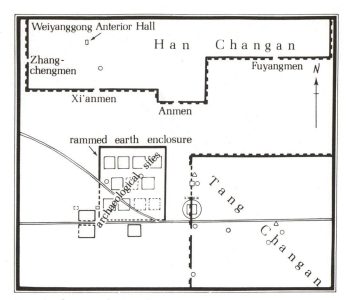

29. Distribution of sites of ritual structures in the southern
suburb of Han Changan

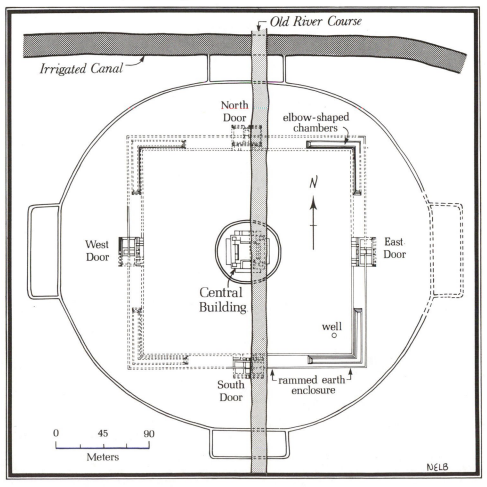

30. Plan of the site of Pi Yong

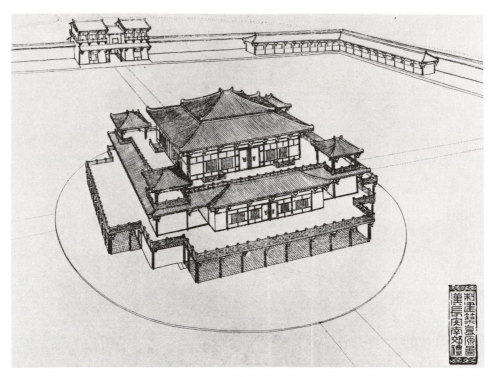

31. Reconstruction of the main central building of Pi Yong

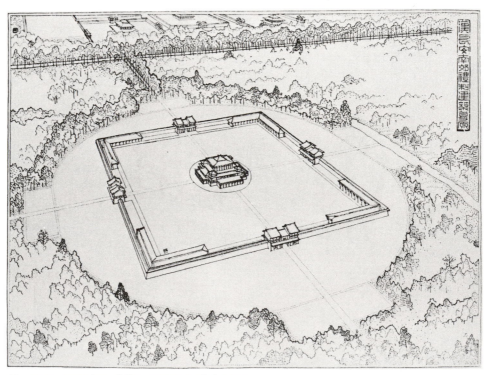

32. Reconstruction of the structure of Pi Yong

33. An eaves tile with a Green Dragon design
(unearthed at site of the ritual structures in the
southern suburb of Han Changan)

34. An eaves tile with a White Tiger design (unearthed
at same site as fig. 33)

35. An eaves tile with a Red Bird design (unearthed at same site as fig. 33)

36. An eaves tile with a Black Turtle design (unearthed at same site as fig. 33)

2 Luoyang: The Capital City of Eastern Han

The remains of the capital of the Eastern Han dynasty, Luoyang 洛阳, are situated approximately 15 km east of the present-day city of Luoyang in Henan. Since the site is bordered on the north by the Mangshan 邙山 Mountains and overlooks the Luo River to the south, it has protective natural barriers and is also at an important junction for transportation and communication (fig. 37). For these reasons, as early as the Western Zhou dynasty a major city, Chengzhou 成周, was constructed there. Chengzhou lasted through Eastern Zhou times. Subsequently, the Western Han city of Luoyang was built on the same site. In other words, the Eastern Han capital of Luoyang was located not only on the site of the Western Han Luoyang but also on that of the Zhou city of Chengzhou.

Architectural traces of Chengzhou are difficult to find now. However, a cluster of Zhou dynasty tombs, which were originally north of the Zhou city, still exists today. The famous Jincun 金村 tombs discovered in 1928 are part of this cluster.[1] From the location of these tombs we can speculate that the area within the boundaries of Chengzhou was much smaller than that of the Eastern Han Luoyang. The Zhou city was closer to the present course of the Luo River and farther removed from the Mangshan Mountains on the north. As for the location and boundaries of the Western Han Luoyang, we can estimate that they must have been roughly the same as those of the earlier Zhou dynasty city. Among the Western Han city's palaces, Nangong 南宫, or South Palace, was the most important. When Emperor Guang Wu 光武, the founder of the Eastern Han, decided to establish his capital at Luoyang in the first year of his reign period Jian Wu 建武 (A.D. 25), he first took up residence in South Palace. Then he embarked on a project to build a new city wall, expanding the boundaries of the old city and enclosing the site of the Zhou dynasty graveyard within the northern section of the new city. Remains that can still be seen today thus confirm the statement from *Diwang shiji* 帝王世纪 quoted in the commentary on the "Treatise on Commanderies and Kingdoms" in *Xu Hanshu* 续汉书 that in the northeastern part of Luoyang of Eastern Han there was a graveyard from the Yin (Shang) dynasty as well as the tomb of King Jing of the Zhou dynasty.

CITY WALL

Today, above ground we still find remains of the eastern, western, and northern walls of the Eastern Han city of Luoyang. When archaeologists went to inspect the site in 1962, there were still walls that stood over 7 m high (fig. 38). As for the southern wall of the city, it was destroyed by water long ago when the Luo River changed its course, so that today no traces of it remain. Fortunately remains of the Ming Tang and the Ling Tai, which were located in the southern suburb of Eastern Han Luoyang, can still be seen. According to *Han guanyi* 汉官仪 and *Luoyang ji* 洛阳记, the distance from these two structures to the southern city wall was approximately 2 or 3 li. Therefore, we can conclude that the southern wall was located in what is now the middle of the Luo River. As in Changan, the Western Han capital, in Luoyang the city wall was constructed out of rammed yellow earth and was extremely sturdy (fig. 39). The thickness of the wall at the base was determined by our test diggings to be about 14 m for the eastern wall, about 20 m for the western wall, and about 25 m for the northern wall—all different. The thickness of the western and northern walls may have been increased for defense purposes during the subsequent Wei and Jin dynasties. Measurements show that the remains of the eastern wall are 3,900 m long, those of the western wall 3,400 m long, and those of the northern wall 2,700 m long. Though the southern wall no longer exists, if we calculate the distance between the southern tips of the eastern and western walls we can determine that it must have been 2,460 m long.[2] Since the southern wall was in the middle of what is today the Luo River, we must add approximately 300 m to the length of both the eastern and western walls to determine their full length. Once we do this, then we can calculate that the total length of the four city walls of Eastern Han Luoyang must have been approximately 13,000 m, or about 30 Han dynasty li. *Diwang shiji*, as quoted by the commentary on the "Treatise on Commanderies and Kingdoms" in *Xu Hanshu*, says "From east to west the city is 6 li and 10 bu 步; from north to south it is 9 li and 100 bu." Also, *Jin Yuankang didao ji* 晋元康地道记 notes that "From north to south the city is 9 li and 70 bu, while from east to west it is 6 li and 10 bu." All these figures coincide with our own measurements. Although none of the existing walls is perfectly straight and both the eastern and northern walls have substantial sections that are curved, the basic shape of the city was rectangular (fig. 37). Since its length, measured north to south, was approximately 9 li and its width, measured east to west, was approximately 6 li, it was known as the "nine-six city." The layout of the Western Han capital of Changan was square, while the layout of the Eastern Han capital of Luoyang was rectangular; this was but one of many differences between the two capitals.

CITY GATES

According to *Luoyang ji* 洛阳记, *Luoyang qielan ji* 洛阳伽兰记, and other documentary sources, Luoyang of Eastern Han had twelve city gates. Although the number of gates was thus the same as in the Western Han capital of Changan, there was an important difference in their location: the Luoyang gates were not equally distributed along the four sides of the city. Instead, the eastern and western sides each had three gates, while there were four gates in the south and only two in the north. The three city gates on the east, from north to south, were Shangdongmen 上东门 Gate, Zhongdongmen 中东门 Gate, and Maomen 旄门 Gate. The three western gates, from south to north, were Guangyangmen 广阳门 Gate, Yongmen 雍门 Gate, and Shangximen 上西门 Gate. The two northern gates, from west to east, were Xiamen 夏门 Gate and Gumen 谷门 Gate. And the four southern gates, from east to west, were Kaiyangmen 开阳门 Gate, Pingchengmen 平城门 Gate, Xiaoyuanmen 小苑门 Gate, and Jinmen 津门 Gate. During the 1962 survey, clear traces were found of all eight gates on the east, west, and north.[3] Even though the four southern gates have been washed away by the Luo River so that no traces can be found, we can still determine their location from the four large avenues that run north to south through the city, which were found during the same survey. From the city plan, as determined by actual measurements, we can see that Shangdongmen Gate and Maomen Gate on the east were directly opposite Shangximen Gate and Guangyangmen Gate on the west. Moreover, Kaiyangmen Gate, Pingchengmen Gate, Xiaoyuanmen Gate, and Jinmen Gate were more or less equidistantly spaced. This arrangement shows a high degree of planning when the city was constructed. Since we have not done excavation, we are not certain about the precise shape and structure of the gates. But the Xiamen Gate at the western part of the northern wall is unusually well preserved. From what can be seen we can conclude that, just as in the case of the gates of Changan, this gate had three separate openings,[4] a fact corroborated by entries found in *Luoyang ji* and other historical records.

CITY STREETS

During our survey, traces of many streets were also found. Most of these streets date from the Northern Wei dynasty.[5] However, we can infer that the layout of streets in the Eastern Han capital was basically the same as that of the Northern Wei city. In other words, the streets of the Northern Wei city followed those of the Eastern Han capital, the only changes being those made to accommodate the relocation of certain palaces and city gates. Therefore, using the remains of the streets found during our survey as a basis, and taking into account what we know about the location of the city gates and the palaces in the Eastern Han city, we can derive the following description of the layout of streets and avenues in Eastern Han Luoyang.

There were five avenues that ran north to south. The first, which we could call Kaiyangmen Gate Avenue, ran north from Kaiyangmen Gate and was 2,800 m long. The second, which we could call Pingchengmen Gate Avenue, ran north from Pingchengmen Gate and stopped at the southern gate of South Palace, a

distance of 700 m. The third, which we could call Xiaoyuanmen Gate Avenue, ran
north from Xiaoyuanmen Gate and stopped at the southern gate of North Palace, a
distance of 2,000 m. The fourth, which we could call Jinmen Gate Avenue, ran
north from Jinmen Gate and was approximately 2,800 m long. The fifth, which we
could call Gumen Gate Avenue, ran south from Gumen Gate, turned eastward
when it met the northern wall of North Palace, then turned southward again,
covering 2,400 m. The street that ran south from Xiamen Gate stopped 100 m
inside the city wall where it met the northern wall of North Palace, hence we
cannot consider it an avenue. There were also five avenues that ran east to west.
The first one, which we could call Shangdongmen Gate Avenue, ran west from
Shangdongmen Gate and stopped at the eastern wall of North Palace, a distance of
600 m. The second, which we could call Zhongdongmen Gate Avenue, ran west
from Zhongdongmen Gate, passing between South Palace and North Palace,
covering approximately 2,200 m. The third, which we could call Shangximen Gate
Avenue, ran east from Shangximen Gate and stopped at the western wall of North
Palace, a distance of 500 m. The fourth, which we could call Yongmen Gate
Avenue, ran east from Yongmen gate and stopped at the Jinmen Gate Avenue, a
distance of about 500 m. The fifth, which we could call Maomen-Gate-to-
Guangyangmen-Gate Avenue, crossed the entire width of the city between those
two gates, a distance of 2,460 m. These various avenues formed a network of
crossroads and T-shaped intersections. If we count the number of avenue segments marked off by the intersections we come up with a total of twenty-four
segments. *Hanyi* 汉仪, as quoted by the commentary on the "Treatise on the
Bureaucracy" in *Xu Hanshu*, says that Luoyang had twenty-four "streets" (*jie* 街);
it is probably these avenue segments that the statement refers to. Except for some
of the smaller avenues that were 20 m wide, most of the avenues measured 40 m
across. Without excavations we cannot have a complete understanding of how
they were constructed. But according to *Luoyang ji* 洛阳记: "The large avenues
within the city and those running through the palace gates all have three lanes.
The middle lane is the imperial by-way and is bordered on either side by a mud
wall that stands over 4 chi high. Only the noblemen and high officials are allowed
to use this middle lane. Pedestrians must use the side lanes, the left-hand one for
entering and the right-hand one for exiting." This passage indicates that the
avenues of Luoyang, with their three parallel lanes, were just like those of the
Western Han capital of Changan.[6]

PALACES

Among the palaces of Luoyang, the most important were Nangong, or South
Palace, and Beigong 北宫, or North Palace. They already existed during the
Western Han dynasty, but then they were much smaller than during the Eastern
Han. Nevertheless, South Palace was already famous during the Western Han and

is often referred to in the historical records. The "Annals of Emperor Gao Zu" in *Shiji* says that in the fifth year of that emperor's reign (202 B.C.), "The emperor held a banquet in Luoyang's South Palace." Again, the biography of Wang Mang in *Hanshu* records that in A.D. 22, "The chancellor, Wang Xun 王寻, led more than ten thousand troops to camp at Luoyang; he occupied South Palace." We can thus deduce that from the beginning to the end of the Western Han dynasty South Palace was the major palace in Luoyang. In 1961, a bronze *zhong*-jar 锺 was found in the ruins of Western Han Changan with the words "South Palace *zhong*" inscribed on it.[7] It must have come from the South Palace of Luoyang of the Western Han[8] (fig. 40). In the first year of the reign period Jian Wu of the Eastern Han (A.D. 25), Emperor Guang Wu decided to establish his capital at Luoyang and took up residence in the Quefei 却非 Hall of South Palace. Quefei Hall must have been part of the legacy of the Western Han Luoyang. Subsequently, with continuous construction, South Palace grew steadily until A.D. 38, when its most important structure, the Anterior Hall, was completed.

Since there has not been thorough excavation, remains of South Palace have not yet been uncovered. But, as mentioned above, we already have some knowledge of the layout of Luoyang's gates and avenues. Based on this, we can make certain general statements about the location of South Palace and its boundaries. From a map based on our measurements, we can tell that in the southern section of Luoyang—that is, south of Zhongdongmen Gate Avenue, north of Maomen-Gate-to-Guangyangmen-Gate Avenue, west of Kaiyangmen Gate Avenue, and east of Xiaoyuanmen Gate Avenue—there was a large rectangular space, which was approximately 1,300 m north to south and 1,000 m east to west. This must have been the location of South Palace. According to the "Treatise on the Five Phases" in *Xu Hanshu*, Pingchengmen Gate was the city gate that faced directly south and also the one that provided access to South Palace. When the suburban sacrifices were held, the emperor's carriage came out from this gate; it was the most important of the city gates. During our test diggings, we found that Pingchengmen Gate Avenue led directly from the southern suburb into the city and continued on into the space we described above, which according to our estimate must have been the location of South Palace. The path of this avenue confirms the accuracy of our estimate.[9]

South Palace was the most important construction project undertaken by Emperor Guang Wu. Under the next emperor (Emperor Ming), North Palace was rebuilt; this rebuilding lasted from A.D. 60 to A.D. 65. Within North Palace, Deyang 德阳 Hall was the most important palace building. It held ten thousand people and stood atop a twenty-chi-high flight of steps, and the Zhuque Que 朱雀阙 in front of the hall was high into the clouds, allegedly visible 40 li away. During our survey, we could not definitely determine the boundaries of North Palace. But from the layout of the avenues, we could determine that North Palace must have been situated north of Zhongdongmen Gate Avenue, east of Jinmen Gate Avenue, and west of Gumen Gate Avenue. This last avenue, Gumen Gate, which ran south from that gate, turned eastward after a short distance; this bend must have been made in order to circumvent the northern wall of North Palace. If this is so, then we could conclude that the northern wall of North Palace was very close to the northern city wall. North Palace was probably even larger than South Palace, and its location was not only north but also slightly to the west. According to textual records, the distance between South Palace and North Palace was 7 li; this figure, however, could not be confirmed by our survey work. Possibly the correct figure was 1 li, which later became corrupted into 7 li. Between the two palaces there were covered passageways, built to provide security for the emperor as he moved back and forth.

In the Western Han capital of Changan, the two major palaces, Changlegong and Weiyanggong, were both located in the southern part of the city, side by side. In the Eastern Han capital of Luoyang, however, the two major palaces were located in the northern and the southern parts of the city, respectively, and had connecting passageways between them. This is another distinct difference in the design of the two Han capitals. Yet from another point of view, the capitals were similar in the respect that their palaces, wherever they were located, occupied over half the entire area of each city. In addition to South Palace and North Palace, Luoyang also had Yongangong 永安宫 Palace, situated northeast of North Palace, near Shangdongmen Gate. Furthermore, in the northwestern part of the capital there was Zhuolongyuan 濯龙园, an imperial park. Southeast of South Palace, near Maomen Gate and Kaiyangmen Gate, stood the ministries of the grand commandant (*taiwei* 太尉), the imperial secretary (*sikong* 司空), and the chancellor (*situ* 司徒). These were the highest administrative bodies of the empire. Northeast of North Palace, right next to the northeastern corner of the city wall, stood the Grand Storehouse (*tai cang* 太仓) and the Armory (*wu ku* 武库). The residential districts of the high officials and aristocrats, such as Buguang 步广 and Yonghe 永和 precincts, were mostly located near Shangdongmen Gate. The residence of Dong Zhuo, for example, was in Yonghe Precinct. As for the common people, they lived outside the city, just beyond the city gates.[10] The residential areas of the commoners were mostly outside the city wall immediately by the gates, similar to those of the Western Han Changan. As for industrial and commercial centers, there were three markets: Nanshi 南市 (South Market), Mashi 马市 (Horse Market), and Jinshi 金市 (Gold Market). South Market and Horse Market were both located outside the city, the former in the southern suburb and the latter in the eastern suburb. Gold Market was located inside the city, northeast of Yongmen Gate, southwest of North Palace and northwest of South Palace. Pan Yue 潘岳 (d. A.D. 300) says in his *Xianju fu* 闲居赋 that he faces the court and has the market at his back. This refers to the fact that Gold Market was located north of South Palace.

In A.D. 25, Emperor Guang Wu Di established his capital at Luoyang. One hundred sixty-five years later, in 190, the rebel Dong Zhuo forced Emperor Xian Di to flee from the city and seek refuge in Changan. We read that Dong Zhuo "burned the palaces, temples, and houses of Luoyang," and "the fire lasted more than three days, until the city of Luoyang was reduced to ruins." In this way, the prosperous Luoyang was totally destroyed. In 196, when Emperor Xian Di returned to Luoyang, we read "the palaces were completely burned, and the officials had to clear away brambles and seek shelter between tumbled walls." There was no building left in which Emperor Xian could reside; he had no choice but to bow to Cao Cao 曹操's wish and move his capital to Xuxian 许县.

LUOYANG IN WEI AND JIN DYNASTIES

Nevertheless, because of Luoyang's strategic location the capital was reestablished there during the succeeding Wei dynasty, ruled by the Cao clan. Emperor Wen of the Wei (Cao Pi 曹丕) rebuilt parts of North Palace. Then, in the year 235, under the direction of Emperor Ming (Cao Rui 曹睿), a major reconstruction was undertaken. Taiji 太极 Hall, Zhaoyang 昭阳 Hall, and other buildings were constructed on top of the old foundations of South Chongde Hall of the Eastern Han. At the same time, several parks, including Fanglinyuan 芳林园, were restored and expanded. Since the destruction at the end of the Eastern Han had been so severe, it was an enormous feat to rebuild the capital on top of the ruins. According to the biography of Gao Tanglong 高堂隆 in *Weizhi* 魏志: "There were tens of thousands involved in the labor. Everybody from ministers of state to students joined in the task. The emperor himself led the others, taking part in the digging." It is safe to assume that the size of Luoyang during the Wei dynasty did not exceed that of the Eastern Han Luoyang. The Western Jin dynasty, which followed the Wei, continued to construct new buildings, but did not make any major changes in the design of the city.

However, it should be mentioned that Emperor Wen (Cao Pi) of the Wei dynasty built Jinyongcheng 金镛城 Fortress at the northwestern corner of the city. (He was following the example of his father, Cao Cao, who had built three defense towers, Tongquetai 铜雀台, Bingjingtai 冰井台, and Jinhutai 金虎台, at the northwestern corner of his stronghold, Yecheng 邺城.) Jinyongcheng Fortress was built for military purposes. Its walls and ramparts were particularly strong. And because it stood against the Mangshan Mountains and was situated on high ground that commanded a view of all of Luoyang, it was of critical military importance. In the final years of the Western Jin dynasty, that is, during the rebellions of the Yong Jia 永嘉 period (307–13), this fortress was fought over intensely by those who were contending for control of Luoyang. At that time, it was known as the Luoyang Rampart. In the survey done in 1962, it was determined that Jinyongcheng Fortress measured 1,080 m from north to south and 250 m from east to west. The fortress consisted of three separate fortifications, whose walls were 13 m thick. The northern fortification and the middle one were outside the Luoyang city wall; the southern fortification was just inside it. These fortifications had connecting doors and ramps.[11] It is also noteworthy that along the walls of Jinyongcheng Fortress there were projecting bastions at intervals of 60 or 70 m. These bastions were about 15 m long and 8 m wide (fig. 41). Similar bastions were found on the northern and western city walls of Luoyang, where they were about 18 m long and 8 m wide, and they were constructed at about 120 m intervals. These bastions, like Jinyongcheng Fortress itself, were apparently constructed during the Wei or possibly the Western Jin dynasty.[12] No other examples of such bastions built on the outer edges of city walls have been found from any remains dating from the Han to the Sui-Tang period, except for those on the fortress walls built in border regions. Such bastions were used again in the Northern Song dynasty capital of Bianliang. In the Song dynasty, they were called "Horse Faces" and were used to supplement the city's defenses, ensuring that enemy forces who approached or scaled the city wall would be attacked from three sides. The appearance of these bastions on the city walls of Luoyang during the Wei and Jin dynasties is indicative of constant fighting during that period. They were an innovation made in response to special military needs.

During the year 311, the Xiongnu 匈奴 chieftain, Liu Cong 刘聪, led his army to invade Luoyang. In the intense battle that ensued, most of its palaces, temples, government offices, and houses were burned down. The Luoyang which had been slowly rebuilt over a seventy-year period during the Wei and Jin dynasties was again reduced to ashes.

LUOYANG IN NORTHERN WEI DYNASTY

One hundred eighty years later, in 493, the Northern Wei dynasty established its capital at Luoyang, the last dynasty to do so. Emperor Xiao Wen 孝文 of the Northern Wei decided to shift his capital from Pingcheng 平城 to Luoyang in that year. Subsequently, after many years of development and reconstruction, Luoyang not only became a prosperous city once again, but also was given a new layout that made it, as the Northern Wei capital, different in many respects from the Luoyang of earlier dynasties. Since the Northern Wei was the last dynasty to make Luoyang its capital and afterward the site was abandoned, the remains are quite well preserved. After our survey, we were able to make a relatively accurate and reliable plan of the city (fig. 42).

The most important change in the Northern Wei Luoyang was the abolition of the custom of having two palaces, the South and the North Palace, which had existed since the Eastern Han. Instead, a single, walled palace was built. This palace was in the northern part of the city, slightly off to the west, built on the foundation of the North Palace of Han and Wei dynasties. It had a neat rectangular plan, enclosed by four walls. The eastern and western walls each measured 1,400 m, and the northern and southern walls were 600 m. The palace occupied approximately one-tenth of the area of the entire city. Near the west end of the southern wall of the palace, the remains of an enormous gate have been found. This was the Chang-hemen 闾阖门 Gate, the main palace gate.[13]

The names of the twelve city gates of Eastern Han Luoyang were all changed by now, with the exception of Kaiyangmen Gate at the east end of the southern city wall. Actually, some of the gate names had already been changed during the Wei and Jin dynasties, some were not changed until the Northern Wei, while still others were changed twice. The former Shangdongmen Gate was now Jianchunmen 建春门 Gate, Zhongdongmen Gate was now Dongyangmen 东阳门 Gate, Maomen Gate was now Qingyangmen 青阳门 Gate, Pingchengmen Gate was now Pingchangmen 平昌门 Gate, Xiaoyuanmen Gate was now Xuanyangmen 宣阳门 Gate, Jinmen Gate was now Jinyangmen 津阳门 Gate, Guangyangmen Gate was now Ximingmen 西明门 Gate, Yongmen Gate was now Xiyangmen 西阳门 Gate, Shangximen Gate was now Changhemen 闾阖门 Gate, Xiamen Gate was now Daxiamen 大夏门 Gate, and Gumen Gate was now Guangmuomen 广莫门 Gate. All twelve gates were rebuilt, eleven of them on their former Han and Wei dynasty sites. But Xiyangmen Gate on the western wall was moved from the old site of Yongmen Gate 500 m to the north, so that it was now directly opposite Dongyangmen Gate on the eastern wall. Furthermore, when Emperor Xiao Wen first arrived at Luoyang, the palaces were not ready, and so he resided temporarily in Jinyongcheng Fortress. While there, he created a new city gate near the fortress at the north side of the west wall of the city. This new gate was called Chengmingmen 承明门 Gate (fig. 43); thus now Luoyang had thirteen city gates.[14]

Since the boundaries of the palaces and the location of some of the city gates had been changed, the streets within the city also underwent changes. For example, because South Palace had been totally demolished, it now became possible for an avenue to span the length of the entire city, north to south, from Guangmuomen Gate to Pingchangmen Gate. Since Yongmen Gate of the Eastern Han no longer existed, Yongmen Gate Avenue was probably also done away with. Due to the opening of Chengmingmen Gate, there was now a new avenue leading from that gate eastward into the city. It should be pointed out that now there was also an avenue that cut across the city in an east-west direction from Jianchunmen Gate to Changhemen Gate. This avenue cut across the walled palace, running through the palace's own east and west gates, dividing it in two halves, north and south. The southern half was used for palace audiences, while the northern half was the site of the imperial residence. More important, since the newly constructed Xiyangmen Gate was directly opposite Dongyangmen Gate, the Shangdongmen Gate Avenue of the Eastern Han was extended to cross the entire city. This was thus a second avenue that cut across the entire city, east to west. This avenue passed by the southern wall of the walled palace and formed a kind of interior boundary within the city. North were the imperial palaces and parks; south were the government offices, the temples, and the houses of the aristocrats. Last, we should note that since the walled palace was in the north of the city, slightly west

of center, and its southern gate, the Changhemen Palace Gate, directly faced
Xuanyangmen Gate on the southern city wall, the avenue that connected the two
gates, Tongtuo 铜驼 (Bronze Camel) Avenue, became a kind of major artery, just as
Pingchengmen Gate Avenue had been during the Eastern Han.[15] All the high
officials' offices, all the temples and ancestral halls, as well as the other important
buildings were arrayed along the two sides of Tongtuo Avenue [16] (figs. 44–46).
The famous Yongning 永宁 Temple was on the west side of the avenue, where
its remains are still preserved today and have recently undergone excavation[17]
(fig. 47). So it was that Xuanyangmen Gate became the most important city gate in
Northern Wei Luoyang, as Pingchengmen Gate had been during the Eastern Han.

As mentioned above, when the Northern Wei rebuilt the Eastern Han city of
Luoyang, it gave the city a new appearance and design. But this new Luoyang we
have been describing so far was actually only the inner city of Northern Wei
Luoyang. Far beyond the old city wall, another wall was erected, known as the
outer city wall, enclosing a much larger area. According to *Luoyang qielan ji*, the
outer city wall was 20 li long from east to west and 15 li long from north to south—
very long indeed. The city within was divided into 220 wards, each of which was
square and enclosed by walls. These ward walls were 300 bu on a side, about one li
by contemporary reckoning. The city had a very exact and neat layout. According
to the "Annals of Emperor Shi" in *Weishu*, the construction of this outer city
began in 501, during the reign of Emperor Xuan Wu 宣武, eight years after
Emperor Xiao Wen moved to Luoyang and made it the site of his new capital, and
the actual construction required tens of thousands of laborers. The wards outside
the inner city were occupied by the common people, who were kept under strict
control and regulation. The markets—that is, the centers of industry and
commerce—were also located in the outer city. The Dashi 大市 (Big Market) was
in the western part of the city, west of the inner city. The Xiaoshi 小市 (Small
Market) was east of the inner city. Sitongshi 四通市 (Four-Way Access Market)
was south of the inner city, just outside Xuanyangmen Gate. Jinshi (Gold Market),
which had been inside the Luoyang of the Han and Jin dynasties, was demolished
and a Buddhist temple was constructed on its former site. These changes thus
ended the Eastern Han tradition of having a market just north of the main palace,
which is evidenced by Pan Yue's observation that "I face the Court and have the
market at my back."[18] In summary, we can say that the structure and layout of
Northern Wei Luoyang, when compared to that of the two Han capitals, shows
epoch-making changes, and established a precedent later adopted for the Sui
capital of Daxing 大兴 and the two Tang capitals of Changan and Luoyang.

RITUAL STRUCTURES

According to the "Annals of Emperor Guang Wu" in *Hou Hanshu*, the Pi Yong
辟雍 (Hall of Learning), Ming Tang 明堂 (Ritual Hall), and Ling Tai 灵台 (Spirit

Terrace) were all built in A.D. 56. All documentary references indicate that the three structures were located just south of Eastern Han Luoyang, outside Kaiyangmen Gate and Pingchengmen Gate. This location has been confirmed by archaeological excavations.[19]

The Pi Yong was situated on the eastern side of the large road outside Kaiyangmen Gate. The remains show that the ground plan was square and that it was surrounded by a wall that was 179 m on each side. Within this large square enclosure there were four clusters of buildings evenly spaced apart. Each cluster consisted of three structures.[20] According to *Han guanyi*, the Pi Yong was surrounded on all sides by a moat, over which there were bridges. However, archaeological excavation has not yet turned up any remnants of such of a moat. During the Wei dynasty and the Western Jin dynasty, the Pi Yong was rebuilt, probably on the site of the Eastern Han Pi Yong. In 1930, a stele was discovered on the site commemorating three visits to the Pi Yong by Emperor Wu of the Jin dynasty (r. A.D. 265–89) (fig. 48), and in recent years the base of this stele has likewise been found. This discovery proves beyond a doubt that the ruins on this site are those of the Pi Yong of the Han and Wei dynasties.[21] During the Northern Wei dynasty, reconstruction of the Pi Yong was undertaken, but it was never completed.

The Ming Tang was located on the western side of the large road outside Kaiyangmen Gate, and was 150 m east of the Pi Yong. The remains show that the ground plan was square and that the building was surrounded on all sides by a wall which was 400 m on a side. Within this large square enclosure there was a round terrace, 62 m in diameter, that was the site of the main structure. Thus, the remains have some correspondence with the description in *Shuijing zhu* 水经注, which states that the design of the Ming Tang was circular at the top and square at the bottom.[22] During both the Western Jin and the Northern Wei dynasties, the Ming Tang was reconstructed on the same site.

The Ling Tai was on the western side of the large road outside Pingchengmen Gate, 80 m east of the Ming Tang. The remains indicate that the Ling Tai also had a square ground plan and a wall around it. The walls on the east and west sides were each 220 m long, while those on the north and south were 200 m long. Within this large square enclosure there was a high terrace that had a square ground plan. Its base was approximately 50 m on a side, and it was the site of the main structure (fig. 49). What remains today of this terrace stands 8 m high. The top has been destroyed. According to historical records, the terrace was flat and had no superstructure on top (fig. 50). Other buildings or structures flanked the terrace on all sides, mainly on two levels. The upper level was 1.86 m higher than the lower level and was approachable by ramps. The structures on the lower level in reality were verandas, whose banks or aprons were covered with oval river stones (fig. 51). The structures on the higher level on each side of the central terrace consisted of five rooms each. The floors of these rooms were lined with rectangular tiles and the walls were painted various colors. The eastern rooms were painted green, the western ones white, the southern ones red, and the northern ones black. Obviously, these colors were related to the Four Deities that the structures represented (i.e., the Green Dragon, the White Tiger, the Red Bird, and the Black Turtle). It is noteworthy that the five rooms on the western side had dark inner chambers that were sunk below the central terrace. In these dark inner chambers the floor was lined with square tiles (fig. 52). According to the "Treatise on Astronomy" in *Jinshu*, Zhang Pingzi 张平子 (Zhang Heng, A.D. 78–139) constructed a bronze armillary sphere in a sealed room; it is perhaps these chambers that the text refers to. During the Wei and the Western Jin dynasties, the Eastern Han Ling Tai continued to be used. But since it suffered severe damage during the fighting of the last years of the Western Jin, it was abandoned during the Northern Wei and a Buddhist pagoda was built on top of the terrace. The Buddhist images carved on bricks which were found during our excavation date from the Northern Wei.[23]

ACADEMIES

The Tai Xue (Imperial Academy) occupied a very large area. Because of the pilfering of stone classics from the Tai Xue site before Liberation, the remains have been severely damaged. But our reconnaissance and excavations showed that it consisted of two distinct sections. The first section was north of the Pi Yong. Its ground plan was rectangular, the eastern and western sides being approximately 200 m long, and the northern and southern sides 100 m long. In the past, fragments of stone classics were mostly dug up just north of this section. Hence, we can assume that this was the most important part of the Eastern Han Tai Xue. The second section was approximately 100 m northeast of the first section, and its remains are very well preserved. Its ground plan was also rectangular. The northern and southern sides were approximately 200 m long; the eastern and western sides 150 m long. It was surrounded by a wall.[24] The construction of the Tai Xue began in A.D. 29. Later, the Tai Xue was expanded several times and it did not reach its completed form until A.D. 32. At that time, the number of students enrolled in the Tai Xue occasionally exceeded 30,000. In 175, Emperor Ling had the Confucian classics cut on stone at the Tai Xue; hence, these works are referred to as the "Xi Ping 熹平 Stone Classics," taking their name from Emperor Ling's reign period (fig. 53). So many people were eager to look at and copy from the stone classics that more than a thousand carriages arrived at the Tai Xue every day, jamming the streets nearby. At the end of the Eastern Han, when Dong Zhuo burned the palaces and temples of Luoyang, the Tai Xue was also damaged. In 224, Emperor Wen of the Wei dynasty rebuilt the Tai Xue on its former site. Sometime between 240 and 249, another set of stone classics was cut in three calligraphic styles (fig. 54). At the beginning of the Western Jin dynasty, the Tai Xue was established in accordance with the Han and Wei precedents. In 276, the Guo Zi

Xue (National Academy) was established to exist side by side with the Tai Xue. Therefore, in his *Xianju fu*, Pan Yue says, "the two academies stand side by side, identical in appearance. The right-hand one is for the descendants of the imperial clan, and the left-hand one for talented common people." Moreover, according to *Shu zheng ji* 述征记, the Tai Xue stood 200 bu east of the Guo Zi Xue. Therefore, we can deduce that the Tai Xue of the Western Jin occupied the northeastern part of the grounds occupied by the Tai Xue during the Han and Wei dynasties. And the southwestern part of the Han and Wei Tai Xue was converted into Guo Zi Xue.

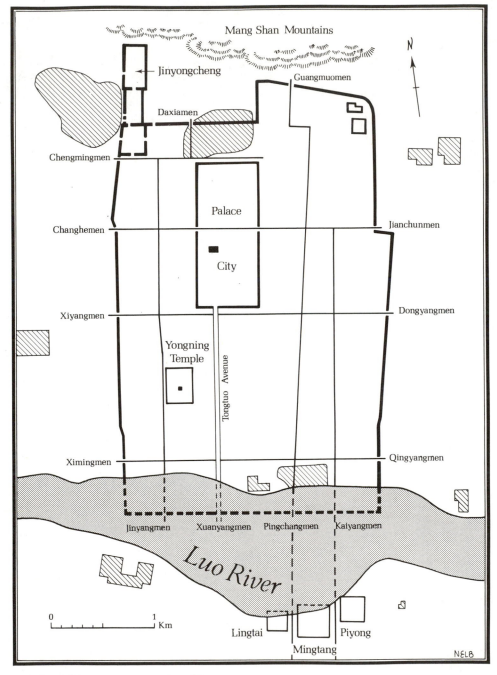

37. Plan of the Eastern Han city of Luoyang

38. Remains of a section of the northern wall of Eastern Han Luoyang

39. Stamped earth layers on a section of the eastern wall of Eastern Han Luoyang

40. "Nangong zhong," a zhong-vessel of the South Palace of Luoyang, unearthed at Sanqiaozhen, Xi'an

41. Western wall of the Jinyongcheng of Luoyang and a bastion (the so-called "Horse Face")

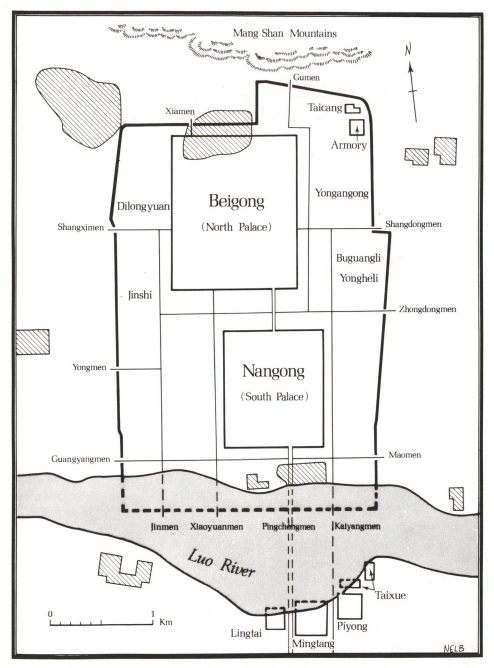

Mang Shan Mountains

Gumen

Taicang

Xiamen

Armory

Yongangong

Dilongyuan

Beigong

(North Palace)

Shangdongmen

Shangximen

Buguangli

Yongheli

Jinshi

Zhongdongmen

Yongmen

Nangong

(South Palace)

Guangyangmen

Maomen

Jinmen   Xiaoyuanmen   Pingchengmen   Kaiyangmen

Luo River

Taixue

0   1
|__|__|__|__|__|__|__| Km

Piyong

Lingtai

Mingtang

NELB

42. Plan of the city of Luoyang during the Northern Wei dynasty (the Jinyongcheng at the northwestern corner was first built during the Cao Wei period)

43. Remains of Chengmingmen Gate of Luoyang during the Northern Wei dynasty

44. Structural remains on the east side of Tongtuo Avenue in the Northern Wei city of Luoyang (possibly a portion of the Zongzheng administrative building or the royal ancestral temple)

45. Eaves tiles unearthed at the structural site on the east side of Tongtuo Avenue in Northern Wei Luoyang

46. Brick engraved with animal face unearthed at the structural site on the east side of Tongtuo Avenue in Northern Wei Luoyang

47. Remains of the base of a pagoda in Yongning Temple in Northern Wei Luoyang

皇帝三臨辟雍皇太子亦再蒞之盛德隆熙之頌

大晉龍興

48. Portion of the inscribed monument commemorating the three visits to Pi Yong by Emperor Wu Di of Jin

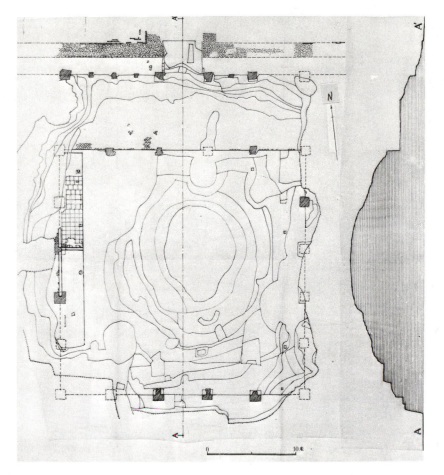

49. Plan and cross section of the site of Ling Tai of Eastern Han Luoyang

50. Main structure of Ling Tai in Eastern Han Luoyang

51. Remains of the stairs on the northern side of the main structure of Ling Tai and of the stone-covered banks of the verandas

52. Brick-paved floor of the "dark room" in the west of the main structure of Ling Tai in Eastern Han Luoyang

53. Fragment of the Stone Classics engraved during the
Xi Ping reign of Han

54. Fragment of the Stone Classics
engraved during the Zheng Shi reign of
Wei

3 Han Dynasty Agriculture

AGRICULTURAL PRODUCTS

We begin our discussion of Han dynasty agriculture by talking about the agricultural products of the period evidenced by archaeological finds.

Remains of agricultural products have been discovered in many tombs dating from the Western Han and the Eastern Han, including tombs found in Luoyang in Henan, Jiangling 江陵 and Guanghua 光化 in Hubei, Changsha 长沙 in Hunan, Xuzhou 徐州 and Haizhou 海州 in Jiangsu, Guixian 贵县 in Guangxi, and Guangzhou 广州 in Guangdong.[1] The tombs that contain the largest variety of agricultural products and the most well preserved products are the Mawangdui 马王堆 tombs in Changsha. Moreover, the pottery models of granaries found in the Shaogou 烧沟 tombs in Luoyang and the bamboo slips contained in the Mawangdui tomb have the names of various agricultural products written on them (fig. 55). To summarize, the most important food products of the Han dynasty were grains such as foxtail millet, rice, wheat, barley, panic millet, and beans. The rices included short-grain, long-grain, and glutinous rice. The beans included soybeans and red beans. In the Yellow River region of the North, the primary products were millet and wheat. A scene of a farmer tilling the soil with an ox-drawn plow found on a pictorial stone in the Mizhi district of Shaanxi has engraved on it a picture of full-grown foxtail millet, which must have been an important grain in that area[2] (fig. 56). We have also found remains of foxtail millet in the tombs in Luoyang, Jiangling, Guanghua, Changsha, Xuzhou, and Guangdong. These finds indicate that the cultivation of foxtail millet was very widespread. Wheat and barley were also cultivated in the Yangtze River region as well as in the Yellow River region. Remains of these were found in the Han Mawangdui tomb. Similarly, rice was cultivated in the Yellow River region (in addition to the South); a grain found in a Han Luoyang tomb has been identified as short-grain rice.[3] Furthermore, the word *shudao* 秫稻 written on the pottery found in that tomb must stand for glutinous rice.[4] In the Yangtze River region and other southern areas, rice was of course the most important grain. It has been determined that the rice found in the Han tomb excavated at Guangzhou was long-grain rice, whereas the rice found in the Mawangdui tomb in Changsha included all three varieties, short-grain, long-grain, and glutinous; references on the bamboo slips of the same tomb corroborate the physical remains.[5] In a

Fenghuangshan 凤凰山 tomb of Jiangling, we found four very well preserved sheaves of rice in a pottery granary. The ears measured 18.5 cm, and every ear had on the average fifty-one grains of rice. They have been identified as a kind of short-grain rice[6] (fig. 57). In addition, it has been reported that remains of sorghum have been unearthed from Han tombs in Luoyang and in Guangdong as well as from a Han village site at Sandaohao 三道壕 in Liaoyang,[7] but they have not been scientifically examined. Besides these grains, there were of course other agricultural food products, including Job's tears, taro, mallow, mustard green, sweet melon, bottle gourd, bamboo shoot, lotus root, and ginger (fig. 58). Among the fruits were the chestnut, Chinese jujube, pear, peach, plum, apricot, Chinese plum, and red bayberry. For weaving cloth, there was hemp, already quite common. In the Shaogou tombs in Henan, a pottery granary had the words "ten thousand piculs of hemp" written on it; and actual remains of hemp seeds have been found in the Han tombs at Changsha Mawangdui and at Luobowan 罗泊湾 in Guizhou.

AGRICULTURAL IMPLEMENTS

One of the distinguishing characteristics of Han agriculture was the widespread use of iron agricultural implements. They have been found throughout the nation; that is, not only the Central Plains area but also on the frontiers. Archaeological excavations have turned up a variety of types of iron agricultural implements, from such distant places as Inner Mongolia and Liaoning in the northeast to Yunnan and Guizhou in the southwest; from Guangdong and Fujian in the southeast to Gansu in the northwest.[8] The types of implements include the spade, shovel, pick, and plow, all used for tillage; the hoe, used for weeding; and the sickle, used for harvesting (figs. 59, 60). Furthermore, two- and three-toothed rakes, used for loosening the soil (fig. 61), have been found in Liaoyang 辽阳 in Liaoning, Mancheng 满城 and Baoding 保定 in Hebei, and Xuzhou in Jiangsu.[9]

The plowshares attached to Han plows were commonly made entirely of iron. They were a vast improvement over the wooden plowshares dating from the Warring States period, whose only iron part was the blade. The Han plowshares varied according to the soil type. Some were small and light, suitable for cultivated soil. Some were sharp and heavy, as would be needed to open uncultivated land. There was also a kind of giant plowshare, found in Sandaohao in Liaoyang, Liaoning, as well as in the village of Changcheng 长城 in Tengxian 滕县, Shandong, and the village of Gangtou 岗头 of Shijiazhuang 石家庄, Hebei. Their length and width exceed 40 cm.[10] The famous Han tomb at Mancheng also contained one of these giant plowshares[11] (fig. 62). Because it was so heavy an enormous amount of power must have been required to move it and it would not have been suitable for normal land conditions. Therefore, some people have speculated that these giant plowshares were used in irrigation projects, in other words, used to dig ditches. However, the "Treatise on Irrigation" in *Hanshu* says that the *cha* 锸 serves to produce "clouds," and that ditches serve to produce "rain." In Yan Shigu's commentary he states, "the *cha* is a spade, to open irrigation ditches"; thus the plow does not seem to have been an important implement in irrigation projects. In excavations in Pucheng 蒲城, Liquan 礼泉, Xi'an, and Longxian 陇县, all in modern Shaanxi, we have found evidence of a technique of using a plowshare crown—that is, of attaching a crown at the leading end of the plow-share to prevent damage to the plowshare itself[12] (fig. 63). Since this crown was narrow and fit only onto the blade part of the plowshare, it must have been relatively inexpensive to make and readily replaceable once worn down.

The use of the moldboard had already begun in the Han dynasty. Moldboards of Han dynasty date have been found in Anqiu 安丘 of Shandong, Zhongmou 中牟 and Hebi 鹤壁 of Henan, and in Changan, Liquan, Xi'an, Xianyang, and Longxian in Shaanxi.[13] Moldboards (*lipi* 犁镴, also called *lijing* 犁镜) were attached on top of the plowshare and used in combination with the plowshare to turn the soil (fig. 64). Among the moldboards found in Shaanxi Province were ones with only a single leaf, used to turn the earth on a single side, as well as ones with double leaves, forming a saddle shape, which were used to turn the soil on both sides. From this evidence we can see that the design of moldboards during that period had already reached a high degree of sophistication.[14]

In the Han dynasty, the use of oxen as draft animals was also widespread. The wooden model of ox and plow (fig. 65) dating from the last years of the Western Han, found in Mozuizi 磨咀子 in Wuwei 武威, Gansu; that depicted in the mural of the Wang Mang period found in the Shanxi village of Pinglu 平陆; that on the engraved stone (fig. 66) of the Eastern Han found at Shuanggou 双沟 in Suining 睢宁, Jiangsu; that on the engraved stone of the Eastern Han found at Hongdao-yuan 宏道院 in Tengxian, Shandong; that on the engraved stone of the Eastern Han found in Mizhi 米脂, Shaanxi; and that in the mural depicting soil tillage of the Eastern Han found in Holingor, Inner Mongolia—all these are valuable sources for the study of the use of oxen as draft animals.[15] In the pictures on the stamped bricks and in the murals, we usually see two oxen pulling a plow. The oxen bear a yoke that draws a plow with a long shaft, which a single farmer holds as he drives the oxen. This is the most common way oxen were used during the Han dynasty. The passage in *Hanshu's* "Treatise on Food and Money" which says, "in the use of the double harness plow, there are two oxen and three men," has been interpreted in several different ways. Yet the archaeological material now available to us leaves no doubt that the so-called "double harness plow" refers to a plow drawn by two oxen. At the end of the Eastern Han, and especially during the Wei and Jin dynasties, technology involving the use of oxen in plowing improved. In Gansu's Jiayuguan 嘉峪关 a mural has been found that shows a single ox pulling a plow.[16]

Another noteworthy matter is the use during the Han dynasty of the seed plow for seeding. In the Wang Mang period mural mentioned above, found in Pinglu,

Shanxi, in addition to the scenes of tillage there are also scenes showing the use of a seeder (fig. 67).[17] Since the mural has become faint the depictions are unclear. The seeder seems to have three legs, but the body is not clearly shown. There is, however, no question that the implement pictured is a seeder. The mural confirms references to such an implement found in entries about sowing in the "Treatise on Food and Money" in *Hanshu* and in Cui Shi 崔寔's *Zhenglun* 政论. Although this is our only archaeological evidence of the use of the seeder during the Han dynasty, there is a feeling among archaeologists that what had seemed to be a small version of an iron plowshare found in the Han sites at Sandaohao, Liaoyang, and in the town of Qinghe 清河, Beijing, and in Fuping 富平, Shaanxi, might actually have been the legs for seeders; if so, these implements could be called "seeder-shares" (fig. 68).[18] In contrast to plows drawn by two oxen, the seeder depicted in the Han mural is drawn by a single ox. Obviously, the power needed to draw a seeder was far less than that required to draw a plow. With a three-legged seeder three rows of seeds could be planted simultaneously. This method was of course much more efficient than sowing seeds by hand, and the results were also superior.

In the Wei and Jin period murals found in Jiayuguan, Gansu, there were also scenes of harrowing and leveling. Both the harrow and the leveler were drawn by oxen. The farmer stood on the implements as they moved, to increase the downward pressure (figs. 69, 70).[19] These murals supply us with our earliest pictorial information concerning the two implements. After the earth was tilled by a plow, the resultant lumps of earth had to be broken up by big harrows with teeth on them. After sowing, the seeds had to be covered; the leveler used in this stage of the process helped to make the soil even more fine while it also pressed and leveled the ground, protecting the soil against erosion. The use of the leveler was confined to the dry fields of the North. The harrow was used not only in the dry northern fields but also in the wet fields of the South. We find this fact attested by the pottery models of plowed and of harrowed fields in the Western Jin tombs excavated at Lianxian 连县, Guangdong.[20] In historical records, the use of harrows and levelers is first mentioned in *Qimin yaoshu* 齐民要术, a text dating from the Northern Wei of the sixth century; the implements are not referred to in Han or Jin writings. But since archaeological evidence shows that their use was already extensive during the Wei and Jin (they have been found even on the distant frontiers) it does not seem impossible that they were first used as early as the Eastern Han.

IRRIGATION

The widespread use of iron implements also permitted developments in irrigation. Large-scale irrigation projects were sponsored and managed by the government. One early example is the Zhengguo 郑国 Canal built during the Qin dynasty in the Guanzhong 关中 area. During the Western Han this canal was renovated and maintained, and a branch canal, the Bai 白 Canal, was added to it. In 1973, archaeologists found remains of the Zhengguo Canal and the Bai Canal in Jingyangxian 泾阳县, Shaanxi. At the head of the Bai Canal, they discovered a "well canal" section, over 300 m long. The well canal was a new development in canal technology during the Han (fig. 71).[21] The Dujiang 都江 Weir built during the Qin dynasty in Guanxian 灌县 of modern Sichuan was also renovated and maintained during the Han. In 1974, a stone statue of Li Bing 李冰, the official in charge of local irrigation in 168 B.C., was found at the bottom of the Dujiang Weir. The statue stands almost 3 m high. It was placed in the middle of the water not only to commemorate Li Bing's deeds but also to serve as a gauge of the water level (fig. 72).[22]

The use of a crossbar and ropes to pull water out of river or well to irrigate farming fields was a common practice during the Han, and it is depicted in engraved stones in tombs.[23] Use of wells for irrigation was extensive in the Yellow River valley and other northern areas. Pottery models showing wells have been found in many places, and in some of them it is clear that the wells were for irrigation. For example, a pottery well excavated from a Han tomb at Luoyang has a well frame complete with winches; two buckets were used alternatively to draw water. Alongside the well there is a long water trough. This model seems to indicate that after water was drawn from the well it flowed through the trough into canals to irrigate the fields (fig. 73). In the Yangtze River valley and other parts of southern China, in addition to the extensive use of river water, artificial ponds with embankments were also built to hold water for irrigating rice fields. In the tombs of the Han and the Wei and Jin periods located at Shaanxi's Hanzhong 汉中, and Sichuan's Chengdu 成都 and Pengshan 彭山, Yunnan's Chenggong 呈贡,[24] and Guangdong's Lianxian, we have found pottery models of ponds with embankments which are connected to rice paddies. Such ponds were artificial reservoirs, which were equipped with sluice-gates in order to regulate the amount of water needed to irrigate the nearby fields (figs. 74, 75). The Shao Embankment built in Lujiangjun 庐江郡 (modern Lujiang, Anhui) in the early years of the Western Han was renovated during the Eastern Han. It was a large-scale irrigation project. The Anfeng 安丰 Pond in Shouxian 寿县, Anhui, is the old site of this Shao Embankment. In 1959, archaeologists also found a weir on that location dating from the Eastern Han. Iron implements used in the construction of the weir were found nearby; among them was an iron hammer incised with the words *Dushuiguan* 都水官 ("Water Conservancy Official"), indicating that the irrigation project was carried out under government supervision.[25]

HARVESTING AND FOOD PROCESSING

To harvest grains, iron sickles were widely used. A pictorial brick of the Eastern Han period excavated from Yangzishan 扬子山 of Chengdu, Sichuan, depicts a rice-harvesting scene. The picture shows very clearly how rice was harvested.[26] First the ears were cut off, then a long-handled, hooked scythe was used to cut the straw (fig. 76).

After grains were harvested, threshing and winnowing had to be done; these are also featured on certain pictorial bricks and murals. It is noteworthy that in the Han tombs in Luoyang and Jiyuan 济源 of Henan we have also found pottery models of winnowing machines (figs. 77, 78).[27] Generally speaking, millet and wheat were planted in the North, and the threshing process was necessary to separate out the chaff; whereas in the South, where rice was cultivated, the winnowing machine was needed to separate out the husks. However, from the Han tombs excavated at Luoyang and Jiyuan, we see that some winnowing machines were also used in the northern Central Plains area.

To process grains, a *jiandui* 践碓 (treadle-operated tilt hammer) was commonly used. It was a simple machine operated by foot whose purpose was to pound grain. Pictures of this machine appear on pictorial stones and bricks as well as in pottery models found in many places (figs. 79, 80). From historical records we know that during the Wei and Jin dynasties there was also widespread use of water-powered tilt hammers. Mills, consisting of two rotating stone slabs, were also common during the Han. Actual mills as well as pottery models of them have been discovered at many Han archaeological sites and tombs (fig. 81). The earliest stone mill was found in a Han tomb in Mancheng. Underneath the mill there was a large bronze bowl, used to catch the flour ground out by the mill (fig. 82).[28] A pottery model of a similar mill has been found in a Han tomb in Yinqueshan 银雀山 in Linyi 临沂, Shandong, which is even older than the actual mill found in Mancheng and probably predates the reign of Emperor Wu of the Han (Han Wu Di).[29] The widespread use and manufacture of such large, rotary stone mills must have been closely tied to the development of iron implements. In the pottery models found in various Eastern Han tombs, we often see the treadle-operated tilt hammer and the mill placed together in a single room to facilitate grain processing.

DOMESTICATION OF ANIMALS AND SILKWORMS

During the Han dynasty, there were also many other, supplementary kinds of food production. The most common was raising domestic fowl and animals. From archaeological evidence we know that the types of domestic fowl that were kept included chickens, ducks, and geese; among domestic animals there were horses, cows, sheep, pigs, and dogs. In pottery models found in Han tombs, pigpens are often connected to the privies, the arrangement indicating that pig excrement was used to fertilize the fields (fig. 83). In addition to these domestic animals, camels were also domesticated in the North to help in transportation. The archaeological evidence for the camel includes, in addition to the camel-shaped handles of some seals, a funerary statue of a man riding a camel, found in 1969 in Dingxian 定县, Hebei, in the tomb of Prince Mu 穆 of Zhongshan (Liu Chang 刘畅), who lived at the end of the Eastern Han, and also images of camels on Eastern Han pictorial bricks found in 1978 in Xinduxian 新都县 of Sichuan Province.[30] At that time hunting also served to supplement agriculture. Wild rabbit and sika deer were among the foods found in the Mawangdui Han tomb of Changsha; the fowls found there included turtledove, wild goose, owl, bamboo partridge, magpie, ringed pheasant, and crane.[31] Hunting scenes have been found on pictorial stones and bricks recovered from many sites, and a pictorial brick from Yangzishan in Chengdu, Sichuan, shows hunting of birds; this is the kind of material that throws much light on contemporary practices.[32] In addition to the fish and other water animals caught from rivers and lakes, fish and turtles were also obtained from artificial ponds. This practice is evidenced by pottery models of ponds found in Hanzhong 汉中, Shaanxi.[33] Archaeological evidence has also been found of the consumption of various kinds of aquatic plants such as lotus root and water chestnut (fig. 84).

The cultivation of mulberries and silkworms was also an important supplementary industry in agricultural villages. As early as the Warring States period two kinds of mulberry trees are found depicted on bronze vessels. The taller kind we could call "mulberry trees," and the shorter kind we could call "mulberry bushes" (figs. 85, 86). The latter were not only easier to pick but also juicier and more tender, hence more suitable for feeding the silkworm. These two different types of mulberries have also been found on pictorial stones and bricks of the Han period. According to the section on methods for improving the mulberry in *Fan Sheng zhi shu* 氾胜之书, mulberry bushes were artificially developed.[34] During the Han dynasty, the cultivation of mulberries and silkworms spread from the Yellow River region to the frontiers. Needless to say, there was abundant production of silk in the area of modern Sichuan. According to the "Treatise on Geography" in *Hanshu*, the region of modern Guangxi and Guangdong also had a silk industry as early as the Western Han. From the biography of Wei Sa 卫飒 in *Hou Hanshu*, we can see that there was mulberry and silkworm cultivation in the Guiyang 桂阳 Prefecture of modern Hunan in the early part of the Eastern Han. The mural in the Holingor Han tomb shows that toward the end of the Eastern Han at the latest Dingxiang 定襄 Prefecture (in the north of modern Shanxi, transferred there from Inner Mongolia) also had mulberry cultivation.[35]

POPULATION AND ECONOMY

Tomb number 10 excavated in 1973 at Fenghuangshan in Jiangling, Hubei, was occupied by a certain Zhang Yan 张偃, who was buried in A.D. 153. He was a landowner and a local official in his hometown of Jianglingxian. His duty was to collect government taxes from the farmers. His tomb contained many bamboo and

wooden slips which were the official records of the local government adminis-
tration. Among them was a group of bamboo slips called "Granary Records of
Zheng 郑 Village," which were local government receipts for grain seeds loaned to
twenty-five families of farmers of Zheng village. These receipts record the amount
of farmed land and the population of Zheng village (fig. 87).[36] According to these
records, the twenty-five families of Zheng village consisted of 105 persons; sixty-
nine of them were capable of agricultural labor. The village had a total of 617 *mou*
亩 of land. Thus, there was on the average 24.6 mou per family, or less than 6 mou
per person (with each mou equivalent to 456 square m).[37] From these figures we
can see that even in the first part of the Western Han period, the average
independent farmer was quite limited in the amount of land he farmed. The
"Zhushuxun" 主术训 chapter of *Huainanzi* 淮南子 says that for middle-quality
fields, the grain produced in a year did not exceed four *dan* 石 (piculs) per mou.
According to the biography of Zhong Changtong 仲长统 in *Hou Hanshu*: "The
harvest from the highest quality fields is about three *hu* 斛 per mou [a hu being
equivalent to a dan picul]." We can determine, therefore, that the average
farmland during the Han dynasty produced three to four piculs per mou.
Therefore, 6 mou of land (the average per person) could only produce about 20
piculs (each picul being equivalent to approximately 20 liters). If we estimate that
a person's daily food requirement is about 5 sheng 升 (or roughly one liter), then
the annual requirement should be 18 piculs. We can thus see that the harvest
realized from a whole year of the farmer's hard labor left him with little surplus in
addition to what was needed to fill his stomach. According to the receipts, there
was a certain farmer named Ye whose family consisted of eight people, and yet he
only had 15 mou of land. This averages out to less than 2 mou per person, which
would have made living conditions harsh indeed.

Furthermore, the farmers were responsible for taxes and corvée labor.
According to the records found in tomb number 10 at Fenghuangshan, these taxes
and corvée labor requirements were quite heavy. Under such circumstances, some
farmers were forced into bankruptcy. Then, the big landowners would take
advantage of the opportunity to buy up the farmland of the bankrupt farmers. In
order to live, the bankrupt farmers had to become tenant farmers or hired laborers
of the landowners; some even had to sell themselves as slaves. In time, these
conditions became more and more severe. Because of this process of land aggrandizement, we read that toward the end of the Western Han, "the wealthy families
owned huge numbers of formerly independent farms." Therefore, there is the
emergence at this time of many privately owned manors.

In the Eastern Han, due to the lenient policies of the Court, the land aggrandizement problem became more severe and the influence of the powerful landowners
increased; manors became both more numerous and larger. Agricultural production on the manors was carried out by the landowners' slaves and others who were
personally dependent upon them; that is, the so-called bond-servants. The salient
point about the economy of the manors was diversification. Agriculture was still

primary, but it was supplemented by related activities and various crafts. The manors became self-sufficient. And one step beyond self-sufficiency was the land-owners' involvement in commercial enterprises, that is, the marketing of a portion of their manors' products.

As mentioned several times before, a tomb in Holingor, Inner Mongolia, was excavated in 1972, the occupant of which had risen to the post of colonel of the Wuhuan 乌丸 army. He was an important official and landowner. Many murals were found in this tomb, among which, on the south wall of the posterior room, was one that depicts in a lively and concrete fashion the activities of the tomb occupant's manor (fig. 88).[38] In the center of the mural are the manor's houses. Far in the northeast corner there is a large field. Farmers hold plows and drive oxen, tilling the land. Closer to the dwellings there are vegetable gardens where two farmers are working intently with hoes. Walls surround the vegetable garden to prevent the fowl and other animals from straying in. Near the dwellings there are stables and pens for oxen and sheep. The presence of young as well as full-grown animals gives evidence of continuous breeding. Outside the pens, there are scattered groups of chickens and pigs. Nearby the dwellings there is a mulberry grove where four women appear, holding ropes, hooks, and nets, picking mul-berry leaves. Close by, there are bamboo baskets and screens used in silkworm cultivation. On the far west side, there are three pools in which bundles of hemp are placed. Workers stand beside the pools, netting the hemp. Nearby, there is also a structure to house vehicles. In addition to this mural on the south wall, murals in the front room of the tomb likewise depict piles of harvested foods, ox-carts used in transporting the food, grain bins for storing the food, and people in the process of hulling the grain with tilt hammers. On the mural found in the middle room, brewing is also shown. This indicates that not not only was food processed on the manor, wine and vinegar were also made there. There are also several murals in the front room depicting the pasturing of horses, cattle, and sheep. These show that aside from agriculture the manors engaged in animal husbandry. This tomb is located in the northern grasslands, where animal husbandry must have been especially widespread (figs. 89, 90).[39]

It is noteworthy that in the center of the mural on the south wall in the rear room of the Han tomb at Holingor there is a watchtower situated beside the dwellings. Similarly, in the upper corner of the mural that depicts sheepherding in the front room there is a walled fort. At the rear of the fort is a tall watchtower at a corner (fig. 91). Hence we can see that the manor's buildings included those used for military or defensive purposes. The farmers who worked on the estate were not only the wards of the powerful landlord, they were also members of his private militia. Many of the historical records corroborate this fact, indicating that especially in the last years of the Eastern Han the men who were attached to powerful landlords had military as well as agricultural duties. From a late Eastern Han tomb at Tianhuishan 天迴山 in Chengdu, Sichuan, archaeologists found clay figures of farmers and soliders; they not only are wearing the same kind of clothes, the farmers are also shown wearing large battle knifes. This evidence further corroborates the military roles of the farmers at that time (fig. 92).[40]

At the end of the Eastern Han when Cao Cao seized control of the government he curbed the power of the landlords, prohibited land aggrandizement, and established the *tuntian* 屯田 ("agriculture colony") system. There were two kinds of *tuntian*, the commoners' and the soldiers'. In the first, common farmers who did not have their own land or oxen were recruited to farm government land under the direction of various agriculture officials. Fifty to sixty percent of their harvest had to be turned over to the government. In the second kind of *tuntian*, soldiers were organized to engage in agricultural production and the harvest was used by the military. In the tomb mentioned above dating from the Wei and Jin period found in the Jiayuguan district of Gansu, there are two extremely precious wall murals depicting a military *tuntian* colony.[41] The first mural shows the military camp. In the middle there is a large tent occupied by a military official, which has guards stationed outside. The guard on the right holds a banner and seems to be the runner. On the right of the tent there are six serrated banners implanted in the ground in two rows. They evidently mark the entrance to the headquarters tent. On the remaining three sides many smaller tents are arrayed in rows. In front of each tent *ji*-halberds and shields stand in the ground (fig. 93). The second mural depicts the cultivation of land by the military. In the center a military officer gallops about on horseback; on each side there is a platoon of foot soldiers marching with *ji*-halberds and shields. Beside each platoon there are two men driving oxen and tilling the land. One of them wears a hat and looks like a member of the Han race. The other, with untied hair, wears the clothes of one of the minority ethnic groups (fig. 94). These two murals, viewed together, provide us with a realistic picture of the military cultivation of land west of the Yellow River during the Wei and Jin dynasties. During the Wei dynasty, military cultivation of land was also widely practiced in the Central Plains area. However, we have not yet uncovered archaeological evidence of it.

55. Names of agricultural products inscribed on pottery granaries unearthed from Han tombs in Luoyang

56. Ox-drawn plow and millet plants on a pictorial stone unearthed in Mizhi, Shaanxi

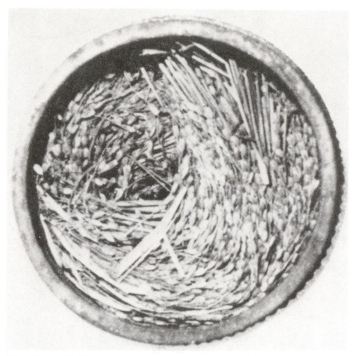

57. Rice ears from a pottery granary unearthed from a Han tomb at Fenghuangshan, Jiangling

58. Remains of Job's tears from a pottery jar unearthed from a Han tomb in Luoyang

59. Iron spade with wooden handle unearthed from the Han tomb at Mawangdui in Changsha

60. Stone human figure holding a spade, unearthed in Pixian, Sichuan

61. Iron rake with two teeth, unearthed from the Han tomb in Mancheng

62. Large iron plowshare unearthed from the Han tomb in Mancheng

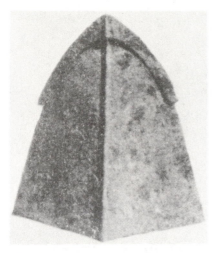

63. Iron plowshare and its crown, unearthed in Longxian in Shaanxi

64. Iron plowshare and moldboard unearthed in Changanxian, Shaanxi

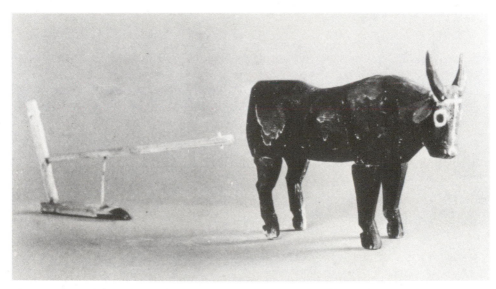

65. Wooden models of oxen and plow unearthed from the Western Han tomb at Mozuizi, in Wuwei, Gansu

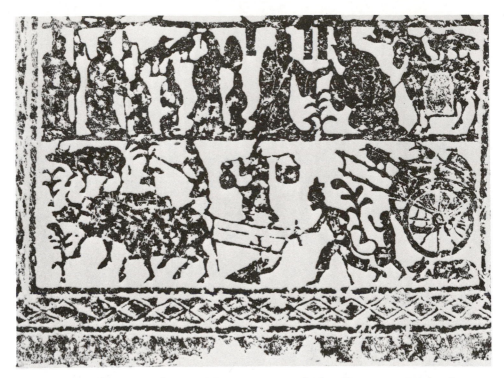

66. Plowing with oxen in the pictorial stone art unearthed at Shuanggou, Suiningxian, Jiangsu

67. Use of a seeder depicted in the wall painting of a Han tomb at Zaoyuancun in Pinglu, Shanxi

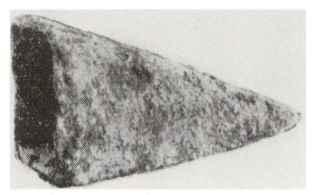

68. Iron blade of seeder unearthed in Fuping, Shaanxi

69. A harrowing scene depicted (in the lower part) on a pictorial brick in a Wei-Jin period tomb at Jiayuguan in Gansu

70. A soil-leveling scene depicted on a pictorial brick in a Wei-Jin period tomb at Jiayuguan in Gansu

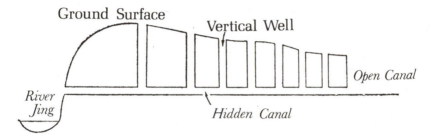

71. Well canal at the head of the Baiqu Canal in Jingyangxian, Shaanxi

72. Stone statue of Li Bing and its inscription, unearthed at the Dujiangyan in Guanxian, Sichuan

73. Pottery models of a well and water trough unearthed from a Han tomb in Luoyang

74. Pottery model of a pond unearthed from a Han tomb in Hanzhongxian, Shaanxi

75. Pottery model of a pond unearthed from a Han tomb in Chengdu, Sichuan

76. Fishing, hunting, and harvesting depicted in a pictorial brick
unearthed from a Han tomb at Yangzishan in Chengdu, Sichuan

77. Pottery models of winnowing machine and treadle-operated tilt hammer unearthed from Han tomb in Luoyang

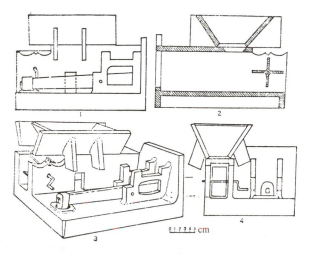

78. Reconstructive drawing of fig. 77

79. Treadle-operated tilt hammer as depicted in pictorial brick unearthed from Han tomb in Pengxian, Sichuan

80. Pottery model of treadle-operated tilt hammer unearthed from Han tomb in Shanxian, Henan

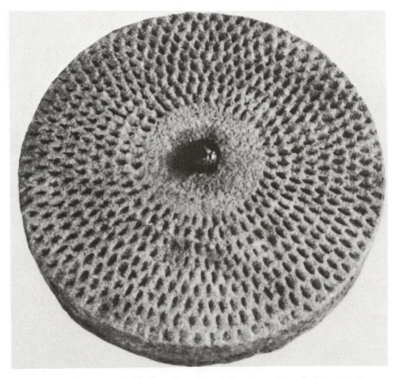

81. Stone quern unearthed at the site of the Han city of Changan in Xi'an

82. Stone quern and bronze receptacle unearthed from Han tomb in Mancheng

83. Pottery model of pigsty and privy, unearthed from a Han tomb in Luoyang

84. Taro harvesting depicted on pictorial brick unearthed in Pengxian, Sichuan

85. Picking tree mulberry leaves depicted on pictorial stone at the Wu Liang Family Shrine in Jiaxiang, Shandong

86. Picking bush mulberry leaves depicted on pictorial brick unearthed in Chengdu, Sichuan

87. "Grain records of Zheng Village"—inscribed bamboo slips (partial) unearthed from tomb number 10 at Fenghuangshan in Jiangling

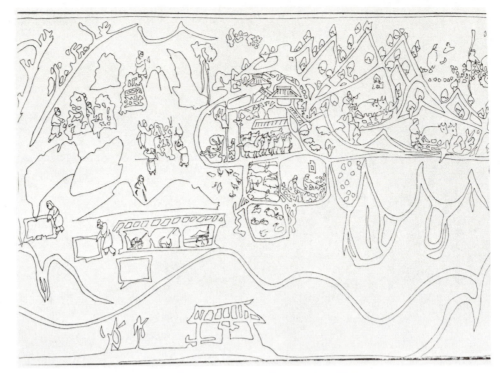

88. A manor depicted in a wall painting in the Han tomb at Holingor in Inner Mongolia (copy)

89. Grazing horses depicted in wall painting in the Han tomb at Holingor in Inner Mongolia

90. Grazing cattle depicted in wall painting in the Han
tomb at Holingor in Inner Mongolia

91. Fortress and watchtower depicted in wall painting in the Han
tomb at Holingor in Inner Mongolia

92. Clay figurine of farmer holding spade and wearing large knife, unearthed from a Han tomb at Tianhuishan in Chengdu, Sichuan

93. A military barracks in a wall painting in a Wei-Jin period tomb at Jiayuguan, Gansu

94. A soldiers' farm in a wall painting in a Wei-Jin period tomb at Jiyuguan,
Gansu

4 Lacquerware

LACQUERWARE BEFORE THE HAN DYNASTY

Archaeology tells us that lacquered wares existed in China probably as early as the Neolithic period. In 1978, many wooden objects were found at the site of Hemudu 河姆渡, Yuyaoxian 余姚县, Zhejiang Province. One of the wooden bowls is covered both inside and out with a bright red pigment that appears to be a lacquerlike substance.[1] The Hemudu site has been dated by radiocarbon to about 7,000 B.P. If the pigment on the bowl proves to be lacquer, then it will be the earliest known lacquered vessel in China.

By the Shang 商 period, the decoration on lacquered vessels was already quite accomplished. Many fragments of lacquered vessels, which included types like basins and boxes, were found in 1978 at a middle Shang site at Taixicun 台西村, in Gaocheng 藁城, Hebei Province. The designs were in black against a red background, and included *taotie*, leaf, thunder-cloud, and dragon motifs, all closely comparable to bronze motifs. Some fragments were even decorated with turquoise inlays or gold sheets. Fragments of lacquered vessels have also been frequently found at Yinxu 殷墟 at Xiaotun 小屯 in Anyang 安阳, Henan, the site of the late Shang dynasty capital, but they are so poorly preserved that neither the vessel shape nor the decoration can be distinguished clearly.[2]

It is, in any event, certain that the production of lacquer wares was quite advanced in the Shang period. As a result of the far-ranging influence of Shang civilization, lacquered vessels were also found in distant regions. For example, a burial belonging to the Lower Xiajiadian 夏家店 culture excavated in 1977 at Dadianzi 大甸子, Aohan 敖汉 Banner, in Liaoning Province, yielded two well preserved red lacquered vessels, somewhat like the Shang bronze *gu* 觚 in shape.[3] Radiocarbon dates place the site at Dadianzi at about 3,500 B.P. These two *gu*-shaped lacquered vessels may be regarded as the earliest well preserved examples of lacquered vessels.

Lacquer vessels are also known from excavated sites of the Western Zhou period. For example, they have been found in the early Western Zhou tombs at Pangjiagou 庞家沟, at Luoyang, Henan, excavated in 1964, and at the late Western Zhou to early Eastern Zhou burials of the Guo 虢 state at Shangcunling 上村岭 in western Henan, excavated in 1956. The vessels from both sites are decorated with inlaid shell discs. The early Western Zhou burials excavated in

1953 at Puducun 普渡村, Changan, in Shaanxi Province, also contained lacquered fragments with what appears to be shell disc inlays.[4]

Rapid and astounding advances in the development of the lacquer industry were made only with the beginning of the Warring States period. Large numbers of well-preserved lacquered vessels were found before Liberation in sites in Changsha, Hunan, and in Luoyang, Henan; and, after Liberation, in Changsha, Jiangling, and in Sui Xian 随县, Hubei, in Xinyang 信阳, Henan, and in Chengdu, Sichuan.[5] In addition to lacquered vessels, these finds included various types of lacquered home furnishings and grave goods, musical instruments, and weapon accessories, indicating that lacquered items were widely used for various aspects of social life. Considering only lacquered vessels, for example, most early Warring States vessels have wood cores, which tend to make them heavy and bulky. From the mid–Warring States period on, vessel cores made with thin wooden sheets or fabric begin to appear. By the late Warring States period, inlaid bronze dics (gold or silver gilded) were added to thin-cored lacquered vessels, making them sturdier as well as more elaborate and beautiful. The painted designs on these are also very rich and elegant. In short, Warring States lacquerware had reached very high standards in every respect. Han period lacquerware represents a further development from the foundations laid in the Warring States period.

HAN LACQUER WARES

Han lacquerware has been discovered at many localities; only the most notable finds will be mentioned here. Finds before Liberation include the large numbers of well-preserved vessels from Pyongyang in Korea and Noin Ula in Mongolia.[6] Many of these are dated by inscription and are extremely valuable for research. Since Liberation, lacquer vessels in various states of preservation have come from Han burial sites in Luoyang in Henan; Wendeng 文登 in Shandong; Yancheng 盐城 and Lianyungang 连云港 in Jiangsu; Ningbo 宁波 in Zhejiang; Changsha in Hunan; Guangzhou in Guangdong; Qingzhen 清镇 in Guizhou; and Wuwei 武威 in Gansu.[7] The lacquer vessels from Qingzhen and Wuwei also carry detailed inscriptions with dates like those from Pyongyang. In the past ten years or so, finds of Han lacquerwork have been virtually innumerable: at Hepu 合浦 and Guixian 贵县 in Guangxi, Haizhou 海州 in Jiangsu Province, Linyi 临沂 in Shandong, Mancheng in Hebei, and Fuyang 阜阳 in Anhui, to name only a few.[8] Particularly notable are the rich finds from the Han tombs at Mawangdui; in Changsha, Fenghuangshan in Jiangling; and at Dafentou 大坟头 in Yunmeng, which yielded large numbers and varieties of lacquered vessels in pristine condition, all of which are valuable new material for the study of Han lacquerware[9] (figs. 95–98).

The core materials used in Han lacquerware are mainly wood and fabric (fig. 99); bomboo cores were also used, but only rarely (fig. 100). The method of constructing the cores has been learned by both observing the excavated examples and experimenting.[10] Wood cores were made in three ways. (1) For circular-shaped objects, a round shape would first be carved with the help of a turntable and then the interior would be hollowed out. This method is generally used to make *ding* 鼎 tripods, boxes, *hu* 壺 wine vessels, and *yu* 盂 basins (fig. 101). (2) For more regularly shaped vessels, the core would still be carved from a single piece of wood, but without using a turntable. Ear-cups (that is, cups with earlike handles), spouted *yi* 匜 vessels, and square wine vessels (*fang hu* 钫壺), low tables, and other noncircular objects would be made by this method (fig. 102). (3) The core would be formed with thin pieces of wood, curved and fitted to each other with wooden nails to form a thin cylinder, with the bottom of the vessel attached as a separate sheet. Cylindrical vessels with straight walls like *zun* 樽 or *lian* 奩 were made in this way. This method requires a covering of hemp cloth to be spread over the thin wood core before lacquering to cover the seams. In fabric-cored vessels, numerous layers of hemp or silk cloth would be built over a model of the vessel constructed of wood or clay. After the layers of fabric had dried and hardened, the inner wood or mud core would be removed, leaving only the fabric armature. This is known traditionally as *tuotai* 脱胎. Generally speaking, the majority of lacquer vessels of the early Western Han period were wood-cored. Among the twenty-odd lacquered vessels from the Han tombs at Fuyang, Anhui, almost half had fabric cores, but among the over-180 lacquer vessels from the early Western Han tomb number one at Mawangdui, Changsha, only a few vessels like *zhi* 卮 and *lian* had fabric cores. From mid-Western Han on, in the lacquered remains from sites such as Changsha, Mancheng, Qingzhen, and Pyongyang, for example, fabric cores were increasingly used for vessels like ear-cups, trays, *zhi*, boxes, and *lian*, although wood-cored lacquer vessels were still common.

Decoration was applied on lacquerware in the following ways.[11] (1) Painting with lacquer: the most common method, which involves the mixing of pigments with the semitranslucent lacquer and applying this mixture to the lacquered surface of the vessel. The colors thus applied are brilliant and durable. (2) Painting with oil: here, pigments were mixed with oil (possibly tung oil) and applied to the lacquered surface of the vessel. The oil and pigment mixture deteriorates with age, and the decoration painted in this way is not very durable and rubs off easily. (3) Incising: decoration is incised into the lacquered surface of the vessel with a pointed needlelike instrument. Bamboo slips from tomb number 3 at Mawangdui, Changsha, record that this method was known as *zhuihua* 锥画.[12] On two lacquered *zhi*-vessels unearthed at a Han tomb at Guanghua 光化 in Hubei, the incised tiger, hare, bird, and other animal and cloud-scroll designs were filled in with gold so that they resemble the gold- and silver-inlaid decorations on bronzes.[13] (4) Finally, individual motifs were cut out from thin sheets of gold or silver and attached to the lacquered surface of the vessel, resembling what was later known as *pingtuo* 平脱[14] (fig. 103).

The most common designs found on Han lacquerware include conventionalized dragon, bird, "scrolling cloud" (*juanyun* 卷云), floral, and geometric motifs, as well as more realistic animal, bird, and fish motifs (figs. 104–05). In general, these designs are all delicate and flowing. The designs on early Western Han lacquer vessels are rich and complex; those on Eastern Han vessels appear simpler. The isolated finds of vessels from Pyongyang decorated with scenes from mythology and stories of filial piety are unusual themes,[15] but they nevertheless are representative of a new trend, or a trend which had existed as early as middle and late Western Han period as shown by the finds from the tomb of Shi Qi Yao 侍其繇 in Haizhou, Jiangsu (figs. 106–07).[16] Gold and silver sheet motifs on lacquerware from places such as Changsha, Hepu, and Lianyungang include a colorful variety of birds, animals, horses and carriages, human figures, and various geometric patterns.[17]

From the late Warring States period on, and especially since mid–Western Han, gilt or silvered bronze mountings were often added to the rims of lacquered *pan* 盘 basins, *zun* 樽 vessels, boxes, and cosmetic boxes; also, gilded buttons were inlaid onto the handles of lacquered cups. These are the so-called "silver rims and yellow handles" referred to in *Yan tie lun* 盐铁论 (*Discourses on Salt and Iron*) or the "button objects" referred to in the "Biography of He Xi Empress Deng" in *Hou Hanshu*. In the Eastern Han period, lacquered cosmetic boxes from Luoyang and Pyongyang carried quatrefoil decorations in bronze, and were even inlaid with crystal or glass beads[43] (fig. 108).

The durability of lacquered wares is illustrated by the discovery of Western Han lacquered vessels in the Eastern Han tombs at Qingzhen in Guizhou Province. In the Western Han tombs at Shiyanli 石岩里 at Pyongyang, lacquered ear-cups dated 85 B.C. and 3 B.C. were found together,[19] clearly indicating that such vessels can last for at least eighty years or more.

In other words, the high level of workmanship, beautiful colors, exquisite designs, and durability of Han lacquer vessels made them the most valuable vessels of the period, and needless to say, the price of Han lacquerware was accordingly high. Hence it was recorded in the *Yan tie lun* that the price of one lacquered cup could purchase ten bronze ones, and that it required a hundred workmen to make one lacquered cup and the effort of a thousand workmen to make one lacquered screen.

Because lacquer goods were so valuable, Han nobles and high-ranking officials often inscribed them with their clan names or official titles as signs of ownership. For example, the lacquer cups from tombs of Wang Xu 王旴 and Wang Guang 王光 at Pyongyang are inscribed with the characters "Li Wang" 利王[20] and "Wang shi Lao" 王氏牢. The lacquered cup in the tomb of Geng Ying in Yanggao 阳高, Shanxi Province, was inscribed with the character "Geng" 耿.[21] The characters "Yang zhu jia pan" 杨主家般 were inscribed on the lacquered *pan* found in the tomb of Liu Jiao 刘骄 in Changsha, Hunan.[22] The lacquered *pan* found from a tomb at Yangjiashan 杨家山 in Changsha, traditionally alleged to be the grave of a queen, was inscribed with the following phrase: "Yang zhu jia pan, jin Changsha

Wang hou jia pan" 杨主家般，今长沙王后家般.[23] Lacquer pieces from the tombs
of the marquis of Dai 轪, his wife and son, buried in tombs number 1, 2, and 3 at
Mawangdui, Changsha, are inscribed with "Dai Hou Jia" 轪侯家, etc. (fig. 109).[24]
Some lacquer items are inscribed with the characters "Shang Lin" 上林 (fig. 110),
signifying that they were used in the Shang Lin Palace.[25] Some are inscribed "Da
Gong" 大官 or "Tang Gong" 汤官,[26] indicating that they were used in the royal
kitchens. Some lacquer vessels carry inscriptions dealing with their actual functions. For example, many ear-cups and *pan* basins from Mawangdui are inscribed
with such auspicious phrases as "Jun xin jiu" 君幸酒 ("Auspicious Drinking")
and "Jun xin shi" 君幸食 ("Auspicious Banqueting"), and lacquered ear-cups
from Han tombs in Ningbo carry "Yi jiu" 宜酒 ("Desirable Wine") inscriptions
(figs. 111, 112).

The eating and drinking vessels of the Han ruling class were often decorated
with gold and silver mounts. A passage in the "Biography of Kong Yu" in *Hanshu*
says: "I once followed His Majesty to the Eastern Palace [Changlegong] and was
given cups and tables, all adorned with gold and silver." A passage in the "San bu
zu" section of *Yan tie lun* notes: "The wealthy today possess *shu* cups with silver
rims, gold handles, and inlays of gold." Another in *Han jiu yi* says, "Gold-
mounted wares are used by the highest officials, and silver-mounted wares by the
middle level and the imperial houshould officials." These texts indicate that not
only were lacquer vessels widely used in royal and noble households, they were
also exquisitely beautiful. Two lacquered *pan* dating to the Wang Mang Interregnum (beginning of first century A.D.) from Pyongyang are inscribed, stating
that they belonged with *pan* nos. 1,450–4,000[27] and 2,173–3,000[28] respectively.
Hence there must have been thousands of *pan* vessels alone in use in the royal
kitchens in the Changlegong, not to mention other vessel types (fig. 113). The
astounding number of lacquered vessels in the royal household illustrates the
extravagance and luxury of the lives of the Han ruling elite, as well as the
advanced state of the lacquer-manufacturing industry in the Han period.

LACQUERWARE INDUSTRY IN THE HAN DYNASTY

In the Han period, lacquer articles were manufactured in many regions. It is
important to note that many of these lacquer workshops were government
managed. Lacquer wares found in an early Western Han tomb at Shitougang
石头冈 in Xicun 西村, Guangzhou, were fire-branded with the characters "Pan
yu" 番禺[29] (fig. 114). Fire-branded characters "Bu shan" 布山 and "Shi fu" 市府
were found on lacquer wares from the early Western Han tomb at Luobowan
罗泊湾 in Guixian, Guangxi.[30] Lacquer wares from the early Western Han tomb
at Yinqueshan in Linyi, Shandong, were fire-branded with the names "Ju shi"
莒市 and "Shi fu" 市府[31] (fig. 115). Fire-branded characters "Cheng shi" 成市
and "Shi fu" 市府 appear on lacquer items from the early Western Han tombs at

Mawangdui, Changsha, and Fenghuangshan, Jiangling.[32] These characters indicate that these lacquer wares were manufactured at Panyu in what was then Nanhai Prefecture (now Guangzhou), at Bushan in Yulin Prefecture (now Guiping in Guangxi), in Juxian in Chengyang Principality (now Juxian, Shandong), and in Chengdu in Shu Prefecture (now Chengdu). These were all administrative seats of prefectures or principalities. They also indicate that these early Western Han lacquer goods were manufactured under the supervision of the Shi Fu, that is, the local department of commerce and handicraft. As the lacquer industry of Sichuan was especially prosperous, large numbers of lacquer goods from Chengdu were sold as far away as Changsha and Jiangling.

Among the numerous lacquer wares unearthed in 1977 from the early Western Han tomb of the marquis of Ruyin 汝阴 at Shuanggudui in Fuyangxian, Anhui Province, many carry incised inscriptions.[33] For example, a lacquered *zhi* 卮 is inscribed "*Zhi* belonging to the marquis of Ruyin, capacity 5 *sheng* 升; made in the third year by the Ku official of Ruyin, named Ji 己, and the workman Nien 年." An inscription on a lacquered *pan* says, "Flat, fabric-cored *pan* belonging to the marquis of Ruyin, diameter one [Chinese] foot three inches; made in the seventh year by the officer Hui 讳 and the workman Su 速." Some vessels are branded with "Ruyin" shopmarks, clearly indicating that they were made locally. References to the same officials and workshops on an inscribed bronze lamp from the same tomb at Fuyang indicate that as early as the beginning of Western Han, local lords often established their own workshops for the production of lacquered and other wares. Since their power extended over rather limited territories one workshop often served to produce all types of wares, and the same officials were put in charge of the production of different types of wares.

According to the "Treatise on Geography" in *Hanshu*, handicraft officials were established in modern-day Luoyang, Wuzhi, Yuxian, and Nanyang in Henan Province, in Zhangqiu and Tai'an in Shandong, in Chengdu and Zitong in Sichuan, and these were directly controlled by the central government. Government-controlled industries were probably founded during the reign of Emperor Jing Di and the early part of Emperor Wu Di's reign. The *Hanshu* ("Biography of Gong Yu") also records that the workshops in Shu 蜀 and Guanghan 广汉 prefectures of Sichuan manufactured both lacquered and gold and silver vessels. Most of the mid–Western Han to early Eastern Han lacquer goods found in Pyongyang, Noin Ula, and Qingzhen are inscribed with the names of the Shu and Guanghan workshops of Sichuan, confirming the textual records. Many of these also carry gilt or silvered bronze mounts, clearly illustrating what was maintained by the *Hanshu*. The workshop of the prefecture of Shu was located in Chengdu and that of Guanghan was in Zitong, which was renamed Zitong during the Wang Mang Interregnum. Hence, lacquer goods made in these two workshops during the Interregnum were inscribed with "Chengdu Jun" and "Zitong Jun."[34]

As previously mentioned, the burials in Mawangdui (Changsha) and in

Fenghuangshan (Jiangling) date from the early Western Han period, and many of the lacquer wares from these burials carry Chengdu workshop marks such as "Cheng shi" and "Shi fu." This evidence suggests that the locally controlled workshops at Chengdu had, by the mid–Western Han period, already passed under the direct control of the central government. These government-controlled workshops at Shu and Guanghan in Sichuan were mainly responsible for the supply of lacquer goods to the royal court and high officials' households; those lacquer goods inscribed with "chenyu" 乘輿 were used specifically by the emperor. The discovery of these lacquer wares as far away as Qingzhen, Pyongyang, and Noin Ula probably indicates they were imperial gifts to officials guarding the frontiers, to the leaders of minority groups, or to foreigners.

The lacquer wares from Qingzhen, Noin Ula, and Pyongyang all carry detailed and dated inscriptions. The earliest is dated 85 B.C., the latest, A.D. 102. These inscriptions mention the year of manufacture, the name of the workshop, the type of vessel and its capacity, and the names of officials and workmen involved; thus, they provide detailed information on the organization of the two largest lacquer workshops at Shu and Guanghan and on the actual processes of production. The inscription on a lacquered cup unearthed in Qingzhen in Guizhou may be given as an example:

> In the third year of reign period Yuan Shi 元始 [of Emperor Ping, A.D. 3], the Guanghan Prefecture official workshop manufactured this Chenyu 乘輿 lacquered, incised, painted, wood-cored, yellow ear-cup, with a capacity of one *sheng* 升, sixteen *yue* 龠. Manufactured by Sugong Chang 素工昌, Xiugong Li 休工立, Shanggong Jie 上工阶, Tongerhuangtugong Chang 铜耳黄涂工常, Huagong Fang 画工方, Diaogong Ping 泪工平, Qinggong Kuang 清工匡, Zaogong Zhong zao 造工忠造, Hugongzushi Hui 护工卒史恽, Shou Chang Yin 守长音, Cheng Feng 丞冯, Yuan Lin 掾林, Shoulingshi Tan zhu 守令史谭主.

From the list of craftsmen named, we can see that there was detailed division of labor between the various workmen and the different stages of lacquer production. First comes the "Sugong," who made the wood core (he would not be mentioned if a fabric core was used); then the "Xiugong" who applied the lacquer. He is followed by the "Shanggong," who was also responsible for the application of lacquer, but in contrast to the "Xiugong," he applied the final layers. It has been argued that the Shanggong attached bronze parts, but since his name also appeared on lacquer items without bronze parts, this interpretation cannot stand. The Shanggong is followed by the workman responsible for gilding the bronze handles of the cup, the "Tongerhuangtugong"; then the workman who painted the decoration, called the "Huagong." The job of the "Diaogong" has been greatly disputed, and he has been thought to have been responsible for carving decoration and inscriptions on the lacquers. However, although many lacquer wares from Dafentou in Yunmeng, Hubei, did not have carved inscriptions, the word "diao" 泪, was still mentioned in the inventory tablet found in the grave.[35]

Hence, it seems likely that his job involved not the carving of decorations or inscriptions but the final polishing and buffing of the lacquered surface to make it shine. He is followed by the "Qinggong" who makes sure it is cleaned—i.e., a kind of product inspector—and, finally, the "Zaogong," the general supervising foreman of the entire workshop. The order presented above suggests that the processes involved were as follows: (1) making of the core; (2) application of the base layers of lacquer; (3) application of top layers of lacquer; (4) attachment of metal parts; (5) painting the surface designs; (6) buffing; (7) final cleaning and inspection. In the earlier lacquer vessels dated to 85 B.C., the only stages named by the inscriptions were the carving of the core, lacquering, and painting, but inscriptions dating from the reign of Cheng Di (late first century B.C.) included also the second lacquering process, the attachment of metal parts, and the final cleaning and inspection. This evidence suggests that the manufacturing process became increasingly more refined.

Among the lacquer wares from Pyongyang and Qingzhen with more complete inscriptions, two were made in A.D. 3 and two in A.D. 4 by the Guanghan workshop, and three were made in A.D. 3 and seven in A.D. 4 by the Shu workshop, as can be seen in table 1 and table 2. Looking at the seven lacquer vessels made by the Shu workshop in the year A.D. 4 alone, we notice that the names of the various workmen are different. Evidently, not only were there different workmen responsible for different stages of lacquer production, but there were also many different workmen trained in a given skill. In general, the largest numbers of workmen were employed in the application of lacquer, followed in number by those in charge of adding bronze parts, painting the designs, and applying the final layers of lacquer. Polishers occupy a relatively small number, probably because the job is relatively simple. There must have been only a few inspectors and foremen, for the same inspector's name, Ping, appeared on all seven lacquers, while the same foreman's name, Zong, appeared on five of the seven lacquer pieces. This evidence supports our interpretation of their responsibilities.

We should note, however, that although there was a clear division of labor among the workmen, many workmen were capable of different jobs. For instance, workman Tan applied the top layers of lacquer as well as painted in designs; the workman Feng carved wood cores, made bronze mounts, painted designs, and polished; the foreman Zong occasionally also helped with lacquer application. And based on information derived from known dated lacquers, each workman functioned over a considerable length of time. For example, the foreman Zong was in charge for eighteen years from 4 B.C. to A.D. 14; and the workman Feng, responsible for wood-core carving, painting, and polishing, worked for as long as twelve years, from 4 B.C. to A.D. 8.[36]

In Han handicraft workshops, the workmen involved in actual production were often from one of three groups. The same division also occurred in the Shu and Guanghan lacquer workshops. They consisted of (1) exiled peasant laborers,

TABLE 1   Titles and Names of Workmen and Officials at the Government Lacquer Workshop at Guanghan Jun in the third and fourth Years of the Reign Yuan Shi (A.D. 3–4) of Emperor Ping Di

Guanghan Jun Workshop 广汉郡工官	Lacquered cup of A.D. 3 (found in Qingzhen) 清镇	Lacquered cup of A.D. 3 (found in Qingzhen) 清镇	Lacquered tray, A.D. 4 (found in Qingzhen) 清镇	Lacquered cup of A.D. 4 (found in Pyongyang) 平壤
Sugong 素工	Chang 昌	Chang 昌		
Xiugong 休工	Li 立	Long 隆	Ze 则	Xuan 玄
Shanggong 上工	Jie 阶	Sun 孙	Liang 良	Hu 护
Huangtugong 黄涂工	Chang 常	Hui 惠	Wei 伟	
Huagong 画工	Fang 方		Yi 谊	Wu 武
Diaogong 泂工	Ping 平	Ping 平	Ping 平	
Qinggong 清工	Kuang 匡	Kuang 匡	Lang 郎	
Zaogong 造工	Zhong 忠	Zhong 忠		Ren 仁
Hugong Zushi 护工卒史	Yun 恽	Yun 恽	Yun 恽	Yun 恽
Zhang 长	Yin 音	Yin 音	Qin 亲	Qin 亲
Cheng 丞	Feng 冯	Feng 冯	Feng 冯	Feng 冯
Yuan 掾	Lin 林	Lin 林	Zhong 忠	Zhong 忠
Ling Shi 令史	Tan 谭	Tan 谭	Wan 万	Wan 万

(2) convicts, and (3) skilled workmen, discussed in detail above. The first two groups were primarily responsible for all the odd jobs and the dirty work around the workshop. Although the workmen of the third group were distinguished by their special skills, they were nevertheless still slave-laborers, with no personal freedom, and hence were hardly different from the other two groups.

Lacquer inscriptions also tell us that there were five administrative posts attached to the lacquer workshops at Shu and Guanghan. They are: (1) the Zhang 长, the chief administrator, and (2) the Cheng 丞, his assistant, with positions and salaries comparable to those of district and assistant magistrates; (3) the Yuan 掾, their subordinate, whose job it was to see that orders were carried out properly (i.e., a type of executive officer); (4) the Ling Shi 令史, in charge of paperwork; and (5) the Hugong Zushi 护工卒史, or head supervisor. This last rank was generally used for rather ordinary supervisory posts throughout the Han administrative system, but since he was sent directly by the prefectural government, and answerable only to it, he possessed authority and power even above the chief administrator (Zhang), and his name was therefore usually placed first in the inscriptions.[37] In the inscription dated to 85 B.C., the name of the head supervisor (Hugong Zushi) was listed after those of the chief and assistant administrators; only in inscriptions dated 23 B.C. and later did his name appear at the head of the list, and this order of listing became the rule thereafter. This development

TABLE 2   Titles and Names of Workmen and Officials at the West Workshop of Shu Jun in the 3rd and 4th Years of the Reign Yuan Shi (A.D. 3–4) of Emperor Ping Di

West Workshop of Shu Jun	Lacquered cup of A.D. 3 (found in Qingzhen)	Lacquered cup of A.D. 3 (found in Pyongyang)	Lacquered cup of A.D. 3 (found in Pyongyang)	Lacquered box of A.D. 4 (found in Pyongyang)	Lacquered tray of A.D. 4 (found in Pyongyang)	Lacquered tray of A.D. 4 (found in Pyongyang)	Lacquered cup of A.D. 4 (found in Pyongyang)	Lacquered cup of A.D. 4 (found in Pyongyang)	Lacquered cup of A.D. 4 (found in Pyongyang)	Lacquered cup of A.D. 4 (found in Pyongyang)
Sugong 素工	Feng 丰	Feng 丰	Jin 禁	Lü 吕	Gong 恭	Shi 石	Yi 舀	Yi 舀	Yi 舀	Yi 舀
Xiugong 休工	Jian 建	Gan 籥	Ji 给	Huo 活	Zhou 周	Tan 谭	Shun 顺	Zong 宗	Li 立	Bian 便
Shanggong 上工	Chang 常	Tan 谭	Qin 钦	Gu 古	Wei 威	Feng 丰	Kuang 匡	Huo 活	Dang 当	Kuang 匡
Huangtugong 黄涂工	Wu 武	Chong 充	Wu 武				Gui 段	Gui 段	Gu 古	Gui 段
Huagong 画工	Dian 典	Tan 谭	Feng 丰	Qin 钦	Fu 辅	Zhang 张	戋	Meng 孟	Ding 定	Feng 丰
Diaogong 汩工	Wan 万	Rong 戎	Yi 宜	Rong 戎	Feng 丰	Rong 戎	Rong 戎	Feng 丰	Feng 丰	Zhong 忠
Qinggong 清工	Zheng 政	Zheng 政	Zheng 政	Ping 平	Ping 平	Ping 平	Ping 平	Ping 平	Ping 平	Ping 平
Zaogong 造工	?	Yi 宜	Yi 宜	Zong 宗	Zong 宗	Zong 宗	Zong 宗	Yi 宜	Zong 宗	Yi 宜
Hugong Zushi 护工卒史	Zhang 章	Zhang 章	Zhang 章	Zhang 章	Zhang 章	Zhang 章	Zhang 章	Zhang 章	Zhang 章	Zhang 章
Zhang 长	Liang 良	Liang 良	Liang 良	Liang 良	Liang 良	Liang 良	Liang 良	Liang 良	Liang 良	Liang 良
Cheng 丞	Feng 凤	Feng 凤	Feng 凤	Feng 凤	Feng 凤	Feng 凤	Feng 凤	Feng 凤	Feng 凤	Feng 凤
Yuan 掾	Long 隆	Long 隆	Long 隆	Long 隆	Long 隆	Long 隆	Long 隆	Long 隆	Long 隆	Long 隆
Ling Shi 令史	Kuan 宽	Kuan 宽	Kuan 宽	Bao 褒	Bao 褒	Bao 褒	Bao 褒	Bao 褒	Bao 褒	Bao 褒

suggests that the central government had tightened its grip over the workshops at Shu and Guanghan from the time of Cheng Di on (late first century B.C.).

As shown in the tables, four lacquer items from Pyongyang and Qingzhen were produced by the Guanghan workshop and ten were produced by the Shu workshop between A.D. 3 and 4. We can also see that the names of the five administrators continue to show up, clearly indicating that there was only one person attached to each administrative post. But on lacquer wares made in more widely separated years, different names usually appear, suggesting that, in contrast to the workmen, who worked in the shops for long years, there was higher turnover in the administrative posts. One Zhang is known to have been in office from A.D. 3 to 8—even so, no more than six years—while other administrators were often transferred after one or two years.

Beside the Shu and Guanghan workshops, lacquer wares were also made at the official workshops at the Western Han capital of Changan (modern Xi'an). Some of the lacquers found in Wuwei, Gansu, and in Pyongyang, Korea, have inscriptions stating they were made by ''Kaogong'' 考工, ''Yougong'' 右工, or ''Gonggong'' 供工. Kaogong and Yougong were workshops under the Department of Imperial Household Supplies; Gonggong is believed by some to be another name for Kaogong, or it may be another workshop under the same department. These Changan workshops manufactured both bronze and lacquer vessels. These lacquer inscriptions contain terms for various workmen specializing in painting, polishing, and lacquering, but usually only a single workman's name is given — the name of the workman comparable to the foreman in the Shu and Guanghan workshops. Among the officials at the workshop were ''Ling'' 令, ''You Cheng'' 右丞, ''Yuan'' 掾, ''Ling Shi'' 令史, and ''Se Fu'' 嗇夫. Some of these titles refer to responsible officials, but only You Cheng were in charge of lacquer working. The relatively few finds from Changan workshops suggest that they might have not been as productive as the Shu and Guanghan workshops.

A passage in the ''Biography of He Xi Empress Deng,'' in the *Hou Hanshu*, relates: ''In A.D. 105, the metal-mounted vessels of Shu and Guanghan and the long swords with silken sashes are no longer available.'' This may indicate that these two famous Sichuan workshops had stopped supplying lacquer wares to the court. As mentioned earlier, the latest inscription on the lacquers found at Pyongyang is dated A.D. 102. This date corresponds well to the *Hou Hanshu* comment. From these data, we may assume that the government-controlled lacquer industry was already in decline from mid-Eastern Han on, its place taken by the privately owned workshops controlled by the local warlords and wealthy landowners.

To summarize, the lacquer industry that began its rapid development only in the Warring States period reached its height in the Han. As with all things that have reached their zenith, the lacquer industry's decline was inevitable. There were many different types of lacquered wares, and the superb quality and beauty of the lacquered food and wine vessels had made them more desirable than bronze vessels. But from the time of the late Eastern Han, Wei, and Jin dynasties, celadon wares became increasingly popular and in many instances came to replace lacquer wares. However, lacquer techniques still continued to develop and advance throughout the post-Han periods.

95. Lacquered ding-tripod unearthed from Han tomb number 1 at Mawangdui, Changsha

96. Lacquered box from Mawangdui Han tomb number 1

97. Lacquered boxes for toilet articles from Mawangdui Han tomb number 1

98. Lacquered tray and plates from Mawangdui Han tomb number 1

99. Lacquered plate with fabric core from Mawangdui Han tomb number 1

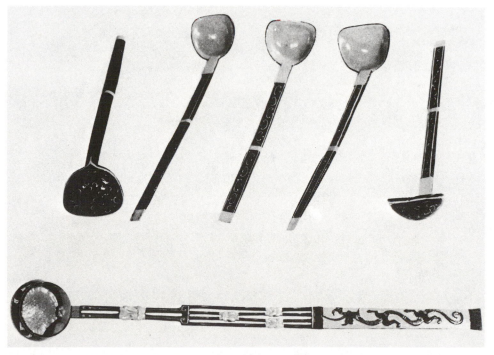

100. Lacquered ladles with bamboo cores from Mawangdui Han tomb number 1

101. Lacquered zhong-vessel from
Mawangdui Han tomb number 1

102. Lacquered fang-vessel from
Mawangdui Han tomb number 1

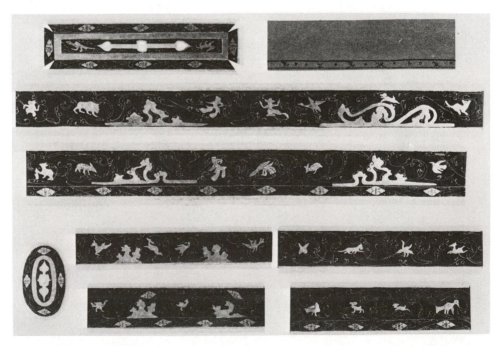

103. Designs of silver sheets attached to lacquerware unearthed from a Han tomb in
Lianyungang, Jiangsu

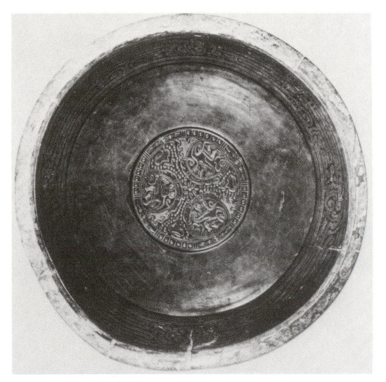

104. Animal designs on lacquerware unearthed from a Han tomb near Pyongyang, Korea

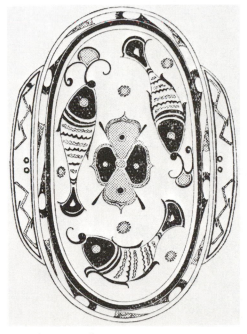

105. Fish designs on lacquerware unearthed from a Han tomb at Fenghuangshan in Jiangling

106. Lacquerware design depicting human figures in a story, unearthed from Shi Qi Yao's tomb from the Western Han period in Haizhou, Jiangsu

107. Lacquerware design depicting human figures in a story unearthed from Shi Qi Yao's tomb from the Western Han period in Haizhou, Jiangsu

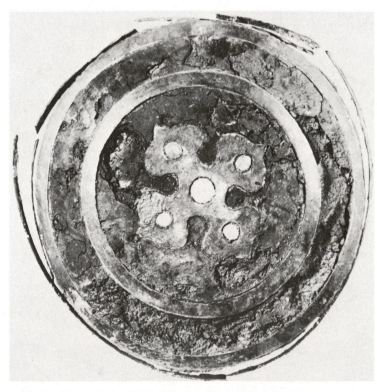

108. Persimmon-butt-shaped bronze decor with inlaid glass beads on a lacquerware unearthed from a Han tomb in Luoyang

109. The inscription "Dai Hou Jia" ("Marquis of Dai's household") on a lacquerware unearthed from Han tomb number 1 at Mawangdui in Changsha

110. The inscription "Shang Lin" on a lacquerware unearthed from a Han tomb at Noin Ula in Mongolia

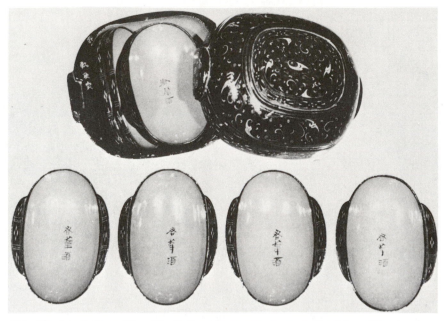

111. The inscriptions "Jun Xin Jiu" on lacquerwares unearthed from Han tomb
number 1 at Mawangdui in Changsha

112. The inscription "Jun Xin Shi" on a lacquerware unearthed from
Han tomb number 1 at Mawangdui in Changsha

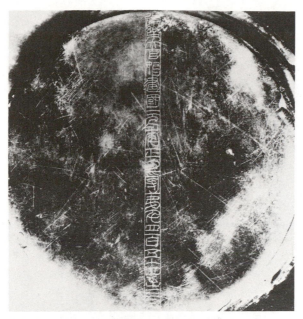

113. Inscription on a lacquered tray unearthed from a Han tomb near Pyongyang, Korea

114. The inscription "Pan Yu" fire-branded on a lacquerware unearthed from a Western Han tomb in Guangzhou

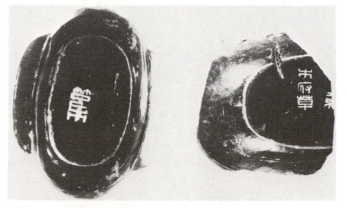

115. "Ju Shi" and other inscriptions fire-branded on lacquerwares unearthed from a Western Han tomb at Yinqueshan in Linyi, Shandong

5 Bronzes

In 1968, in Mancheng, Hebei Province, a large number of valuable bronze vessels were excavated from the tombs of Prince Liu Sheng 刘胜 and his wife Dou Wan 窦绾 of the Western Han period.[1] Among them was a *zhong* 锺 inscribed "Chu da guan zao zhong" 楚大官糟锺 and gilded with shining gold and silver, with four golden dragons coiled around it and clouds in the background (fig. 116). Another item was the "Changle culinary officer's *zhong*" (*Changle shiguan zhong*) 长乐饮官锺. On it golden or silver stripes dotted with silver beads formed diamond or triangular shapes in which pieces of green glass were inlaid. It is an extremely colorful and pretty work of art (fig. 117). There were also a pair of *hu* 壶 covered with characters in seal script, each character decorated with bird or insect motifs. The characters are decorative, but they also form a literary composition of mysterious content (fig. 118).[2] Another item was a *bo shan lu* 博山炉, an incense burner. The burner and its lid were made in the form of layers of mountains with trees, animals, and hunters on them. These decorations were patterned with gold threads, some of which were as thin as fine hair. The details of animals, human figures, trees, and hills were delicately depicted with these golden lines (fig. 119). The best-known item among them in the Mancheng find was the Changxin 长信 Palace lamp, gilded with bright gold, in the form of a kneeling palace maid holding the lamp in her hands. Not only was the palace maid beautifully sculptured, the lamp and its cover were cleverly designed so that both the lamp's illuminating power and the direction of its rays were (and still are) adjustable. Since the smoke was absorbed into the body of the maid through her arms, it was in fact an antipollution design (fig. 120). In short, it can be said that the bronzes in the tombs of Liu Sheng and his wife represent the epitome of Han bronze craftsmanship.

The Spring and Autumn–Warring States era was a transitional period for Chinese bronzes. The Warring States bronzes had changed from the solemn, heavy, solid, and archaic style of the Shang and Western Chou periods to a new style, which was delicate, lively, and full of variation. The new techniques of gold- and silver-gilding and inlaying with gold, silver, and precious stones made bronzes more colorful and attractive. In the light of the treasures found in the Mancheng Han tombs, we can conclude that the Western Han bronze craft represents a step forward from that of the Warring States period. Forms became more suitable to the needs of real life and decorations became richer and more handsome.

It should be pointed out that the bronzes found in the tombs of Liu Sheng and Dou Wan were objects available only in palaces or residences of princes. For example, the *Chu da guan zao zhong* was originally owned by the household of the prince of Chu, Liu Jiao 刘交. In 154 B.C., the grandson of Liu Jiao participated in the rebellion of the seven feudatories and was killed. This *zhong* was confiscated and later given to Liu Sheng by the central court. The same is true for the Changxin Palace lamp. It originally belonged to the marquis of Xinyang 信阳, Liu Jie 刘揭. Confiscated in 151 B.C. together with his other property and his title, the lamp was turned over to the Changxin palace due to an offense committed by the marquis' son. Later the lamp was probably given to Dou Wan by her relative the empress dowager Dou.[3] As for the two *hu* vessels with bird-seal inscriptions, although they contained no inscriptions about their owner or the craftsman who made them, because the bird-pattern seal characters were popular in the South during the Spring and Autumn–Warring States periods, it was likely that they were in the collection of the prince of Wu 吴 or that of the prince of Chu. They were perhaps given to Liu Sheng after being confiscated from their previous owners as a consequence of the latter's participation in the rebellion of the seven feudatories. The bronze known as the Changle culinary officer's *zhong* was originally an item in the imperial palace, and it must have been given to Liu Sheng by the empress dowager. The changing of hands of these items tends to indicate that even in the imperial palace or in the palaces of princes, these beautifully made bronzes were rare, highly valued items. Probably because most of these bronzes were made during or before the reign of Han Wen Di, they preserve a certain likeness in decorative technique to the Warring States bronzes on the one hand, and, on the other, they indicate that new techniques were developed. The similarity in form, pattern, and decorations between the Changle culinary officer's *zhong* and a bronze *hu* found in 1928 in Jincun 金村, Luoyang, in a Warring States tomb is obvious evidence of this transition.[4]

Generally speaking, after the mid-Western Han, sophisticated patterns and rich decorations on bronzes gradually became rare; instead, plain bronzes became popular—even the imperial utensils of the palace were no exception. In 1961, twenty-two bronze pieces were found buried in Sanqiaozhen 三桥镇, in the city of Xi'an in Shaanxi Province. They included ten basins, five *ding*-tripods, five *zhong*, one *fang*, and one *juan* 䦼 (fig. 121).[5] With only one exception, all have rather detailed inscriptions. They were imperial utensils of the Shanglinyuan imperial park located near the capital city of Changan. The characters "Chen yu" 乘舆 inscribed on one of the five tripods make it clear that it was an imperial vessel (fig. 122). They were made in the middle to late Western Han period (i.e., 97–18 B.C.). Most of them were made in Changan, some were from Taishan 泰山 Prefecture (today's Taian 泰安 district in Shandong), some were from Dongjun 东郡 (today's Puyang 濮阳 in Henan) or from the palaces in Luoyang. Some were tributes from the provincial officials of Dongjun 东郡, Yingchuan 颍川 (today's Yuxian, Henan), or Jiujiang 九江 (today's Shouxian, Anhui) (fig. 123).[6] We notice that despite their being used in the palace, they were all plain bronzes, with little pattern or decoration. In fact, except for the very special treasures made in the earlier period, those zhong and fang 钫 that were made during the later years of Liu Sheng's life and those fang and juan acquired by his palace officials from Hedong 河东 (today's Xiaxian 夏县, Shanxi) and Luoyang were plain bronzes similar to the ones excavated in Sanqiaozhen in X'ian (figs. 124, 125). The popular plain Han bronzes have often been considered an indication of a decline in bronze craftsmanship. This plainness, however, may be due to the fact that as the delicate and handsome lacquer wares became more efficient utensils for daily use than bronze vessels, the ruling class began to prefer lacquerware to bronzes. On the other hand, the plain and simple patterns of the bronzes might have been a new fashion of the time.

Despite the simplification of the patterns and decorations of the bronzes, the scale of the Han bronze industry was by no means reduced. On the contrary, it was further developed. The items found in Sanqiaozhen provide very good evidence of this development. According to the inscriptions on the eight basins made by the craftsmen who produced for the Shanglinyuan palace, we know that during the ninth month in the first year of Yang Shuo (24 B.C.) craftsman Yang Zheng 杨政 had made ten pieces; as of the fifth month in the fourth year of Yang Shuo (21 B.C.) craftsman Li Jun 李骏 and Zhou Bo 周博 had made 240 pieces each; as of the sixth month in the second year of the Hong Jia reign (19 B.C.) craftsmen Yang Fang 杨放 and Zhou Ba 周霸 had made 300 pieces each; as of the fourth month in the third year of Hong Jia (18 B.C.) craftsmen Huang Tong 黄通 and Zhou Bo 周博 had made 84 pieces each. Within the seven years from 24 to 18 B.C., 1,258 bronze basins were made, certainly an amazing number (figs. 126, 127). Regarding ding-tripods, in 51 B.C., craftsman Wang Yi 王意 made 116 pieces, and as of the sixth month in 19 B.C., craftsman Zuo Yun 左恽 made 200.[7] Needless to say, the numbers of other utensils made were also large. Bronzes were used not only in the palaces; they were popular among the nobility, bureaucrats, and even middle and small landowners. Their popularity has been substantiated by the excavation of many Han tombs. It is fair to say that precisely because of the simplification of bronze patterns it was possible to produce large quantities of bronzes, thus making them widely popular during the Han.

Compared with bronzes of the previous period, Han bronzes had undergone many changes. The food vessels fu 簠, gui 殷, dui 敦, and dou 豆, popular in the Zhou dynasty, had already disappeared by the Han. Instead, ding 鼎, zhong 锺, hu 壶, and fang 钫 were the main vessels used at the time. They inherited the form and style of those of the previous period, with some variation. Fang was popular during only the Western Han, and had disappeared in the Eastern Han. Among other vessels, juan, xi 洗, wu 鍪, zun 樽, pan 盘, zhi 卮, bei 杯, jiao dou 鐎斗, fu 釜, and zeng 甑 were the most frequently seem vessels, apart from the four main ones mentioned above. All types bear Han characteristics, and some were first introduced during the Han (fig. 128). Lamps, incense burners, tables, irons, stoves, and dripping jars became popular during the Han, but had not yet appeared or were rare during the pre-Han period (figs. 129, 130). This evidence indicates that, apart from being used for the serving of drink and food, storage, and cooking, bronzes had also been put to use in other areas of daily life. Among them, in particular, were lamps and incense burners, often elegantly made. In addition to the Changxin palace lamp mentioned above, from the Han tombs in Mancheng came the "red bird lamp" (fig. 131), the "sheep lamp" (fig. 132), and the "danghu 当户 lamp." There were also the "phoenix lamp" found in the Han tomb in Hepu in Guangxi and the "twelve-branch lamp" found in the Leitai 雷台 Han tomb in Wuwei in Gansu Province (fig. 133).[8] Of clever and innovative design, these were at the same time very efficient utensils. Although bronze lamps existed during the Warring States period, Han lamps greatly exceeded those of the Warring States in variety, quantity, and popularity.

Although plain bronzes became prevalent after the mid-Western Han, gilded bronzes were also quite popular, and some bronzes had patterns composed of thin engraved lines. A *zun* 樽 wine jar excavated in a late Western Han tomb in Changsha is covered with an elegantly engraved cloud pattern. Its detail and flowing style resemble lacquerware.[9] A *hu* with loop handle, a *pan* with three legs, and other bronzes discovered in the late Western Han tomb in Hepu in Guangxi are all decorated with various types of geometric patterns, as well as phoenixes, deer, or other animals (fig. 134). All patterns were compositions in which thin, engraved lines depict details.[10] A bronze table from an Eastern Han tomb in Wuzhou, Guangxi, is decorated with a similar pattern (fig. 135).[11] This kind of pattern engraved on bronze vessels had first appeared in the Warring States period; it was further developed during the Han and was popular mainly in the South. In addition, it should be especially mentioned that in 1962 two gilded bronze goblets were found in Youyuxian 右玉县 in Shanxi Province, both bearing inscriptions testifying that they were made in Western Han in 26 B.C. On the goblets, lively patterns of monkey, camel, ox, rabbit, sheep, deer, tiger, fox, bear, wild goose, crow, goose, duck, and other animals and birds were cast in relief instead of being engraved. This relief casting has not been found among pre-Han bronzes (fig. 136).[12] In short, although the Han bronzes showed signs of decline in pattern and decoration, they nevertheless displayed certain innovations. Nor was the technique of inlaying with gold, silver, and precious stones lost during the Han. In recent years, in an Eastern Han tomb in Xuzhou in Jiangsu, we have found an ink-stone box which was inlaid corals, turquoise, and blue gems (fig. 137).[13] A gilded bronze goblet found in an Eastern Han tomb in Leitai in Wuwei, Gansu, had on it pictures of strange birds and animals with clouds and mist, composed of inlaid silver threads (fig. 138).[14] However, there is no denying that these are extremely rare finds for that period.

Apart from the utensils that were intended for practical use, many bronze models of carriages, horses, and mounted horsemen—which were made particularly for funeral purposes—have been found in Leitai in Wuwei, Gansu, in 1969. The casting technique reached a highly advanced level (figs. 139, 140). This sophistication is fully demonstrated in the "Flying Horse," now known throughout the world, a running horse with a bird underneath one of its hooves (fig. 141). The date of the Leitai tomb was late Eastern Han. Utilitarian bronzes found in the same tomb include *hu*, *pan*, *wan*, *jian*, *xi*, *jiaodou*, *yundou*, as well as the aforementioned lamp and wine goblet; the abundance and diversity of types indicate that bronzes were popular throughout the Han dynasty.[15] It is evident, however, that bronzes declined after the Wei-Jin period. This decline could have been caused by the flourishing of porcelain, which took the place of bronze in daily life.

China is one of the first civilizations to invent the bronze mirror. According to recent excavations, we are now certain that bronze mirrors already existed during the Shang dynasty. By the Warring States period the technique for making mirrors was developing rapidly, and Han mirrors, which had proceeded a step further from those of the Warring States period, became quite widespread. As opposed to ancient Japan, where in Yayoi culture and Tomb culture imported mirrors were considered sacred treasures, in China mirrors have always been mainly utilitarian objects. Because the form and decorations of mirrors changed continuously from one period to another, providing significant chronological data, bronze mirrors have become important objects for archaeological study.

The form and decoration of mirrors of the Warring States period were preserved in those of the early Western Han period. The most common mirror is the type with a *panchi* ("intertwining serpents") design on a ground pattern and with a belt like knob. The mirrors found in the Han tombs at Mawangdui, Changsha, are of this type (fig. 142).[16] Unlike the mirrors of the Warring States period, mirrors after the beginning of the early Western Han began to bear inscriptions. The early Han mirrors, strictly speaking, still belong to the Warring States style. The "Han style" mirror began to appear in mid-Western Han during Wu Di's reign. The earliest type is the so-called grass-leaf pattern mirror, such as those found in the Mancheng tomb (fig. 143).[17] A later style is the so-called star-cloud pattern mirror, also called the "hundred nipple" mirror. The design on this mirror was probably developed from the early Western Han *panchi*-pattern mirror, but the ground pattern had disappeared, as it had in the grass-leaf pattern mirrors (fig. 144). The mirrors most typical of late Western Han were the "*Riguang*" mirror and the "*Zhaoming*" mirror. They were so named because of their inscriptions. Their designs are characterized by regularity and simplicity. The handle now becomes a hemispheric knob (fig. 145). During the Wang Mang Interregnum the Taoist ideology of the *yin yang wu xing* school was reflected in the design of bronze mirrors. A large number of mirrors have as their pattern the Four Deities (Green Dragon, White Tiger, Red Bird, and Black Turtle) and also the duodenary cyclical characters.This type is known as the "guiju" 规矩, or "elbow ruler", mirror (in the West it is sometimes called the TLV mirror). The designs of these mirrors were relatively complicated. They were popular up to the mid-Eastern Han period (fig. 146). Mirrors with dated inscriptions began to appear during the Wang Mang Interregnum and became more and more popular in the course of the Eastern Han dynasty. A new style appeared after mid-Eastern Han. The decorative designs of these mirrors were in relief, and they depict either deities and spiritual beasts or human figures and horses and carriages. The former mirrors are referred to as "immortal and animal" mirrors and the latter, as "pictorial" mirrors. Their designs were becoming increasingly lively at the same time that the the hemispheric knobs on them were becoming larger and larger (figs. 147, 148). It should be noted that at least since the mid-Western Han, the style of bronze mirrors was uniform throughout the empire, but the "immortal and animal" and the "pictorial" mirrors that appeared after the mid–Eastern Han were first developed in the Zhejiang area, to the south of the Yangtze River. Thus, in late Eastern Han and the Three Kingdoms periods, there was a certain degree of difference between the northern and southern mirrors. According to the inscriptions on mirrors excavated in Japan, the craftsmen of Luoyang enjoyed the highest reputation, but those of Kuaijijun (modern Shaoxing in Zhejiang) were almost comparable. These inscriptions thus indicate that without question by late Eastern Han Kuaiji had become a mirror production center.[18]

The inscriptions on mirrors made around the time of Wang Mang often contain a line reading, "good copper produced from Danyang 丹阳." Danyang Prefecture, with its capital located in today's Xuancheng, Anhui Province, was thus the location of the most famous copper mine during the Han. According to the "Treatise on Geography" in the *Hanshu*, the Han government had established the post of copper official in Danyang Prefecture. A mirror of the Wei-Jin period unearthed in Liaoyang of Liaoning and many mirrors excavated in Japan bear a different line reading "copper produced in Xuzhou."[19] Xuzhou was located in present-day southern Shandong and northern Jiangsu, with its capital in modern Xuzhou, Jiangsu, and these inscriptions furnish evidence that it was a well-known copper production center during the Wei-Jin period. However, in point of fact, no copper mines are actually known in this area and the problem is yet to be solved. To be sure, many copper mines were actually explored during the Han; and, according to historical records, Sichuan and Yunnan also had rich copper mines.

In 1953 an investigation of a Western Han copper-mine site in Xinglong 兴隆, Hebei Province, disclosed shafts, ore-selection ground, and smelting workshops. The mine shafts were more than 100 m below the ground surface, and led to spacious mining areas. Iron hammers and pegs found near the shafts were the mining tools. Tunnels were dug around the mining area. Ores were selected near the exits of the tunnels and then taken to four nearby smelting workshops. The furnaces seem to have been round brick structures, according to what is left of them. The finished product was in the form of large disc-shaped ingots, each weighing from 5 to 15 kg. The characters meaning "East 60" or "West 53" were incised on the ingots. "East" and "West" could refer to the location of the workshop, and the numbers might indicate serials. Some ingots bear the characters "Second year," perhaps indicating that the ingots were made before the reign title system was established by Han Wu Di (fig. 149).[20] In 1955, ten rectangular copper ingots were found at a site near the Han capital Changan, each weighing 34 kg, containing 99 percent copper, and all inscribed with weight and serial number. One has a line reading, "Sold by Tian Rong 田戎 of Wanli 宛里 in Fupo 富波 district in Runan 汝南 Prefecture." The inscription indicates that the government not only ran copper mines itself but also made purchases from private miners in order to satisfy its demand for bronze manufacturing and cash minting.[21]

The scale of the production of bronze objects under Han-government management was quite large. Government-managed production supplied mainly the palace and other government offices. Two subordinate officials, of the Shaofu qing 少府卿 (Lesser Treasury Ministry) in the central government the Shangfang ling 尚方令 (Shangfang Office) and the Kaogong ling 考工令 (Kaogong Office) were in charge of bronze production for imperial and governmental uses at the capital. The Shangfang Office, according to inscriptions, was by the time of Wu Di's reign already divided into the three offices of Left, Right, and Center, and this division continued into Eastern Han. The Central Shangfang Office had the largest capacity in terms of variety of products. The bronzes it produced included *ding*-tripods, *zhong*, *hu*, *chiao*, *dou*, lamps, and so on. The crossbow was an item produced by all three offices. The Kaogong Office (which by Eastern Han became subordinate to the Taipu Qing 太仆卿 [The Grand Servant] produced more or less the same items as produced by the Central Shangfang Office with the exception of mirrors, which were made only by the Shangfang Office. Another subordinate office of the Lesser Treasury Ministry called The Yougongshi 右工室 also produced some bronzes. Both the Kaogongshi and the Yougongshi also produced lacquerware.

Bronzes were also produced by some of the workshops run by the prefectural manufacturing offices of the Han central government. For example, the manufacturing offices in Shu and Guanghan prefectures, apart from making lacquerware, were also famous for the bronzes they produced. According to the "Biography of Gong Yu" in *Hanshu*, "Shu and Guanghan produce mainly golden and silver wares." However, archaeological excavations have shown that the manufacturing of golden and silver wares was not that popular in Han. We therefore suspect that what are here referred to as "golden and silver wares" in fact were bronze vessels and utensils gilded with gold or silver. The Palace Museum in Beijing has in its collection a bronze goblet with a saucer. The set was made in A.D. 45 by the Western Manufacturing Office of Shujun. Both the goblet and its saucer were gilded with gold. Turquoise and crystal were inlaid on the goblet and on the three bear-shaped legs of the saucer (fig. 150).[22] There is a detailed inscription on the saucer that reads: "In the twenty-first year of the Jian

Wu reign, the Western Manufacturing Office of Shujun made an imperial goblet
with saucer. The saucer is decorated with carved bear-shaped legs. [Both] were
inlaid with turquoise. The diameter of the bronze saucer is 2 *chi* 2 *cun*. [The set]
was made by these craftsmen: Chong 崇, coppersmith; Ye 业, carver; Kang 康,
metalsmith; and Ye 业, artisan; [they were] under the supervision of [the following manufacturing officials]: Yun 恽, craftsman supervisor; Fan 氾, superintendent; Meng 萌, assistant director; Xun 巡, secretary; and Yun 郿, director." The
format and the titles of craftsmen and craft officials in this inscription were similar
to those on lacquerware. This similarity indicates that the same manufacturing
office produced both lacquerware and bronzes.

In 1925, a lacquer cup made in A.D. 52 by the same manufacturing office
was excavated in Wang Xu 王肝's tomb in Pyongyang in Korea. The inscription
on it reads: "In the twenty-eighth year of the Jian Wu reign, the Western
Manufacturing Office of Shujun made an imperial soup-cup, with a capacity of 2
shen 2 *he*. It was made by craftsmen: Hui 回, molder [?]; Wu 吴, lacquerman; Wen
文, polisher; Ting 廷, lacquerman; and Zhong 忠, artisan; [they were] under the
supervision of the following manufacturing officials: Han 旱, craftsman supervisor; Fan 氾, superintendent; Geng 庚, assistant director; Xi 翁, secretary; and
Mao 茂, director."[23] Comparing the two inscriptions, we find that the lacquer cup
was made seven years later than the bronze; thus, names of many of the manufacturing officials were different. However, the name of the superintendent, Fan,
was still found in the later inscription. This evidence indicates that Fan served for
quite a long time, at least seven years, and that the same manufacturing officials
were in charge of both bronze and lacquerware production.

Private bronze-making workshops were also quite numerous. Inscriptions on
some privately produced bronzes mark their prices. Eight hundred and forty
copper cash was the price of a bronze *juan* bought from Hedong Prefecture by
officials of the prince of Zhongshan, whose tomb was excavated in Mancheng
(fig. 151). Another bronze *fang* produced in Luoyang was also bought by officials
of the prince of Zhongshan. Both are believed to be products of private manufactories.[24] Private mirror producers often made use of mirror inscriptions to
advertise the superior quality and elegant design of the mirrors they made. The
contents of the inscriptions often claimed that the user of the mirrors "will live
long, will continue to enjoy wealth and prestige." To cite some examples: "The
substance of this mirror is pure and bright; the rays it radiates could be compared
to those of the sun and moon"; "The mirrors made by the Ye family are handsome
and great. They are as bright as the sun and the moon; indeed, they are rare to
find!"; "I record here the mirrors I made; they will make the user live longer,
likewise his sons and grandsons." It is evident that these mirrors were produced
for the market. Many of them, nevertheless, although produced by privately
owned workshops, bear inscriptions reading "Made by [the imperial workshop]
Shangfang Office," in order to heighten their value. This was probably a cus-
tomary practice among the private producers.

116. Zhong-vessel inscribed with "Chu da guan zao zhong," unearthed from Han tomb in Mancheng

117. Zhong-vessel inscribed with "Changle shiguan zhong," unearthed from Han tomb in Mancheng

118. Hu-vessel decorated with bird-seal-script characters, unearthed from Han tomb in Mancheng

119. "Bo shan" incense burner with gold inlays, unearthed from Han tomb in Mancheng

120. The Changxin Palace lamp unearthed from Han tomb in Mancheng

121. Bronze jian-basin for use at Shanglinyuan Park, unearthed at Sanqiaozhen in Xi'an ("Manufactured at Dong Jun in the third year of Chu Yuan")

122. Bronze ding-tripod with the inscription "Chen yu," unearthed in Sanqiaozhen, Xi'an

123. Bronze zhong-vessel with the inscription "Jiu jiang gong," unearthed in Sanqiaozhen, Xi'an

124. Bronze fang-vessel unearthed from Han tomb in Mancheng

125. Bronze juan-vessel unearthed from Han tomb in Mancheng

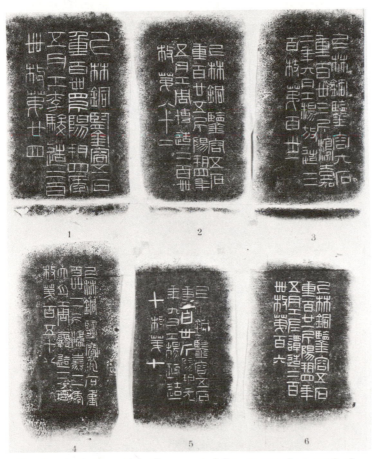

126. Inscriptions on Shanglinyuan Park bronze vessels unearthed
in Sanqiaozhen, Xi'an

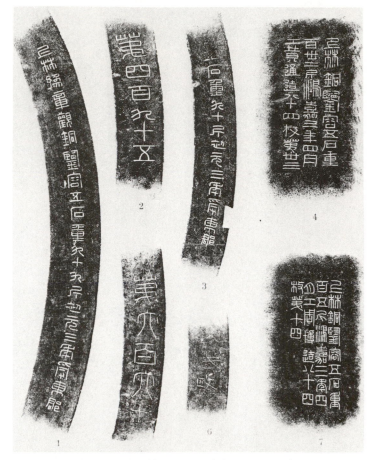

127. Inscriptions on Shanglinyuan Park bronze vessels unearthed in Sanqiaozhen, Xi'an

128. Bronze wu-vessel unearthed from a Han tomb in Pingle, Guangxi

129. Square stove of bronze, unearthed in Xi'an ("Manufactured in the second year of Gan Lu")

130. Dripping jar of bronze, unearthed in Yikezhao Leaque in Inner Mongolia

131. Bronze lamp in the shape of the Red Bird, unearthed from Han tomb in Mancheng

132. Bronze lamp in the shape of a ram, unearthed from the Han tomb in Mancheng

133. Twelve-branch lamp of bronze, unearthed from the Han tomb at Leitai, in Wuwei, Gansu

134. Incised designs on a bronze tray with three legs, unearthed from a Han tomb in Hepu, Guangxi

135. Incised designs on a bronze table unearthed from a Han tomb in Wuzhou, Guangxi

136. Gold-gilded wine zun-cup of bronze, unearthed in Youyu, Shanxi

137. Gold-gilded ink-stone box of bronze, unearthed from a Han tomb in Xuzhou, Jiangsu

138. Gold-gilded wine zun-cup of bronze, unearthed from Han tomb at Leitai in Wuwei, Gansu

139. Bronze model of horsedrawn carriage, unearthed from the Han tomb at Leitai in Wuwei, Gansu

140. Bronze figure of warrior on horseback,
unearthed from the Han tomb at Leitai in Wuwei,
Gansu

141. The "Flying Horse," bronze galloping horse stepping on
flying bird, unearthed from the Han tomb at Leitai in Wuwei,
Gansu

142. Bronze mirror with designs of intertwining serpents, unearthed from the Han tomb of Mawangdui, Changsha

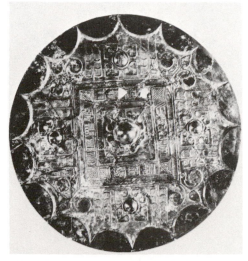

143. Bronze mirror with grass-leaf designs, unearthed from the Han tomb in Mancheng

144. Bronze mirror with designs of stars and clouds, unearthed from Han tomb in Nanchang, Jiangxi

145. Bronze riguang mirror unearthed
from Han tomb in Xi'an

146. Bronze mirror with designs in the
shape of measuring rules ("Elbow ruler"),
unearthed from Han tomb in Xi'an

147. Bronze mirror decorated with design
of spiritual beast, unearthed from Han
tomb in Shaoxing, Zhejiang

148. Bronze mirror with pictorial designs,
unearthed from Han tomb in Shaoxing,
Zhejiang

149. Bronze ingot of Han dynasty date,
unearthed in Xinglong, Hebei

150. Gold-gilded bronze wine zun-cup and tray inscribed with manufacturing date (the twenty-first year of Jian Wu), in the collection of the Palace Museum

151. Inscription on the bronze juan-vessel unearthed from Han tomb in Mancheng

6   Iron Implements

According to archaeological excavations, Chinese iron metallurgy began in the late Spring and Autumn period. By the Han dynasty, the use and manufacture of iron implements had become common and widespread. It can be said that iron tools became indispensable for every aspect of daily life and production. As we have mentioned earlier, farm tools like the plow, the pickax, the spade, the shovel, the hoe, and the sickle were widely used in all parts of China, and their use caused a noticeable increase in agricultural productivity (fig. 152). According to a historian's estimate, at the end of the Warring States period the total population of the seven major states was about twenty million.[1] It increased drastically after mid-Western Han. According to the "Treatise on Geography" in *Hanshu*, the population reached almost sixty million by the end of the Western Han dynasty. This population growth would have been inconceivable had it not been for the widespread use of iron tools both in farming and in waterworks, the latter which greatly increased productivity of food crops and other farm products.

Craftsman's tools—such as the ax, the adz, the hammer, the chisel, the knife, the saw, the awl, nails, and so on—increasingly raised the efficiency of carpenters, bamboo craftsmen, stonemasons, and earth builders, making possible completion of large-scale construction projects (fig. 153). Concurrent with increasing water transport during the Han dynasty, the shipbuilding industry developed rapidly. In 1975, a shipyard of the late Qin or early Han period was excavated in Guangzhou. The yard comprised three building platforms.[2] These are estimated to have been capable of building large wooden ships 30 m long, 8 m wide, with a weight capacity of 60 metric tons.[3] The discovery offers us a glimpse of the scope of the Han shipbuilding industry, which cannot be separated from the use of iron tools. The rotary quern, a small hand mill for grinding grain, was an important tool that concerned the daily life of everyone. Without iron tools, the widespread use of this particular device would have been impossible. Masterpieces of stone, such as the carved pictorial stones and the gate towers and stone animals often found erected in front of Eastern Han tombs, were also the result of skillful application of fine quality iron tools by artists.

The superior quality of iron became all the more evident when it was used in weapons. By the early Western Han period, long iron swords had completely replaced the short bronze swords of the Warring States period. The length of the Warring States bronze sword was in general less than half a meter, whereas the length of the Han iron sword often measured about one meter. The superiority of steel was able to lengthen the sword blade by a hundred percent. In Western Han, a large iron knife with a ring at the end of its handle appeared. Its length was also one meter. This new weapon, unknown to previous periods, became one of the major weapons of the Eastern Han period. Fighting soldiers holding a shield in one hand and this kind of knife in the other are often depicted on pictorial stones. Although the form of bronze ge-halberd of the Shang and Zhou periods changed in the course of time, they were still being made and used in the Western Han; but before long, they also were completely replaced by iron spears and ji-halberds. The length alone of the iron spearheads and ji-halberd heads was about half a meter, and the total length of these weapons, including their wooden shafts, could reach more than 2.5 m.[4] While arrowheads were still made of bronze in the Han dynasty, the stem of the arrowhead was made mostly of iron. However, gradually arrowheads made wholly of iron became popular, and finally they came to replace bronze ones. Due to the advancement in iron technology, the quality of armor improved noticeably. Archaeologists have excavated quite a number of specimens of Han iron armor. Among the best-preserved specimens are one excavated at the site of a frontier town in Dingxiang 定襄 Prefecture (its capital located in present Holingor, Inner Mongolia) and another found in the tomb of Liu Sheng, the Han prince Jing of Zhongshan, in Mancheng, Hebei.[5] The latter was an example of so-called fish-scale armor; it was made of more than 2,800 small iron plates (figs. 154, 155). As a defensive device, large numbers of barbed iron balls were made to be placed on the ground outside the city walls. The thorny iron balls were so devised that no matter how each piece was placed, there was always one sharp thorn pointing upward. Their function was to deter marching soldiers and horses (fig. 156).[6] It was precisely these sorts of superior iron weapons that made it possible to deal with the powerful horsemen from the northern tribes. When Tao Cuo 晁错 analyzed the military situation between the Han and the Xiong Nu during the reign of Emperor Jing Di of Western Han, he pointed out that one of the advantages the Han had over the Xiong Nu was superior weaponry. The fact that the Han dynasty, following Qin, was able to establish a united empire over such a vast area was, in addition to social, economic, and other factors, also closely related to the application of superior iron weaponry in military affairs.

Let us now turn to household utensils. Iron also played an important role in everyday life. Iron provided material for making ding-tripods, stoves, cooking pots, belt buckles, tweezers, fire tongs, scissors, kitchen knives, fishhooks, and needles (figs. 157, 158). The widespread use of iron cooking pots greatly facilitated household cooking. A huge iron pot, with a diameter measuring about 2 m, was found in Wafangzhuang 瓦房庄, Nanyang 南阳, Henan Province; it was possibly used for boiling salt.[7] The kitchen knife—especially made to meet culinary needs—become differentiated from other knives. The Han scissors, like primitive scissors of other civilizations, were made of a bent iron rod with its two sharpened ends facing each other. The resilient nature of steel makes them operable. The convenience offered by scissors in cutting cloth and hair cannot be overemphasized. The iron needle was an indispensable item in the daily life of the Han people. Unfortunately, due to their small size and propensity to rust, needles are difficult to find. Up until today, the needle found in tomb number 167 at Fenghuangshan in Jiangling, Hubei Province, is the only example we have of Han needles. It was this kind of iron needle that was used in sewing and embroidering.[8] Rulers for measuring also were often made of iron. The marks and decorative patterns on a iron ruler found in the Mancheng Han tomb were inlaid with gold threads.[9] In Eastern Han, iron lamps were as popular as bronze lamps. An iron "twelve-branch lamp" found in a Han tomb in Luoyang exhibits the clever and elegant style of the artisan (fig. 159).[10] Even iron mirrors are often found in late Eastern Han tombs. Unfortunately, because of their tendency to rust, they have received much less attention than bronze mirrors. In fact, some of their decorative patterns are quite attractive. For example, through X rays we found that the decoration on the iron mirror discovered in the Han tomb at Leitai, in Wuwei, Gansu, was elegantly inlaid with gold and silver threads in a phoenix design[11] (figs. 160, 161). It should not surprise us that when Cao Cao presented gifts to the emperor, he preferred iron mirrors to bronze.

In short, during the Han dynasty iron implements were closely related to national defense, on the one hand, and to economic life of the country, on the other. Therefore, the iron-manufacturing industry came to be an increasingly important sector of the economy, over which the ruling class found it essential to have control. According to the records in the "History of the Southern Yue' in *Shiji* and in the "Biography of the King of South Yue" in *Hanshu*, in early Western Han when Prince Zhao Tuo 赵佗 of Nan Yue advocated separatism and independence, Empress Dowager Lü Hou 吕后 ordered that shipment of iron implements to that area be banned. The court's punitive move brought on a drastic reaction from Zhao Tuo: he led an army and marched toward Changsha, threatening the central government. This incident demonstrates the importance of iron at that time. In early Western Han, the iron industry was sometimes controlled by the central government and sometimes by provincial lords and principalities. Each lord or prince installed his own iron officials to control iron manufacturing. For example, in the Linzi 临淄 area of Shandong Province, seals have been found with such inscriptions as "The Seal of Qi Iron Office," "Qi Iron Officer," "Qi Iron Office Deputy," and "Iron Deputy of Linzi" (figs. 162–65). In addition, rich merchants, in an attempt to increase their wealth, ran privately owned iron manufactories. Thus, strong competition for control over the iron industry existed between the central government, the principalities, and the wealthy merchants. The strength of the central government greatly increased after the rebellion of the seven states in the Wu and Chu area was crushed by Emperor Jing Di. Eventually, in Wu Di's reign, the central government was able to monopolize the iron industry completely. Like salt, iron implements were manufactured and distributed by government offices.

According to the "Treatise on Geography" in *Hanshu*, more than forty iron offices were established, and they were located as far as Shandong and Jiangsu in the east, Gansu in the west, Liaoning in the northeast, and Sichuan and Yunnan in the southwest, covering a vast area. Inscriptions sometimes can be found on the objects made by the official manufactories. To mention some examples from the excavated finds, those made in the manufactories of the Henan Prefecture (present Luoyang) have the inscriptions "He 河 1," "He 2," "He 3"; those from the Nanyang Prefecture bear the characters "Yang 1," "Yang 2"; those from the Hedong Prefecture (present Xiaxian, Shanxi Province) have "Dong 2," "Dong 3". The characters "He," "Yang," and "Dong" represent names of prefectures, while the numbers "1," "2," and "3" designate the particular manufactory or workshop of that prefecture (fig. 166).[13]

Extensive investigations carried out since the Liberation have uncovered many iron foundry sites in Qinghezhen 清河镇 in Beijing, Tengxian 滕县 in Shandong, and Liguoyi 利国驿 in Xuzhou in Jiangsu.[14] Especially in Henan Province in the Central Plains area, more than a dozen such workshops and foundries have been found. Of these, large-scale excavations were carried out in the site located at Tieshenggou 铁生沟 in Gongxian 巩县 and the one at Wafangzhuang 瓦房庄 in Nanyang 南阳.[15] The former is dated from mid-Western Han to the Wang Mang period, the latter, from mid-Western Han to Eastern Han.

Tieshenggou iron foundry is located in a basin at the foot of Mount Song. There were workshops for smelting, casting, and forging. Only a few kilometers away in the mountains was a rich iron mine from which ore was obtained. Thus, this manufactory in fact encompassed facilities for the whole process from mining and smelting to manufacturing. Within the 2,000 square m already excavated, we have found an ore-dressing yard, eighteen smelting furnaces, one crucible furnace, and one forging furnace, as well as mixing pools, storage pits, and other auxiliary facilities (figs. 167, 168). From the excavated remains and objects, we can see that the ore was first delivered to the dressing yard, where it was crushed by hammers and screened so that the ore pieces were more or less the same size. After that, a certain proportion of limestone as a flux was mixed with the ore in the mixing pool. The mixture was then put in the smelting furnace, together with the fuel. The eighteen smelting furnaces can be divided into several types according to their different structures and functions. Some could be called "solid reduction furnaces." In this type of furnace the iron ore was reduced at low temperatures into spongelike bloom iron pieces. Others could be called "blast furnaces," where liquid cast iron was produced at high temperatures. There is another type that could be called a "steel puddling furnace." Smelted cast iron was put in this type of furnace. When it melted, the liquid was constantly stirred by the founder. Steel or wrought iron could be produced by this process. Most of the smelting furnaces were semisubterranean with walls made of refractory bricks, and both the bricks and the bottom of the furnace were covered with refractory clay. The smelted iron blooms produced were stored in the storage pit. The function of the "crucible furnace" was to melt cast iron. Various clay molds were found near it. They were used for casting various tools and utensils. Near the "forge furnace," used in tempering bloom iron and making implements, an iron anvil and a quenching pool were found. Three types of fuel were used: wood, coal, and coal cakes. The coal cakes were made of coal powder mixed with clay and quartz.[16] We found at this site many smelting furnaces, but only a few forging and crucible furnaces and casting molds, so we concluded that the main function of this foundry was smelting, and that forging and casting were secondary.[17]

The iron foundry at Wafangzhuang in Nanyang was located in Wanxian, the administrative seat of Nanyang Prefecture.[18] The iron office of Nanyang Prefecture was the most famous of its time. The Wafangzhuang site is probably one of the many foundries under the Nanyang iron office. Because the remnants of the ancient city walls of Wanxian still stand, we know that this foundry was located in the central part of the walled city. Because its location was far from the mines, its main function was to cast and forge, using cast-iron ingots smelted elsewhere or recycling old and worn-out iron utensils. Its main function was to manufacture various implements and utensils, just the opposite of the Tieshenggou foundry. Within the 3,000 square m already excavated, sixteen furnaces have been found. Some were crucible furnaces to melt cast iron for casting. At the site a large number of clay molds were found, including molds for vessels, such as *ding*-tripods, pots, and basins; agricultural implements and tools, such as pickaxes, spades, shovels, plowshares, axes, adzes, hammers, and chisels; and such carriage parts as axle-pins and bearings. It is evident that this foundry had a remarkable capacity, casting large numbers of a variety of items. Some furnaces were steel stirring furnaces, in which cast iron was melted and stirred into steel or wrought iron and was then forged into various tools and utensils. A large number of hammers and anvils for forging as well as many finished products like knives, sickles, and spearheads were also found. Unlike the Tieshenggou foundry, the sole fuel used here was wood.[19]

In recent years, excellent results have been achieved by the combined research efforts of archaeologists and metallurgists, especially of metallurgists in analyzing archaeologically excavated iron implements.[20] It has been shown that by the Spring and Autumn period at the latest (late sixth century B.C.) China had already employed the method of reducing iron ore with charcoal at relatively low temperatures ($800°-1,000°$ C) to a relatively pure but spongelike iron bloom. This method is called the "low temperature—solid reduction," or "bloom smelting," method. The product is called bloom-smelted iron (commonly known as wrought iron) and it can be forged into implements. A short piece of iron bar found in 1974 in a tomb of the late Spring and Autumn period in Liuhexian in Jiangsu was forged from this type of bloom-smelted iron.[21] By the late Warring States period, ironsmiths already knew how to produce steel out of wrought iron by the method of solid state carburization of the wrought iron. The technique was to heat pure iron in charcoal for an extended period of time at a temperature above $900°$ C, or to keep heating the iron in charcoal while forging. As a result, when enough carbon was absorbed by the iron, it turned into steel. A late Warring States sword excavated in 1973 in Yanxiadu in Yixian, Hebei, was made of steel produced by this method.[22]

In the two centuries following the late Warring States period, along with accumulated experience, forging technique also improved. The main technique was repeated forging. By means of repeated beating of the heated metal, the carbon content was evenly alloyed with the metal and impurities were reduced, thus greatly improving the quality of the steel. This early technology was known as "hundred-time forged steel." The sword worn by Liu Sheng and later found in his tomb was a product of this technology during its early stage (fig. 169). The new technology of the mid-Western Han was developed from the old technique known as the "solid state carburization method" of the late Warring States period. The cast iron and the carbon infiltration method of the Han period were similar to the material and technique of the late Warring States, the difference being that the Han method extended the hammering and heating process. The hammering process not only forged the metal into the desired shape; it also reduced the number and size of impurities and alloyed them evenly with the metal, thus raising the quality of the steel produced. If we compare the Yanxiadu 燕下都 sword from the Warring States period mentioned above and the Han sword found in Liu Sheng's tomb, we find that the raw materials were both solid-state carbon-infiltrated steel, but the former has an unevenly alloyed carbon content and a high content of larger-sized impurities, whereas the latter has an evenly distributed carbon content with fewer and smaller impurities. The main reason for the difference was that the latter had been produced by a repeated hammering and heating process. This is considered a major development in the history of metallurgy occurring between the late Warring States period and mid-Western Han.

In order to increase its sharpness, Liu Sheng's sword had also undergone the processes of "surface carbonization" and blade-edge quenching. Quenching was a technique of dipping heated steel in cold water in order to increase the strength and hardness of the metal. Only the edge of the blade of Liu Sheng's sword was treated with the quenching process. The result is that only the blade edges are hard and sharp while the body of the sword (the middle thicker part) remains relatively elastic and nonbrittle. The same idea was applied in the surface carbonization process so that only the outside of the sword was hardened.

Other weapons such as the knife, the *ji*-halberd, and the short sword excavated from the Han tomb in Mancheng also indicate a higher quality (fig. 170). A beautifully made desk knife inlaid with gold thread was also found there. Its forging process was similar to that of Liu Sheng's sword, only the body of the blade was made of a steel with lower carbon content and thus of a lesser hardness. By reducing its hardness, the craftsman was able to carve the knife and inlay it with gold thread. However, since the blade edge had been infiltrated with carbon and quenched, the knife was hardened and the edge could easily be sharpened.[23]

On the other hand, as early as the early Warring States period in the fifth century B.C., shortly after the bloom smelting technique was developed, the Chinese founder invented a technique which produced cast iron that had more than 2 percent carbon content. An early Warring States iron adz excavated in Luoyang in 1975 was determined to be the earliest tool made of this kind of cast iron.[24] This is 1,800 years earlier than the development of similar techniques in other civilizations. The main factor in founding cast iron is high temperature. Because of the long history of bronze technology and improvements made in the bellows systems, it became possible to bring temperatures up to 1,100–1,200° C or more. At this high temperature the charcoal-reduced iron would rapidly absorb carbon, thus greatly lowering its melting point. When the temperature exceeds 1,146° the iron with more than 20 percent carbon content begins to melt and its speed of carbon absorption increases. When the process accelerates, the result is completely melted cast iron. This kind of cast iron has a lower content of silicon, and no graphite. It is called white iron because its fracture appears white. It is hard but brittle in character.

In order to improve the quality of white iron, the early Warring States artisans treated it with an extended heating process, causing graphite to separate from the carbonized iron. The resulting cast iron, called elastic cast iron, was not brittle. This kind of iron was widely used for farm tools and weapons in the middle and late Warring States period. A great number of these were found in Warring States period sites and tombs in Changsha of Hunan, Daye of Hubei, and Yanxiadu in Yixian of Hebei. Many iron tools found in the Mancheng Han tomb of mid-Western Han were also made of this elastic cast iron.[25]

It is noteworthy that gray iron pieces were also found in the Mancheng Han tombs. These are the earliest gray iron items ever found in China. The gray iron was produced by raising the heating temperature and speeding up the cooling process. During the treatment, the carbon content in excess of 2 percent would be separated from the cast iron in the form of thin graphite pieces. Gray iron is so named because the color of its fracture is gray. Its hardness is lower than white iron, but it is not as brittle. It stands up to wear and its surface can be smoothened. The pickax in the Han tomb of Mancheng was made of elastic cast iron, while the carriage bearings were made of gray iron, indicating that the characteristics of various kinds of cast iron were understood and utilized accordingly.[26]

The agricultural implements, tools, utensils, and weapons that were described initially can be divided into forged and cast items. Until mid-Western Han, forged items and cast items were invariably made of "bloomery iron" and cast iron, respectively. Cast items became more and more popular as the size of the furnace became larger and the bellowing system improved. However, the brittleness of cast iron greatly limited its use. On the other hand, the carburization method involved a great deal of labor in forging and both productivity and efficiency were low. In this situation a new technique was invented to induce decarbonization of cast iron in solid state to become steel. An iron chisel excavated from Wafangzhuang in Nanyang has the appearance of a cast item. However, the structure of surface metal of the chisel, according to metallographic analysis, was clearly steel. Another chisel shows a carbon content of 0.6 to 1 percent. At the current technological level, a temperature above 1,500° C could not have been achieved. Moreover, there was no refractory material which could withstand such heat. Therefore this steel could not have been liquid. Hence we concluded that this type of steel must have been produced by decarburization in the solid state by some kind of heat treatment.[27] Because an arrowhead excavated from the Mancheng Han tomb was also made of this type of cast steel, we are quite sure this new technique had been developed by mid-Western Han.[28]

A more important new technique developed in late Western Han was the "puddling" steel method. Cast iron was heated into a semiliquid state. By constant agitation in an oxidizing atmosphere the hot metal could be decarburized. Wrought iron or steel, depending on the level of carbon content, could be produced by this process. Using cast iron, which could be easily produced in large quantities, as material for producing steel was a revolution in metallurgical history. Thus "hundred-time forged steel" could be obtained either by puddling cast iron into wrought iron and then carbonizing and forging it into steel, or by puddling cast iron until the desired carbon content was reached and then forging it into steel implements. A large iron knife excavated in a Han tomb at Cangshan in Shandong has a gold-inlaid inscription which reads "thirty-time forged large knife" and is dated the sixth year of Yong Chu (A.D. 112) (fig. 171).[29] Metallurgists who made analyses of this knife concluded that it was made of puddled steel.[30]

From Emperor Wu Di to the end of Western Han, the iron industry was a monopoly of the state. Among those who worked in the government-run industrial mines and foundries, apart from the specialized artisans, were convicted criminals and corvée laborers. The large scale of the Han iron industry is shown by the fact that, according to the records in the "Biography of Gong Yu" in *Hanshu*, more than a hundred thousand miners were mobilized every year to mine copper and iron ores for the purpose of minting coins and smelting iron. In the late Western Han period, ironworkers in Yingchuan Prefecture (modern Yuxian, Henan) and Shanyang Prefecture (in today's Jinxiangxian, Shandong) rebelled in protest of repressive measures against them. In the early Eastern Han period, following the Western Han system, the government still monopolized the iron industry. But influential local power-holders often operated private foundries. The government was unable to enforce the law. Finally, in A.D. 88, Emperor He Di gave in and lifted the ban on private iron and salt production. From then on, both the iron and salt industries gradually were further controlled by local powers.

The Shandong Provincial Museum in its collection has a carved pictorial stone that depicts an iron foundry.[31] Among the twelve artisans shown working, four are bellowing the furnace with leather bellows, the rest are hammering and forging (fig. 172).[32] The stone was excavated at Hongdaoyuan in Tengxian,

Shangdong, in 1930. Its date indicates it was made after the ban was lifted. It appears that the tomb's occupant, a powerful landlord, was engaged in the iron industry and for that reason had the manufacturing scene carved on the wall of his tomb. This stone not only provides us with a vivid depiction of iron manufacture, it also may furnish evidence that iron industry was then controlled by privately owned enterprises. However, it is also possible that this scene was carved on the walls of the tomb of a former iron official of the state.

152. Han dynasty iron implements unearthed in Luoyang, Gongxian, and other localities in Henan

153. Han dynasty iron implements unearthed in Luoyang, Hebi, and other localities in Henan

154. Iron armor plates unearthed at the Han city site in Huhehaote, Inner Mongolia

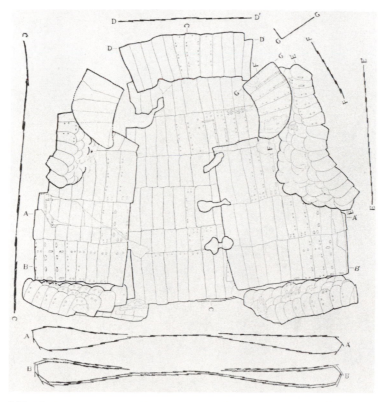

155. Reconstruction of the iron armor plates unearthed at the Han city site in Huhehaote, Inner Mongolia

156. Barbed iron ball unearthed at the site of the Han city of
Changan in Xi'an

157. Iron stove and tray unearthed from a Han tomb in Luoyang

158. Iron cooking pot unearthed from a Han tomb in Luoyang

159. Iron lamp with twelve branches, unearthed from a
Han tomb in Luoyang

160. Iron mirror unearthed from the Han tomb at Leitai in Wuwei, Gansu

161. Reconstructed decorative designs on iron mirror unearthed from the Han tomb at Leitai, in Wuwei, Gansu

162. Clay seal impressed with the inscription "Seal of Qi Iron Office," unearthed in Linzi, Shandong

163. Clay seal impressed with the inscription "Qi Iron Officer," unearthed in Linzi, Shandong

164. Clay seal impressed with the inscription "Qi Iron Office Deputy," unearthed in Linzi, Shandong

165. Clay seal impressed with the inscription "Iron Deputy of Linzi," unearthed in Linzi, Shandong

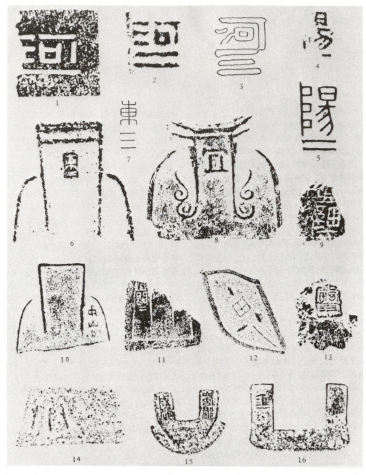

166. Inscriptions cast on Han dynasty iron implements unearthed in Shaanxi, Henan, Shandong, and other provinces

167. Remains of the smelting furnace at the Han dynasty iron foundry at Tieshenggou in Gongxian, Henan

168. Remains of the mixing pool at the Han dynasty iron foundry site at Tieshenggou in Gongxian, Henan

169. Liu Sheng's personal sword and its accessory jade ornaments, unearthed from the Han tomb in Mancheng

170. Iron knife with gold inlays, unearthed from the Han tomb in Mancheng

171. Iron knife and its gold-inlaid inscription, unearthed from a Han tomb in Cangshan, Shandong

172. Iron founding as depicted in a pictorial stone of Han dynasty discovered at Hongdaoyuan, in Tengxian, Shandong

7 Ceramics

GRAY POTTERY

In the realm of gray pottery, which already had a history stretching back to the Shang and Zhou periods, the Han potters attained an unsurpassed level of quality, basing their work on the achievements of the Warring States period. It is no exaggeration to say that in succeeding periods the techniques of gray pottery manufacture did not advance beyond the level attained by the Han potters. Their improvements in techniques of gray pottery firing are manifest in the pottery's color, which is gray; the firing, which was even and uniform; the firing temperature, which was above 1,000 degrees C; the clay ware, which is hard; as well as in the increase in the number of large vessels. As to the last named—that is, large vessels—this statement is borne out by pottery *weng* 瓮 from Han tombs in the vicinity of Luoyang, which often stand more than 50 cm in height, and *jiugang* 酒缸 from the Han tombs at Mancheng, which often reach more than 70 cm in height[1] (figs. 173, 174). Such aspects as hardness of ware and greater numbers of large vessels cannot be explained apart from improvements in the kilns. In 1956 more than twenty kilns from the Warring States, Western Han, and Eastern Han periods were excavated at the site of the old city of Wuji 午汲 in Wu'anxian 武安县, Hebei Province; a comparison of these kilns reveals that the Han kiln chambers are larger, their fire tunnels longer, and their chimneys much improved in design[2] (figs. 175–77).

The bodies of all of the rounded Han dynasty gray pottery vessels were turned on the potter's wheel. Vessel shapes are regular and their surfaces are relatively smooth. In general, with the exception of occasional parallel bowstring lines incised on the wheel and some localized incised geometric designs and stamped patterns, the vessels lack decoration and can be called "plain" (figs. 178–80). In the early Western Han period a few vessel types, such as the *weng* and the *guan*, were still occasionally decorated with faint cord patterns;[3] but from the middle Western Han period onward, few vessels have cord marks. Popular for more than three thousand years—from Neolithic times down to the early Han—the cord pattern finally died out (except in pottery roof tiles). The decline of the cord pattern must be considered one of the important characteristics of Han ceramics.

In Han tombs of all areas, pottery vessels with decoration painted in colors can be found. These wares also belong to the gray pottery family, the painted decoration having been applied after firing. Several pottery *hu* vessels have been discovered in Han tombs in Luoyang and a number of pottery *hu* and *pen* vessels have been recovered from the Han tombs at Mancheng.[4] The colors are bright and the painting refined; all are handsome works of art (figs. 181, 182). Since the decoration was applied only after the vessels were fired, however, the pigments tend to flake readily. These painted wares have been found only in tombs; not a single one has been recovered from a residential area. Thus, we can surmise that they were made for funerary use only. In addition to the painted wares, there are also gray pottery vessels of the Han period whose surfaces were coated with lacquer, in imitation of (true) lacquerware vessels. A number of gray pottery vessels coated with thick black or brown lacquer have been discovered in Han tombs in Yinqueshan 银雀山 in Linyi, Shandong Province; in Shuanggudui 双古堆 in Fuyang, Anhui Province; and in Dafentou 大坟头 in Yunmeng, Hubei Province.[5] All of these closely resemble lacquerware (figs. 183–85). A lacquer-coated pottery *hu* from the Han tomb at Dafentou is called a *xiuhua waweng* 鬃画瓦瓮, or "lacquer-painted pottery vessel," in the inventory tablet of that tomb.

In terms of shape, among the few early Western Han vessels with cord-marked decoration, such as the *weng* and *guan* mentioned above, are ones which have rounded bases[6] (fig. 186). From the middle Western Han period on, however, almost all of the pottery vessels have flat bottoms, with the exception of three-legged and ring-footed vessels. Already at some time before the advent of the Han dynasty, the pottery *li* 鬲—current from the Neolithic through the Shang and Western Zhou periods—had disappeared. The pottery *dou* 豆, which was popular in the Warring States period, was still frequently seen in the early Western Han, but not long thereafter it too disappeared. The pottery *fang* 钫 did not appear until in the late Warring States period; it was most popular in the Western Han period but is very seldom seen in the Eastern Han. In both the Western and the Eastern Han, the pottery *ding* and *zhong* are the most commonly encountered bronze-derived shapes. Even these, however, were seldom seen from the Wei and Jin periods onward, subsequent to the decline of bronze vessels. In addition to these, there is the *yadanhu* 鸭蛋壶, or "duck-egg jar," a vessel of unusual shape which appeared in the closing years of the Warring States period. It continued to be an important and popular shape in the Qin and early Western Han periods (fig. 187) but then disappeared in the middle Western Han. The forms of the various other members of the gray pottery family—such as the *weng*, *guan*, *he* 盒, *zun* 樽, *pen*, and *wan* 碗—also changed through time, never ceasing to evolve. In short, in Han dynasty gray ceramic wares, the types are numerous and the functions varied; their popularity was not restricted to the Yellow River valley or even to the North in general, but spread to all parts of the country. They were the mainstay of Han ceramics.

HARD POTTERY

At the same time, however, to the south of the Yangtze River, in that vast area including Guangdong, Guangxi, Hunan, Jiangxi, Fujian, Zhejiang, and southern Jiangsu, there was another common type of ceramic ware called *ying tao* 硬陶, or "hard pottery," coexisting with the gray pottery described above. These hard pottery pieces were made from a dense and strongly adhesive clay native to the South. In contrast to gray pottery, hard pottery vessels were fired at a higher temperature and the ceramic paste was much harder. On the surface of the vessels there is often a stamp-impressed checkerboard pattern, or there may be an incised wave or sawtooth pattern, in marked distinction to the plain, undecorated gray pottery vessels discussed above (figs. 188–91). Vessel types include the *weng*, *guan*, *hu*, *he*, and *wan*. But, in comparison with the various types of the gray pottery family, the hard pottery pieces have their distinctive style. In the Guangzhou area, for example, there is a type of *hu*, called the *pao hu* 匏壶, or "gourd-shaped jar," whose shape resembles a gourd (*pao-gua* 匏瓜) (fig. 192). And in Guangzhou and Changsha there are the *silianguan* 四联罐, or "four-linked *guan*," and *wulianguan* 五联罐, or "five-linked *guan*," in which four or five small *guan* vessels are connected (fig. 193). A number of vessels have loop handles at their shoulders or waists for tying cords. And there are also a few small *he* and *guan* with three short legs attached at their bases[7] (fig. 194). In short, the ceramic paste, the firing, the decoration, and the shapes of the vessels all reveal that this hard pottery from the Jiangnan ("South of the Yangtze") area inherited the traditions of the so-called "hard pottery with impressed geometric patterns" which had been developing in that area since late Neolithic times. In the Han dynasty it established itself as a separate tradition.

GLAZED POTTERY

A new invention of the Han dynasty potters was a ceramic ware with a thick brown or green glaze. This ware began to appear in the late middle Western Han period, especially around Guanzhong 关中 in Shaanxi Province and Luoyang in Henan Province.[8] Afterward it developed rapidly, and by the late Western Han period it was already common, being used throughout a larger area. By the Eastern Han not only had it spread throughout the entire Yellow River valley and the North of China in general, it was often seen in the Yangtze River valley as well. Generally speaking, the brown glazed ware appeared earlier, the green glazed ware later. However, the green glazed ware enjoyed great popularity during the Eastern Han and became much more widespread than the brown glazed ware. Its glaze contains a large amount of oxidized lead and its firing temperature was relatively low—no more than about 800° C—so it is often called "lead glazed" or "soft glazed" ware. And since it was popular mainly in the Yellow River valley and in the North of China, it can also be termed "Northern glazed ware". The types include the *ding* and *zhong* and a few other bronze-derived shapes. In addition, there are models of granaries, stoves, water wells, and towers, as well as images of such animals as the chicken and dog (figs. 195–97). For several reasons these are considered to have been made for funerary purposes only, not for actual use: first, the red core of this ware, usually of brick, is not too hard; second, the glaze readily flakes or deteriorates; and, especially, they were buried in tombs, almost never being found in residential areas.

Although China has had glazed ceramics ever since the Shang and Western Zhou periods, the glazes of those early wares are all light green ones fired at high temperatures, unrelated to the low-fired brown or green lead glazes discussed above. Thus, it was once assumed that the sudden appearance of lead glazes in the late middle Western Han period might be attributable to the influence of glazed wares from Western Asia that were transmitted to China at the time of Han Wu Di, who sent envoys to the West to establish relations and trade. It is widely known that, as early as the Assyrian empire and the Achaemenid empire of Persia, numerous types of glazed ceramic wares had appeared in the area of such modern West Asian countries as Iran and Iraq. By the time of the Parthians, who were contemporaneous with the Han dynasty, vessels with monochrome glazes in green or brown had gained currency; green glazes especially were often used for ceramic coffins. This Parthian glazed ceramic ware was also low-fired, and in appearance it bears a strong resemblance to that of the Han dynasty wares. The "Xi yu" section of the *Hanshu* relates that after the Han envoys crossed Central Asia and established ties with Parthia, Parthian articles of various types flowed into China. Thus, the appearance of lead glazes in the late middle Western Han period might be the result of influence from Parthian glazed wares. However, another school of thought believes that the Chinese must have invented lead glazes first, without reference to West Asian glazed wares, even though the latter and the Han dynasty lead wares are both low-fired; this is because the components of the glazes are not identical and the appearance of Chinese lead glazes might date as early as the Warring States period.[9] But, from a great number of Warring States and Western Han period tombs excavated since the Liberation, we know that lead glazed vessels may not necessarily have appeared so early as the Warring States period. An answer to the question of whether or not West Asian glazed ceramics and Han dynasty lead glazed wares are physically identical will have to await further research and analysis. Archaeological excavations have revealed that, although lead glazes continued to be used through the Wei, Jin, and succeeding periods, their quality declined significantly. The art of lead glazing was revived in the Tang dynasty, whereupon great progress was made and glorious achievements attained.

Hard pottery pieces coated with a thin layer of glaze have been discovered in many places in the South, but this glaze is quite different from the lead glazes of the Northern glazed wares. Whether yellow or green, the color is always light. The pieces are always very high-fired, and they belong to the family of celadon (or light green) glazed wares. Moreover, *ping* 瓶, or bottles with two ears or handles, have been found in late Western Han tombs in such places as Changsha in Hunan Province and Haizhou in Jiangsu Province.[10] The clay body of these is purplish brown in color and extremely hard. The green glaze on the neck and shoulder portions of these *ping* tends to be relatively thick. These pieces also belong to the Southern group of glazed wares (fig. 198). In addition, several identical glazed bottles, perhaps imported from the South, have been discovered in late Western Han tombs in Luoyang[11] (fig. 199). These hard-bodied glazed potteries, which were popular mainly in the South, are most certainly related to celadon glazed stonewares of the Wei and Jin periods. All characteristics considered, however, there is still a great distance between the glazed hard potteries of the South and the celadon glazed stonewares.

CELADON

It was formerly believed that true celadon, or green-glazed stoneware, first appeared in the state of Wu during the Three Kingdoms period and that the various types of green-glazed stoneware vessels unearthed from tombs in the area of Wuchang and Nanjing—the capital area of the state of Wu—dating to A.D. 227, 251, and 265 are standard examples of that ware.[12] From recent investigation, excavation, and research, however, we now believe that green-glazed stoneware vessels had already appeared as early as the late Eastern Han period, first in Zhejiang Province in the region of Shaoxing and Shangyu. Archaeologists have investigated many old kiln sites in the Shangyu area, among which are a number that belong to the Eastern Han; their shape and structure are those of the so-called dragon kilns. In this type of kiln, which was built on the side of a small hill, the kiln chamber is low and narrow, but quite long, a shape advantageous in circulating the air, and thus, in elevating the temperature. In the sherds unearthed at the kiln sites, the glaze is light green in color, and after careful scrutiny it shows all the characteristics of standard stoneware. A complete *sixiguan* 四系罐—that is, a *guan* with four loops for tying a cord—from the late Eastern Han period was obtained near one of the kiln sites, and it is typical of the green-glazed stoneware of the period.[13] Similar *sixiguan* have also been recovered from late Eastern Han tombs in Luoyang, Henan Province, and in Boxian, Anhui Province;[14] their shape implies that they also belong to the Southern group. Preserved in tombs of relatives of Cao Cao discovered in 1977 in Yuanbaokengcun and Dongyuancun, Boxian, are a large number of green-glazed stoneware vessels characterized by the *sixiguan*. Their shiny glaze and the absence of impurities in their bodies indicate that by the late Eastern Han the technique of manufacturing green-glazed stoneware vessels was already quite advanced.[15] In summary, the development of green-glazed stoneware must be considered another important mark of the creativity of the Han dynasty potters.

POTTERY TYPES

Another distinguishing characteristic of Han dynasty ceramics is the extreme variety of articles produced. In general, pottery containers of the Han dynasty can be divided into two categories. The first category—vessels derived from bronze shapes—includes the *ding, dou, zhong, fang,* and other such vessels; in general these shapes gradually declined in importance during the course of the Han dynasty. The second category—articles for daily use—includes the *weng, guan, ping, he, pen, wan,* and other such vessels; the types are varied and the shapes complex. In addition to these, there are a number of pottery articles generally for daily use, but not for food or drink and not for storage, articles such as tables, lamps, censers, and money jars (fig. 200–02). From the middle Western Han period onward, one of the most important characteristics of the potter's art was the prevalence of various types of pottery *mingqi* 明器, or burial articles, for funerary use—a reflection of changes in burial customs. The variety of types and the quantity of objects were staggering. The first to appear were models of granaries and stoves. They were already present in tombs of the early Western Han period, but they gained widespread popularity after the middle Western Han. Other models were also made—water wells, millstones, pigsties, towers, buildings for grinding grain, paddy fields, and fish ponds—as well as images of such animals as pigs, sheep, horses, dogs, chickens, and ducks. In short, almost any object that could be named was likely to have been crafted in clay. As time progressed, the types became more numerous, especially after the Eastern Han. Pottery figurines were also buried in great numbers. These pottery burial articles were often exquisitely crafted; for example, a number of lively, painted pottery figures on horseback have been unearthed from a Western Han tomb in Yangjiawan in Xianyang, Shaanxi Province.[16] (fig. 203). And pottery dogs and sheep (from an Eastern Han tomb in Baiquancun, Huixian, Henan Province) were sculpted with such verisimilitude that they must be called masterworks of the sculptor's art[17] (figs. 204, 205).

CERAMIC INDUSTRY

The most widely used articles of daily life were pottery. They are comparatively easy to make and most must have been made by small, privately operated workshops. But, during the Han dynasty, many local governments also owned their own workshops and pottery articles from them often have stamped marks. To give some examples: vessels stamped ''He ting 河亭 and ''He shi'' 河市,

unearthed from the site of the Han city of Henanxian in Luoyang (fig. 206); vessels stamped "Shan ting" 陝亭 and "Shan shi" 陝市, unearthed from Han tombs in Shanxian, Henan Province (figs. 207, 208); vessels marked "Han ting" 邯亭, recovered from Han-dynasty sites in Handan, Hebei Province (fig. 209); and vessels stamped "An ting" 安亭, unearthed from the site of the Han city at Anyi in Xiaxian, Shanxi Province[18] (fig. 210). From excavations at the site of the Han city of Henanxian we have learned that those vessels marked "He ting" are earlier and belong to the early Western Han, while those marked "He shi" are later, belonging to the late Western Han.[19] The characters "ting" 亭 and "shi" 市 in the marks refer respectively to the craft and commercial districts of the cities, which in Han times were under the supervision of the local governments. The marks just discussed indicate that these ceramic vessels were made by workshops belonging to the government agencies which supervised crafts and commerce.[20]

A piece of clay with an impressed seal reading "An cheng tao wei" 安城陶尉 provides the best insight into the government-controlled workshops[21] (fig. 211). The characters on the seal indicate that at that time Anchengxian in Runanjun (modern Zhengyang, Henan Province) had an official solely responsible for supervising the ceramic industry.[22] It is important to note that the last character in the seal, "wei" 尉, is a military title. That a military official was supervising the ceramic workshops most probably indicates that in the government-operated kilns many workers were convicted criminals who had been organized for work along military lines.

BRICKS

The manufacture of bricks and pottery roof tiles was an important aspect of the Han dynasty ceramic industry. In ancient China, the earliest bricks were exceptionally large, most of them measuring more than a meter in length. The interior of these bricks is hollow, so they are called *kongxinzhuan* 空心砖, that is, "hollow core bricks," or simply "hollow bricks" (fig. 212). They began to appear late in the Warring States period and were limited in area of use to the Central Plain. They were not used in building houses, but rather in constructing tombs. Hollow bricks were most commonly used in the Western Han period. More than half of the many Western Han tombs excavated in such areas as Baisha in Yuxian and Shaogou in Luoyang (both in Henan Province) were constructed with these hollow bricks.[23] Throughout the Western Han, hollow bricks were used in tombs only, their use not being further extended. And the area in which they were commonly used was also still limited to the region including present-day Henan, central Shaanxi, and southern Shanxi. Although the great majority are rectangular, a few of the Western Han hollow bricks are triangular or long and striplike, convenient shapes for constructing tomb entrances. The decorative motifs on the bricks were designed to enhance the tomb interiors, and they were impressed one by one with a stamp. In addition to geometric patterns, the motifs include numerous varieties of plants and animals as well as human figures, horses and carriages, and buildings.[24] With the coming of the Eastern Han, the use of hollow bricks suddenly declined and eventually died out.

True bricks appeared in early Western Han. They were one of the Han dynasty's great contributions to architecture. In contrast to the hollow bricks discussed above, they were all small, solid, and rectangular or square, the length usually ranging between 20 and 30 cm. We call them "small bricks" to distinguish them from the large, hollow bricks discussed above (fig. 213). They were used in all types of buildings, the rectangular bricks predominating over the square ones. Square bricks were used only for paving floors (fig. 214). In order to meet architectural needs, the size of the bricks had to be regularized. The length, width, and thickness of the rectangular bricks followed a standard formula, the width being one-half the length and the thickness one-fourth the width. Once the small bricks appeared, they were used extensively, quickly spreading to all parts of the country. As the findings from excavations at the Han city site at Henanxian in Luoyang reveal, small, rectangular bricks were used in constructing all types of dwellings and granaries and were also used in lining the walls of water wells[25] (fig. 215). At the Han site of Changan in Xi'an, they were used in constructing underground water drain holes.[26] In the Han dynasty, they were *not*, however, used for building city walls. In the Yellow River valley, small bricks were widely used in constructing tomb chambers as early as the middle and late Western Han period. And by the Eastern Han, their use in constructing tomb chambers had already spread to all parts of the country. With the introduction of small bricks, arch-building technique also became extensively used. Most rectangular bricks can be used in making arches. But in order to reinforce the top of the arch, Han builders used *xiexingzhuan* 楔形砖, that is, "wedge-shaped bricks" or voussoirs, and *zimuzhuan* 子母砖, or bricks with mortise and tenon arrangements, both of which were used only in constructing arches[27] (figs. 216, 217). Most of the rectangular bricks are undecorated, but there are some which have decorative motifs stamped on their sides. The patterns are usually geometric, though other patterns do occur. Most of the square bricks used in paving floors have stamped geometric patterns on their tops. In addition, in Eastern Han pictorial bricks, called *huaxiang zhuan* 画象砖, were also in use. Both square and rectangular bricks sometimes exhibit figural motifs showing scenes of Han social life and daily work. These were mainly used in constructing and decorating tomb chambers, and, in general, their use was limited to Sichuan Province[28] (fig. 218).

TILES

In China, pottery roof tiles, or *wa* 瓦, were in use long before bricks. Archaeological excavations have shown that pottery roof tiles had already appeared as early as the early Western Zhou period. A great many were recovered at the site of Kexingzhuang 客省庄 in the vicinity of Xi'an.[29] In the Spring and Autumn and Warring States periods the production and use of roof tiles spread rapidly; furthermore, the tiles were distinguished according to function into flattened ones and cylindrical ones. The flattened ones were placed on the lower level and the cylindrical ones overlapped them on top. In the Warring States period, the faces of the cylindrical tiles (also called eaves tiles, or *wadang* 瓦当) usually were semicircular. Some of the faces were left plain, but others were decorated. Each of the seven states of that period had its own distinctive style of decorating eaves tiles.

By the Han dynasty, the manufacture and use of pottery roof tiles had progressed greatly and technical improvements had occurred. Both flattened and cylindrical tiles were becoming regularized in shape as well as in stamped, cord-pattern decor. Finds from the excavations at the Han city site at Henanxian reveal that in early Western Han many eaves tiles were semicircular, but from the middle Western Han period onward semicircular tiles were gradually replaced by ones with full, circular faces.[30] During the Han dynasty, decoration on the faces of eaves tiles became uniform throughout China. From the great metropolitan cities of Changan and Luoyang to the small towns on the distant frontiers, the geometric patterns on the roof tiles all came to follow the *juanyun* or "scrolling cloud" motif, almost without exception (figs. 219–22). Moreover, from the Western Han period onward auspicious phrases such as "Chang le wei yang" 长乐未央 ("Profound happiness without end"), "Chang sheng wu ji" 长生无极 ("Long life without limit"), "Qian qiu wan sui" 千秋万岁 ("A thousand autumns, ten thousand years" or "everlasting life"), and "Yi nian wu jiang" 亿年无疆 ("A hundred million years without limit") were impressed on tiles as decoration (figs. 223–26). On eaves tiles found in the towns near the northern frontier other phrases such as "Shanyu tian jiang" 单于天降 ("Heaven-descended khan") and "Shanyu he qin" 单于和亲 ("The khan in quest of marriage with China") were applied[31] (figs. 227, 228). In Xihaijun 西海郡 (a commandery established by Wang Mang of the Xin 新 dynasty) in the vicinity of Qinghai Lake, eaves tiles have been found with impressed characters reading "Xihai anding" 西海安定 ("Pacified Xihai")[32] (fig. 229). During the reign of Wang Mang, designs of the so-called *sishen* 四神 or Four Deities—the Green Dragon, the White Tiger, the Red Bird, and the Black Turtle—appeared on eaves tiles intended for buildings of a ceremonial nature.[33]

It is important to note that in the Han dynasty eaves tiles with impressed character decoration were used for palaces and government buildings in the capital, Changan, and in the *san fu* 三辅—the three military districts contiguous with and immediately surrounding the capital (namely, Jingzhao 京兆, Fengyi 冯邑, and Fufeng 扶风). The characters used in the decoration indicate the names of the buildings. Many examples have been found. In the Shanglinyuan garden complex in the suburbs of Changan, for example, eaves tiles were stamped with characters reading "Shang Lin" 上林 (fig. 230). In the Yidang Hall 骀荡殿 and

Zhefeng Tower 折风阙 of the Xijianzhang Palace 西建章 in Changan, eaves tiles were stamped with characters reading "Yidang wan nian" 骀荡万年 ("Yidang ten thousand years") and "Zhefengque dang" 折风阙当 ("Eaves tile of Zhefengque"), respectively (figs. 231, 232). In the Huangshan Palace 黄山 in Huailixian 槐里县, You Fufeng 右扶风, eaves tiles were stamped "Huangshan" 黄山 (fig. 233). In the Lanchi 兰池 Palace in Weichengxian 渭城县, You Fufeng 右扶风, eaves tiles were stamped "Lanchigong dang" 兰池宫当 ("Eaves of Lanchigong") (fig. 234). And in the Zongzheng 宗正 government building, within the city of Changan, eaves tiles were stamped with "Zongzhengguan dang" 宗正官当 ("Tile of the Zongzheng official [building]")[34] (fig. 235). The examples cited above indicate that at that time the government had established special ceramic workshops to supply bricks and roof tiles for use in palaces and government buildings. In the excavations of the Han capital at Changan, there were found a number of eaves tiles impressed with characters reading "Dusikong wa" 都司空瓦 ("Tile of Dusikong") (fig. 236), as well as tiles impressed with characters reading "Dusikong" 都司空, "Baocheng Dusikong" 保城都司空, "Youkong" 右空, and "Du Jian Ping sannian" 都建平三年 (a date equivalent to 4 B.C.), "Du Yuan Shou ernian" 都元寿二年 (equivalent to 1 B.C.), and "Du Yuan Shi wunian" 都元始五年 (equivalent to A.D. 5) (figs. 237–39). Here, the character du 都 is an abbreviation of Dusikong 都司空, the name of a government bureau which was changed to Baocheng dusikong 保城都司空 for a brief period during the reign of Wang Mang. It can be concluded, therefore, that the manufacture of these tiles was supervised by officials from the Dusikong bureau of the Zongzhengqing 宗正卿 and by officials from the Zuosikong 左司空 and Yousikong 右司空 of the Shaofuqing 少府卿.[35] According to the Hanshu, The Dusikong, Zuosikong, and Yousikong were bureaus in charge of both construction and convicted criminals. Since these bureaus supervised the manufacture of bricks and tiles, the evidence from the Hanshu reveals that, in the Han dynasty, numerous prisoners were employed in the government-operated ceramic workshops.

173. Large pottery urn unearthed from Han tomb in Luoyang (height: 50 cm)

174. Large pottery urn unearthed from Han tomb in Luoyang (height: 64 cm)

175. Pottery kiln of Han dynasty excavated from
the site of the old city of Wuji in Wu'anxian, Hebei

176. Pottery kiln of Han dynasty excavated from
the site of the old city of Wuji in Wu'anxian, Hebei

177. Pottery kiln of Han dynasty excavated from the site of the old city of Wuji in Wu'anxian, Hebei

178. Gray pottery jar unearthed from Han tomb in Luoyang

179. Gray pottery jar unearthed from Han tomb in Luoyang

180. Gray pottery ding-tripod unearthed from Han
tomb in Luoyang

181. Painted pottery jar unearthed from Han
tomb in Luoyang

182. Painted pottery basin unearthed from Han tomb
in Mancheng

183. Lacquered pottery jar unearthed from Han
tomb at Yinqueshan in Linyi, Shandong

184. Lacquered pottery ding-tripod unearthed from Han tomb
at Yinqueshan in Linyi, Shandong

185. Lacquered pottery box unearthed from Han tomb at Yinqueshan in Linyi, Shandong

186. Round-based pottery urn unearthed from Western Han tomb in Guanghua, Hubei

187. "Duck-egg jar" unearthed from Han tomb in Xinxiang, Henan

188. Hard pottery jar with impressed designs, unearthed from Han tomb in Mawangdui, Changsha

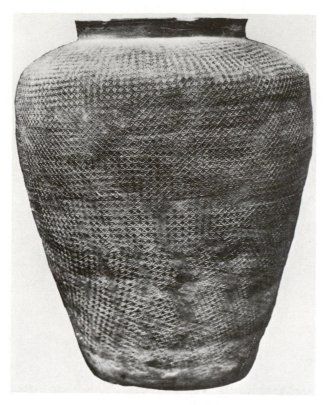

189. Hard pottery jar with impressed designs, unearthed from Han tomb in Shaoxing, Zhejiang

190. Hard pottery jar with impressed designs, unearthed from Han tomb in Shaoxing, Zhejiang

191. Hard pottery jar with impressed designs, unearthed from Han tomb in Shaoxing, Zhejiang

192. Gourd-shaped jar unearthed from Han tomb in Guangzhou

193. Jar with four interconnecting parts, unearthed from Han tomb in Guangzhou

194. Pottery jar with three legs, unearthed from Han tomb in Guangzhou

195. Pottery jar with green glaze of Han dynasty, in the collection of the Palace Museum

196. Pottery model of granary with green glaze, unearthed from Han tomb in Shaanxi

197. Pottery model of storied building with green glaze, unearthed from Han tomb in Lingbao, Henan

198. Hard pottery jar with green glaze and purple core, unearthed from Han tomb in Changsha

199. Same as fig. 198, from Luoyang

200. Pottery lamp unearthed from Han tomb in Luoyang

201. Pottery incense burner unearthed from Han tomb in Luoyang

202. Pottery money jar unearthed from Han tomb in Luoyang

203. Pottery human figure on horseback, unearthed from Han tomb at Yangjiawan in Xianyang, Shaanxi

204. Pottery dog unearthed from Han tomb at Baiquan, in Huixian, Henan

205. Pottery sheep from same site as fig. 204

206. The names "He ting" and "He shi" stamped on pottery unearthed from the site of the Han town of Henanxian in Luoyang

207. The name "Shan ting" stamped on pottery unearthed from Han tomb in Shanxian, Henan

208. The name "Shan shi" stamped on pottery unearthed from Han tomb in Shanxian, Henan

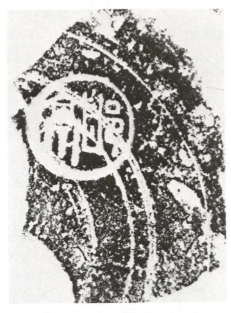

209. The name "Han ting" stamped on pottery unearthed from a Han dynasty site in Handan, Hebei

210. The name "An ting" stamped on pottery unearthed from a Han dynasty site in Xiaxian, Shanxi

211. Clay seal impressed with the inscription "An cheng tao wei"

212. Hollow bricks of Han dynasty, unearthed in Henan

213. Small, rectangular brick of Han dynasty, unearthed from Han tomb in Luoyang

214. Square bricks unearthed at the site of the Han city of Changan in Xi'an

215. Granary built with small, rectangular bricks, excavated at the site of the Han town of Henanxian in Luoyang

216. Wedge-shaped brick unearthed from Han tomb in Luoyang

217. Bricks with tenons and mortises, unearthed from Han tomb in Luoyang

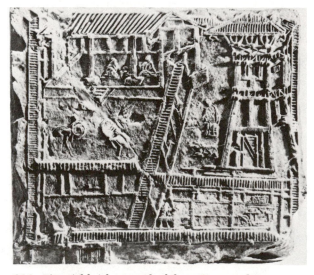

218. Pictorial brick unearthed from Han tomb in Chengdu, Sichuan

219. Eaves tile with "scrolling cloud" design, unearthed from the site of the Han city of Changan in Xi'an

220. Eaves tile with "scrolling cloud" design, unearthed from the site of the Han city of Changan in Xi'an

221. Eaves tile with "scrolling cloud" design, unearthed from the site of the Han city of Changan in Xi'an

222. Eaves tile with "scrolling cloud" design, unearthed from the site of the Han city of Changan in Xi'an

223. Eaves tile with the inscription "Chang le wei yang," unearthed at the site of the Han city of Changan in Xi'an

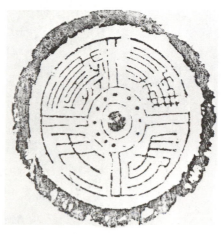

224. Eaves tile from the same site as fig. 223, with the inscription "Chang sheng wu ji"

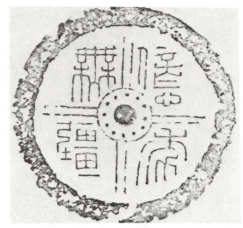

225. Eaves tile from the same site as fig. 223, with the inscription "Qian qiu wan sui"

226. Eaves tile from the same site as fig. 223, with the inscription "Yi nian wu jiang"

227. Eaves tile with the inscription "Shanyu tian jiang," unearthed from Han tomb in Baotou, Inner Mongolia

228. Eaves tile with the inscription "Shanyu he qin," unearthed from Han tomb in Baotou, Inner Mongolia

229. Eaves tile with the inscription "Xihai anding yuanxing yuan nian zuo dang," unearthed at a Han dynasty site in Haiyan, Qinghai

230. Eaves tile inscribed with the name "Shang Lin," unearthed at the site of the Han city of Changan in Xi'an

231. Eaves tile with the inscription "Yidang wan nian"

232. Eaves tile with the inscription "Eaves Tile of Zhefengjue"

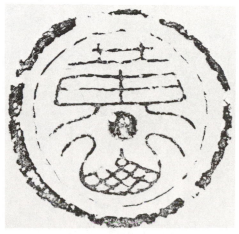

233. Eaves tile with the inscription "Huangshan"

234. Eaves tile with the inscription "Eaves Tile of Lanchigong"

235. Eaves tile with the inscription "Eaves Tile of the Zongzheng Official," unearthed at the site of the Han city of Changan in Xi'an

236. Eaves tile from the same site as fig. 235, with the inscription "Tile of Dusikong"

237. Tile from the same site as fig. 235, with the inscription "Shi Jian Guo Si Nian Baocheng Dusikong"

238. Tile from the same site as fig. 235, with the inscription, "Du Jian Ping sannian"

239. Tile from the same site as fig. 235, with the inscription, "Du Jian Ping sannian"

8 Tombs—I

Han dynasty tombs have been encountered in the course of industrial or agricultural construction as well as during archaeological investigations and excavations with great frequency. This stems from several factors. First, the Western and Eastern Han dynasties lasted for more than four hundred years. During that time China was a unified empire, its political situation relatively stable, its economy relatively prosperous, and its population dense. Han landowners and officials were fond of furnishing their graves richly; consequently, in their graves there are large numbers of many kinds of objects. Burial chambers, furthermore, were often built of brick and stone, which helped to preserve the remains. We estimate that since the Liberation at least ten thousand Han dynasty tombs have been found as a result of archaeological work throughout the country. These discoveries have made possible a relatively good understanding of the mortuary institutions and customs of the Han dynasty.

CHARACTERISTICS OF HAN TOMB CONSTRUCTION

Compared with tombs of previous periods, Han dynasty tombs have many distinctive features. Prior to the Han, during the Neolithic, Shang, and Zhou periods, tombs were mostly placed in rectangular earthen pits. Of varying sizes and depths, these pits were excavated from the ground downward and are referred to as "vertical pits." Beginning in middle Western Han in the Yellow River valley the custom originated of digging the burial chamber laterally or horizontally underground, resulting in "horizontal pits." In the Western Han period, large hollow bricks were used to build the burial chamber, mainly in the Central Plains area. In the Eastern Han, throughout China, in the Central Plains and in the northern and the southern border regions, small bricks were universally used to build a burial chamber with arches and a domed top. Tombs of stone began in the Eastern Han. In addition, during both Western and Eastern Han, horizontal burial chambers were excavated into mountain cliffs in some regions. In short, the principal formal and structural features of Han dynasty tombs that distinguish them from those of earlier periods are, first, the use of horizontal pits for burial and, second, the use of bricks and stones for the construction of the tomb chamber. These features came from an effort to imitate the houses of the living.

175

It should be noted that such changes in tombs began in the middle Western Han period, starting in the Yellow River valley and then spreading throughout the country. Previously, in early Western Han, members of the ruling class were still entombed in the vertical pit graves with wooden encasements that continued from the Warring States period. In fact, this older style of tomb, known as the "vertical pit–wooden chamber grave," continued to be built into late Western Han or even early Eastern Han in the Yangtze River valley and in the southern and northern border regions.

Examples of these vertical pit–wooden chamber graves of early and middle Western Han are the tombs found at Mawangdui (Changsha), Fenghuangshan (Jiangling), and at Dabaotai 大葆台 (Beijing). Construction of the coffins and wooden chambers in these graves still followed the older customs of the Zhou dynasty. Both *Zhuangzi* 庄子 ("Tianxiapian" 天下篇) and *Xunzi* 荀子 ("Lilunpian" 礼论篇) describe burial caskets of varying degrees of elaborateness, as follows: "The caskets of the emperor are of seven layers; of the feudal lords, five layers; of the Da Fu 大夫 class, three layers; and of the Shi 士 class, two layers." Han tomb number one of Mawangdui was the tomb of the wife of Li Cang 利苍, marquis of Dai 軑, and her caskets consisted of four coffins and one wooden encasement, the prescribed number for a feudal lord (fig. 240). In Han tomb number 168 at Fenghuangshan in Jiangling was buried a certain Sui Shaoyan 遂少言, a Da Fu of the fifth rank. His rank was the ninth grade on a scale of twenty, corresponding to that of a county magistrate, and his grave contained two coffins and one wooden encasement (fig. 241). Tomb number 1 of Dabaotai in Beijing was probably the tomb of the prince of Yan. What survives of his caskets appears to be the remains of five coffins and two outer encasements, a burial which corresponds to the grade of emperor, a full grade higher than a feudal lord (fig. 242). It goes without saying that rules for burial according to rank could not have been strictly followed at all times. Li Cang, the marquis of Dai, who was buried in tomb number 2 of Mawangdui, was himself buried within two coffins and one outer encasement.[1]

Good examples of the new horizontal pit graves that appeared in middle Western Han dynasty are the tombs of Prince Jing of Zhongshan 中山靖王, found in Mancheng, Hebei, and of Prince Lu of Qufu 曲阜 in Shandong.[2] In both cases the tomb chambers were caves dug into cliffs, and the caves were divided into several compartments, such as side chambers, frontal hall, and rear hall. In the tomb of Liu Sheng, Prince Jing of Zhongshan, the southern side chamber was for horses and carriages (fig. 243). The northern side chamber was for storage, and large numbers of pottery vessels were placed there (fig. 244). The front hall is of large dimensions, and in it were placed drapes and the principal grave goods (fig. 245). The rear hall was an interior room where the coffin was placed. Within the front hall and the side chambers, houses made of timber had been erected, with tiles on the roofs. In the rear hall, stone slabs had been used to build another house, which had two stone doors. In short, the form and the structure of the tomb imitated residential architectures above ground: thus the term, "underground palaces" *dixia gongdian* 地下宫殿[3] (fig. 246). In this new kind of tomb, the coffins also assumed new settings. In fact, the wooden outer encasements in the tomb of Liu Sheng were basically different from those of Zhou tombs, for they were no longer linings of pits and became in fact outer caskets. It follows also that the number of casket layers is no longer an indication of the status of the master of the grave. Since this new burial custom adopted by Liu Sheng and other nobles is evidently different from the older burial customs continued from the Zhou dynasty as adopted by Li Cang and other nobles, some scholars have maintained that Liu Sheng represented the Legalists, who were progressive and innovative, and that Li Cang represented the Confucians, who were conservative. Actually, tomb customs cannot be related to the Legalist-Confucian struggles; Liu Sheng was not a Legalist, and Li Cang was not necessarily a Confucian.

Another manifestation of the new burial customs of the Han dynasty is the emergence of hollow-brick tombs in the Central Plains area (fig. 247). The Han dynasty hollow-brick tombs differed from the hollow-brick tombs of the Warring States period in that the Han tombs were generally built within horizontal pit caves. These tombs were usually of moderate scale and possibly belonged to members of the middle and small landowner class. In early Western Han, the burial chamber of the hollow-brick tomb was rectangular, shaped like the wooden chamber that it replaced. In middle and late Western Han, the typical hollow-brick tomb was shaped more like a house, with gabled roof and door-shaped front wall [4] (fig. 248). The hollow bricks were often stamped with designs and scenes which constituted the interior decoration of the burial chamber. Polychromic murals begin to appear in some of the tombs. A hollow-brick tomb found in Luoyang has murals with images of sun and moon, of Green Dragon, White Tiger, and Red Bird, and of Fu Xi and Nü Wa[5] (figs. 249–51). Another tomb found in Luoyang not only has sun, moon, and stars depicted in its murals, some of its pictures even depict historical stories such as "Using two peaches to kill three gentlemen," and "The banquet at Hongmen"[6] (figs. 252–54). The mural scenes and stone engravings in tombs of the Eastern Han dynasty develop even further these sky charts and representations of the Four Deities, myths, and historical stories.

Sometime after the middle Western Han, tombs with arches built of small bricks began to appear in the Central Plains and in central Shaanxi; these we refer to as "brick chamber tombs" to distinguish them from the hollow-brick tombs. As soon as it appeared on the scene, the brick chamber tomb became rapidly adopted everywhere, replacing the hollow-brick tombs in the Central Plains and replacing the vertical pit—wooden chamber graves in the Yangtze River valley and the southern and northern border regions. By Eastern Han dynasty, brick chamber tombs were the prevailing form of burial throughout the country (figs. 255, 256). The brick chamber tombs of high nobles—such as the tomb of Prince Jing of Pengcheng 彭城靖王 in Xuzhou, Jiangsu, and the tomb of Prince Jian of Zhong-shan 中山简王, in Dingxian, Hebei—are of large scale and complex construction, with a layout similar to the mansions these princes inhabited during their lifetimes.[7] Some of the brick chamber tombs also were decorated with frescoes, the well-known ones including those found in the family tomb of the marquis of Fuyang 浮阳侯, in Wangdu 望都, Hebei, and in the family tomb of Hongnong Taishou 弘农太守 in Mixian 密县, Henan. The Wangdu tomb has murals depicting the various officials and attendants of the tomb master (fig. 257), causing the chamber to look like his official quarters.[8] The Mixian tomb has murals depicting processions of horses and carriages and scenes of banquets and entertainments, fully attesting to the luxurious life of the tomb master[9] (fig. 258).

A huge brick chamber tomb was excavated in 1972 at Holingor in Inner Mongolia. The master of the grave was a military colonel of the Wuhuan district, and the murals in the tomb mainly illustrate the history of his official career through scenes of horse and carriage processions. From the inscriptions that accompany the various segments of the murals, we know that he was a native of Dingxiangjun 定襄郡, where he qualified for officialdom by being selected as a Xiaolian 孝廉 candidate. Then he was assigned various administrative positions until he finally reached the military colonelcy of the Wuhuan district. The murals show scenes of the various towns in which he had worked—their streets, official buildings, warehouses, and markets—and various activities in which he had engaged in during his career (figs. 259–61). At the time, high officials also were owners of large manors. In the murals is a scene of a manor, depicting such productive activities as cultivating fields, preparing tree nurseries, raising cattle, feeding animals and picking mulberry leaves. Possibly the occupant-to-be of the tomb had retired to his manor, but in any event the manor was in all likelihood his home. The Holingor murals were indeed an unprecedented discovery, fully exemplifying such murals and their objectives and significance.[10]

Beginning in the early Eastern Han, a new kind of tomb known as the "stone chamber grave" came upon the scene, and it became even more popular after the middle Eastern Han. The burial chamber was constructed with neatly dressed stones on which were engraved designs and scenes—thus the name, the "tomb with pictorial stones" *hua xiang shi mu* 画象石墓 (fig. 262). Seen mostly in Shandong, northern Jiangsu, Henan, and northern Hubei, these tombs also occur in northern Shaanxi and western Shanxi. During the past centuries many of them were destroyed and the stone reliefs scattered about. Since Liberation a few have been archaeologically excavated. Some of these, such as the Han tombs in Tanghe (Henan) and in Anqiu, Cangshan, and Yinan (Shandong), are preserved well enough to show that again the layout of the burial chamber imitated the house of the tomb master in his real life[11] (fig. 263). The most obvious case is the Han tomb in Yinan, excavated in 1954. A scene in the tomb depicts the courtyard house in which the master lived during his lifetime, and the layout of the tomb is identical with the layout of the house (fig. 264). Many scenes are depicted in the engravings, all pertaining to scenes of his life and his career history. The master of the Yinan tomb was probably a military general. Above the tomb entrance, in a most prominent location, a battle scene was engraved in fine detail. In it a squad of Han dynasty foot soldiers is in the act of defeating mounted and foot soldiers from a northern nomadic group. The occupant of the tomb, standing in a carriage, is seen behind the soldiers supervising the battle. Obviously this must have been the most memorable scene in his career[12] (figs. 265–67). The Yinan tomb with stone reliefs and the fresco tomb of Holingor may be called the two best examples of the tomb art of Eastern Han.

During the Eastern Han period, many of the brick chamber tombs in the Sichuan region had a kind of pictorial brick fitted on to the walls of the burial chamber. The pictorial bricks are square or rectangular; the square ones are found mostly near Chengdu, but the rectangular ones are widely seen. The designs were either stamped on the bricks before they were dried or painted after the bricks were fired. They depict such life scenes as lectures, banquets, musicales and dances, and carriage processions. Such productive activities as harvesting, hunting, mulberry-leaf picking, taro digging, pestling of rice, wine making, and salt making are also shown—the latter scenes full of local flavor (figs. 268–72). These pictorial bricks were mass-produced, and identical scenes are often seen at tombs in different places. For this reason, it is clear that the scenes shown on these bricks were not directly related to the individual occupants of tombs.[13] In addition, in various places in Sichuan there were many cliff burials during the Eastern Han period. Excavated into high mountain cliffs, these were of varying scales and sizes. Sometimes several tens of tombs have been found clustered together, forming a large cemetery.[14]

BURIAL MOUNDS

All that has been described above pertains to the underground portion of the burial chamber. The portion of the tomb above ground in Han tombs also has distinctive features. During the Shang and Western Zhou periods, even large tombs were not covered with an earthen mound above ground. As *Li ji* 礼记 ("Tan gong" 檀弓) states, "In the past the tombs were without mounds." Earthen mounds began to be built in the Warring States period, such as the mounds over some of the Chu tombs in Jiangling in Hubei,[15] but they were not yet widely distributed. But during the Han dynasty, earthen mounds became universal. The tombs of the emperors and the upper nobility were, *Yan tie lun* records, covered with accumulated earth as tall as a hill. To build them required a vast outlay of manpower and much time.

FUNERARY SHRINES

In the Warring States period funerary shrines were built atop the tombs of some feudal lords. The Wei 衛 tomb at Guweicun 固围村 in Huixian 辉县, Henan, and the tomb of the king of Zhongshan in Pingshan, Hebei, are examples.[16] In the Han dynasty, funerary shrines and monumental towers became very popular, especially in Eastern Han. In his *Shuijingzhu* 水经注, Li Daoyuan 郦道元 makes mention of many Han funerary shrines and monumental towers. Since most of these were built of masonry, some survive to this day. The better-known ones are the Guo lineage shrine at Xiaotangshan 孝堂山 in Feicheng 肥城, Shandong; the Wu 武 lineage shrine and monumental tower in Jiaxiangxian 嘉祥县 (now Jining 济宁); and the funerary tower at Wang Zhizi's 王稚子 tomb in Xindu 新都 and that at Gao Yi's 高颐 tomb in Ya'an 雅安, both in Sichuan[17] (fig. 273). In front of some of these tombs were erected stone sculptures. Stone animal sculptures occur in front of the Wu family tomb and the Gao Yi tomb mentioned above, and additional finds have been made in recent years.[18]

STELES

Beginning in Eastern Han, a stone stele was sometimes erected in front of the tomb, with inscriptions describing the birth and death dates of the persons buried and their life histories.[19] Tomb inscriptions, the preparation of which became popular in Wei and Jin dynasties, were a further development of the Han dynasty tomb steles. The earliest tomb inscriptions, such as the inscribed bricks of 287 and the inscribed stone of 297, both found in Luoyang, were very similar to Han tomb steles in shape.[20] The difference was that the Han tomb steles were large and placed on the ground, whereas tomb inscriptions were written on small tablets placed inside the tomb.

CASKETS

In ancient China, *guan* 棺 and *kuo* 椁, or inner and outer caskets, were both used, and this practice continued into the early Western Han in the vertical pit–wooden chamber graves of that time. However, as stated earlier, in the horizontal pit graves (after the middle of Western Han), and especially in the brick chamber and the stone chamber tombs (of the Eastern Han), the burial chamber itself functioned as an outer casket. It may be referred to as the brick *kuo* or the stone *kuo* (as against the wooden *kuo*), and within the chamber there was only an inner casket but no *kuo* or outer casket. The coffins themselves are of wood and are mostly wider and higher in the front than in the rear—except for the coffins found in wooden chambers, which are of equal width and height from front to rear. In the Western Han dynasty the wooden coffins were put together with tenons and mortises, and the lid was secured onto the coffin by means of hourglass-shaped wooden wedges placed into notches on both lid and coffin, but in the Eastern Han iron nails were universally used. Liu Xi 刘熙 of the Eastern Han said, in his *Shiming* 释名 ("Shi sang zhi" 释丧制): "in the past the coffins were not nailed." The coffins for the nobility were beautifully and elaborately made, as illustrated by the two lacquered coffins in tomb number one at Mawangdui. *Qianfulun* 潜夫论 ("Fuchipian" 浮侈篇) states that "to make a coffin required the labor of thousands and tens of thousands." This has indeed been borne out[21] (figs. 274, 275).

FUNERARY BANNERS

Han practice continued the Zhou custom of using a funerary banner in funerary processions. At the time of burial the banner would be placed over the coffin. The typical banner is over 2 m long, identical with the length of the coffin. These banners have been found at tomb number one of Mawangdui, Changsha, Hunan, number 3 of Mawangdui, and number 9 at Jinqueshan 金雀山 in Linyi, Shandong. The Mawangdui banners are slightly wider at the top, forming a T shape (fig. 276), and the Jinqueshan banner is rectangular, with the top and bottom of equal width. They are all of silk and are painted with fine colored pictures. The picture is divided into three sections, depicting, from top to bottom, heaven, man's world, and the underworld. Both heaven and the underworld are represented by mythological images; the heaven picture has sun, moon, and sometimes stars, and the sun has a golden crow and the moon has a toad and a white rabbit, and sometimes a picture of Changeh, the goddess of the moon (fig. 277). The underworld picture shows various aquatic animals, representing an aquatic palace at the bottom of the sea. As for man's world, the picture depicts scenes from daily life and also a portrait of the master of the tomb (fig. 278). The three banners from Mawangdui and Jinqueshan have elaborate pictures and are valued as art objects. Similar, but much coarser, banners have been found in the Han tombs at Mozuizi in Wuwei, Gansu; some were made of silk, others hemp. All were covering coffins. Some of them have no pictures, others were painted only with the sun and the moon, but all bear inscriptions containing the names and the homeplaces of the masters of the tombs (fig. 279), the inscriptions substituting for the portraits of the silk paintings.[23] Presumably the funerary banners were widely used in Han dynasty funerary rituals, but few of them have survived because they were made of perishable materials such as silk and hemp. They did survive at Mawangdui and Mozuizi because the former tombs had special preservation conditions and the latter tombs were in an especially dry region.

JADE SHROUDS

The emperor and nobles of Han were buried wearing jade shrouds. Made from small square jade plates these shrouds had small holes at the corners, through which gold, silver, or copper threads were strung in order to piece them together to form shrouds with gold, silver, or copper threads.[24] Since Liberation, more than ten jade shrouds have been discovered from Han dynasty tombs, and five have been completely restored. Of the five, two were found at Mancheng, Hebei; one was worn by Liu Sheng, the prince Jing of Zhongshan of the Western Han, and one by his wife Dou Wan (fig. 280). One was worn by Liu Xing, the prince Xiao of Zhongshan of the Western Han; it was found in Dingxian, Hebei (fig. 281). One was worn by Liu Gong, the prince Jing of Pengcheng, of Eastern Han; it was found in Xuzhou, Jiangsu (fig. 282). The last was worn by a Mr. Cao of late Eastern Han, a lineage relative of Cao Cao; it was found in Boxian 亳县, Anhui.[25]

The two Mancheng shrouds are excellent examples. The Liu Sheng shroud consisted of 2,498 jade plates and used 1,100 grams of golden threads, and the Dou Wan shroud used 2,160 jade plates and 700 grams of golden threads. The man-power and wealth represented by these figures are astonishing. Combining evidence from archaeological finds and historical records, we believe that Western Han jade shrouds used golden threads, and Eastern Han jade shrouds used golden, silver, or copper threads. According to *Xu Hanshu* ("Li Yi zhi"), for the emperor golden threads were used, for imperial princes and first-generation feudal lords, silver threads, and for others, copper threads. The Dingxian shroud used copper threads gilded in gold[26], which probably corresponded to silver in quality. So far the earliest complete jade shrouds to be discovered are the two from Mancheng, but shroud fragments have occurred in tomb number five at Yangjia-wan, in Xianyang, Shaanxi, which dates from Wen Di or Jing Di[27]. It appears that jade shrouds began to be used in early Western Han, and their use continued until the end of Eastern Han. The latest shroud is the one found in Boxian, worn by Mr. Cao. It is recorded in *Sanguozhi* 三国志 ("Wei zhi") that Cao Pi, Emperor Wen Di of Wei, banned the use of jade shrouds in A.D. 222. Archaeological excavations have failed to uncover any shroud remains from Wei or Jin sites. The use of the jade shroud seems clearly confined to the Han dynasty. The Eastern Han court occa-sionally presented jade shrouds as gifts to the chiefs of minority groups. It is stated in *Weizhi* ("Fu Yu zhi") that the king of Fu Yu was buried in a jade shroud and that the Han court stored a jade shroud at Xuantujun 玄菟郡, where it would be picked up when the king of Fu Yu died. When Sima Yi 司马懿 exterminated Gongsun Yuan 公孙渊 of Liaodong, a jade shroud was found in the warehouse at Xuantujun. This incident happened after the ban by Cao Pi. Perhaps this was an exceptional situation involving policy toward minority groups. The purpose of using jade for funerary shrouds was to preserve the body. *Hou Hanshu* (the "Biography of Liu Penzi") claimed that the bodies in jade shrouds in the imperial mausoleums of the Western Han were all so well preserved that they looked like living people. This is, of course, not true. Cao Pi was perhaps more on the mark when he said, in banning the practice, that the use of jade shrouds was a "stupid and vulgar act."

INVENTORIES OF GRAVE GOODS

Many early Western Han tombs, such as the Han tombs at Mawangdui in Chang-sha and at Fenghuangshan in Jiangling, have yielded books of bamboo slips that give an inventory of the grave goods—their names and quantities. These are called *qian ce* 遣策, or inventory slips, from the phrase, "inscribe the grave goods on slips," in *Yi li* ("Jixili")[28] (fig. 283). Within some other Han tombs, such as the ones at Dafentou in Yunmeng, Hubei, and the tombs of Huo He and Shi Qi Yao in Haizhou, Jiangsu, rectangular wooden tablets were found, on which are inscribed the names and quantities of the grave goods.[29] These were called *feng fang* 赗方, or inventory tablets, following the statement, "inscribe grave goods on tablets" in *Yi li* ("Jixili") (fig. 284). By consulting these inventories, archaeologists may be able to achieve an understanding of the names and uses of a variety of objects from the Han era.

240. Top view of wooden chamber of Han tomb
number 1 at Mawangdui, Changsha

241. Top view of wooden chamber of Han tomb
number 168 at Fenghuangshan, Jiangling

242. View of the entire burial chamber of the Han tomb at Dabaotai, Beijing

243. The southern side chamber and remains
of carriages and horses in the tomb of Liu Sheng in
Mancheng

244. The northern side chamber with its furnished pottery vessels, in the tomb of Liu Sheng in Mancheng

245. The anterior chamber of Liu Sheng's tomb in Mancheng

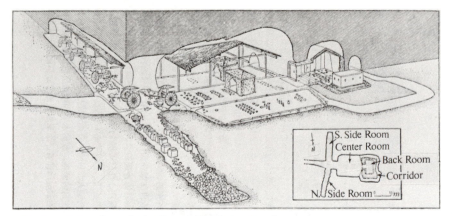

Within the diagram labels:

N
S. Side Room
Center Room
Back Room
Corridor
N. Side Room   5 m

246. Reconstruction of Liu Sheng's tomb in Mancheng

247. Hollow-brick tomb of Western Han, excavated at Shaogou, Luoyang

248. Structure of the top of the hollow-brick tomb of Western Han, excavated at Shaogou, Luoyang

249. Green dragon and white tiger in the murals of a Han tomb (tomb of Pu Qianqiu) in Luoyang

250. Portrait of Fu Xi in the mural of a Han tomb
(tomb of Pu Qianqiu) in Luoyang

251. Portrait of Nü Wa in the mural of a Han tomb
(tomb of Pu Qianqiu) in Luoyang

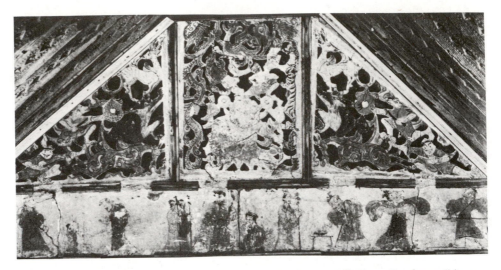

252. Mural scene depicting the story "Using Two Peaches to Kill Three Gentlemen" in a Han tomb in Luoyang

253. "The Banquet at Hongmen" (right half) in the mural of a Han tomb in Luoyang

254. "The Banquet at Hongmen" (left half) in the mural of a Han tomb in Luoyang

255. Brick chamber tomb of Eastern Han, excavated in Luoyang

256. Structure of the top of a brick chamber tomb of Eastern Han, excavated in Luoyang

257. Subordinates, servants, and other human figures in the wall painting of a Han tomb in Wangdu, Hebei

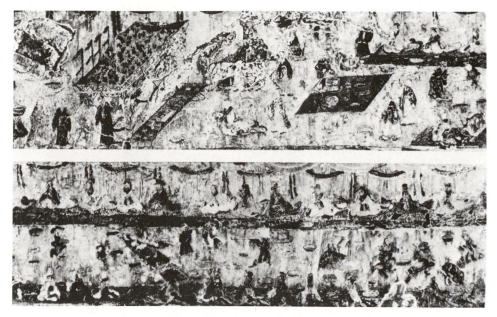

258. A feast and a performance in wall painting of a Han tomb at Dahuting in Mixian, Henan

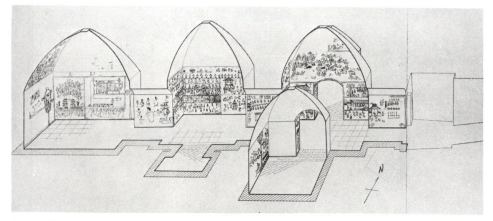

259. Diagram of the chamber of the Han tomb in Holingor, Inner Mongolia

260. Scene of Ningcheng (partial) in the wall painting of Han tomb in Holingor, Inner Mongolia

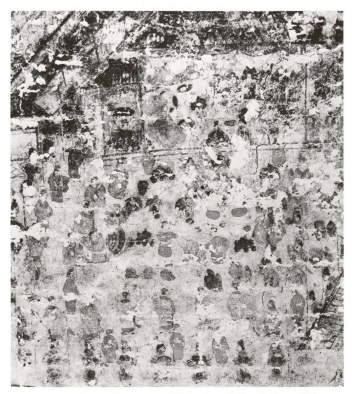

261. Scene of Ningcheng (partial) in the wall painting of Han tomb in Holingor, Inner Mongolia

262. Structure of the burial chamber of the Han tomb in Anqiu, Shandong

263. The doors of the Han tomb in Yinan, Shandong

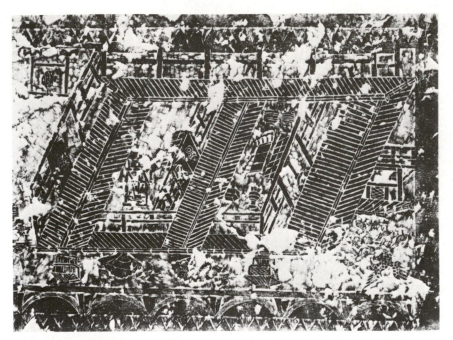

264. Rubbing of the courtyard scene in the stone engravings in the Han tomb in Yinan, Shandong

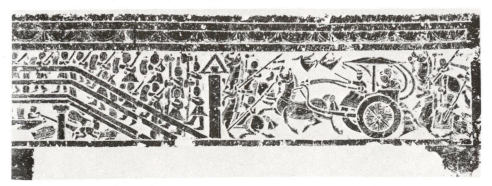

265. Rubbing of the right third of the battle scene in the stone engravings in the Han tomb in Yinan, Shandong

266. Rubbing of the middle third of the battle scene in fig. 265

267. Rubbing of the left third of the battle scene in fig. 265

268. Pictorial brick depicting a lecture scene, unearthed in Deyang, Sichuan

269. Pictorial brick depicting a feast scene, unearthed in Chengdu, Sichuan

270. Pictorial brick depicting music and dance, unearthed from Han tomb in Chengdu, Sichuan

271. Pictorial brick depicting carriages and horseback riding, unearthed from Han tomb in Chengdu, Sichuan

272. Pictorial brick depicting salt making, unearthed in Chengdu, Sichuan

273. Monumental tower (jue) in front of the grave of
Gao Yi in Ya'an, Sichuan

274. Painted lacquered coffin from Han tomb number 1 at Mawangdui,
Changsha

275. Second painted lacquered coffin from Mawangdui

276. Funerary banner
unearthed from Han tomb
number 1 at Mawangdui,
Changsha

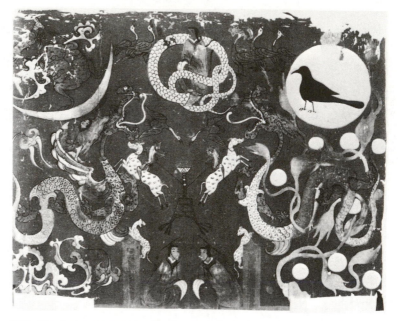

277. The heaven scene in the funerary banner unearthed from Han tomb number 1 at Mawangdui, Changsha

278. Portrait of the tomb master in the funerary banner unearthed from Han tomb number 1 at Mawangdui, Changsha

279. Funerary banner unearthed from Han tomb at Mozuizi, in Wuwei, Gansu

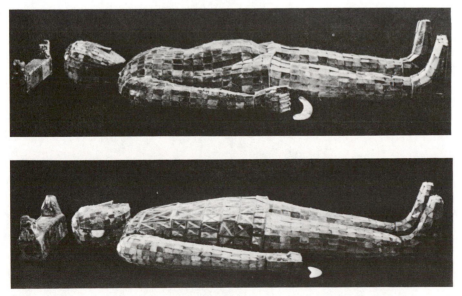

280. Jade mortuary shrouds with gold threads, unearthed from Han tomb in Mancheng (upper: Liu Sheng's; lower: Dou Wan's)

281. Jade shroud with gold threads, unearthed from Han tomb number 40 in Dingxian, Hebei

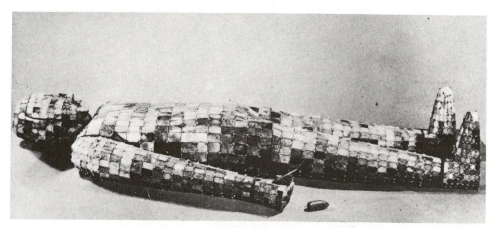

282. Jade shroud with silver threads, unearthed from Han tomb in Xuzhou, Jiangsu

283. Details of "qian ce," or inventory slips, unearthed from Han tomb number 1 at Mawangdui, Changsha

284. "Feng fang," or inventory tablet, unearthed from the tomb of Shi Qi Yao of Western Han in Haizhou, Jiangsu

9 Tombs—II

GRAVE GOODS

One of the central ideas of the funerary rites prevailing among the landowners and bureaucrats of the Han dynasty was that the dead should be treated in the same way as the living. As stated in "Bozangpian," *Lun heng* 论衡, "treat death as life." Consequently, not only did the form and the structure of the burial chamber imitate a real-life house, the grave was also provided with as complete a complement of furnishings and provisions as possible. No utensils and objects that were used by the living were barred from the tomb.

First off, in order that the dead person be able to continue a comfortable life in the other world, foods of various sorts were supplied as the principal grave goods (figs. 285–86). Take tomb number 1 of Mawangdui as an example. The following food items were discovered in the tomb: cereals and legumes including rice, wheat, barley, panic millet, foxtail millet, soybeans, and red beans; fruits and vegetables including melons, jujubes (Chinese dates), pears, plums, Chinese strawberries, malva, mustard greens, lotus roots, and bamboo shoots; animals including pigs, cattle, sheep, dogs, deer, and rabbits; birds including chickens, ducks, cranes, pigeons, owls, wild geese, magpies, sparrows, Mandarin ducks, bamboo pheasants, and pheasants; fish including carp, crucian carp, two other kinds of carp, perch, and bream.[1] These foodstuffs were prepared into cooked cereals, cakes, and various other dishes, with the addition of condiments such as sweetener, honey, soy sauce, salt, and several kinds of wine. The names of the dishes were listed on *qian ce* inventory slips in the tomb; the classes were complex and the names numerous.[2] Liu Sheng, Prince Jing of Zhongshan, buried in the Han dynasty tomb of Mancheng, was famous for his fondness of drinking. In the tombs in which he and his wife were buried there were more than thirty large pottery urns, each 70 cm tall. Some of the urns were inscribed in red on the outside: "15 piculs of Grade A panic millet wine"; "15 piculs of sweet liqueur"; "11 piculs of rice wine"; and the like. Traces of wine were still visible inside the urns at the time of excavation. It is estimated that more than 5,000 kg of wine—a remarkable amount—were contained in these urns[3] (fig. 287).

Another major part of the grave goods of that time consisted of various garments and fabrics. The clothing from tomb number 1 of Mawangdui included padded robes, double-layered robes, single-layered robes, single-layered skirts, shoes, socks, and mittens—most of them made of silk (figs. 288, 289). In addition, many silk fabrics were placed in large bamboo-matted suitcases, including warp-patterned fabric and embroidery, common silk, damask and brocade, the leno (or gauze) weave—their quality excellent, their colors bright, and their designs beautiful[4] (figs. 290, 291). Presumably clothing and fabrics were placed in many other Han dynasty tombs, but elsewhere the conditions for preservation have not been as favorable and they have not survived. But inventory tables (*feng fang*) in some of these tombs, such as the tombs of Huo He 霍贺 and Shi Qi Yao 侍其繇, in Haizhou, Jiangsu, listed names and quantities of clothing, although very little of the clothing itself has survived.

Bronze, lacquer, and pottery items were the most common Han grave goods. Most of these were containers in which food and drink were originally placed. Utensils such as lamps, incense burners, irons (for ironing clothes), toilet article boxes, mirrors, as well as weapons such as knives and swords, were also commonly found in tombs. Ornaments were found also: various beads and pendants of such materials as jade, opal, amber, quartz, gold, and silver. In short, so numerous were the grave goods that they cannot be exhaustively listed. They varied in quality and quantity from grave to grave, depending upon the status and wealth of the grave's occupant; on the other hand, their characteristics changed along with changes in social conditions and manners and customs. In general, in early and middle Western Han, what the nobility and the bureaucrats would place in tombs were the real thing—various valuable objects that they would use in real life. But after middle Western Han fashions changed, and mortuary pottery made specifically for burial purposes increased in quantity. The earliest to appear were pottery granaries and pottery stoves; they had appeared in early Western Han and became popular in middle Western Han. After that, pottery models of wells, querns, pigsties, multistoried buildings, pestling shops, and farm fields, along with pottery images of domestic animals and fowl such as pigs, dogs, sheep, chickens, and ducks, made a gradual appearance. The later the grave (especially after Eastern Han), the more numerous were these pottery models (figs. 292, 293). In Eastern Han tombs, the grave goods consisted mostly of pottery vessels and such pottery mortuary models as described above. There was a decrease in the more valuable utilitarian vessels of bronze and lacquerware. Even the large graves of bureaucrats and nobility are no exception. What is indicated is that, with the development of the manorial economy, the ideology pertaining to grave goods among the members of the landowning class underwent a significant change. They may have felt that, rather than placing valuable objects of limited quantity underground, it might be better to make symbolic pottery models of everything in the manor and to place them in the tomb.

What is amply reflected in the grave goods is that landowners of the Han dynasty paid special attention to the possession of land. In tomb number 167 at Fenghuangshan in Jiangling, which is dated to early Western Han, was found a piece of hardened clay wrapped in dark red silk. This was referred to as "bu tu"

簿土 on the *qian ce* found in the same grave, meaning that it was a legally owned piece of land that had been officially registered. This piece of clay is rectangular, 20 by 14 by 12 cm. Placed in the tomb, it probably symbolized the continued possession of this piece of land by the master of the tomb.[5] The use of pottery models of farm fields in Eastern Han probably carried the same implication (fig. 294).

During the Shang, Western Zhou, and Eastern Zhou dynasties, graves of rulers were often accompanied by nearby pit burials of horses and chariots or of carriages. Real carriages and horses were still used in some tombs of the nobility in middle Western Han, examples being the tombs of Prince Jing of Zhongshan in Mancheng and Prince Lu in Qufu.[6] Special pits containing chariot and horses were placed in front of the burial chamber of the tomb of the prince of Yan at Dabaotai in Beijing, a continuation of the traditional Shang and Zhou custom[7] (fig. 295). But in late Western Han and Eastern Han, wooden and pottery models of carriages and horses replaced real ones. The burial of human victims as part of grave furnishings was by then legally banned, as recorded in *Hanshu* ("Biography of Prince Jingsu of Zhao") and other texts. Therefore, with a few exceptions, human victims no longer are found in Han tombs, and wooden or pottery figurines take the place of servants and maids (fig. 296).

Tombs number 4 and 5 found at Yangjiawan, in Xianyang city of Shaanxi, are dated to emperors Wen Di and Jing Di of Western Han; their occupants probably were important military generals. Some archaeologists speculate that these were the tombs of Zhou Bo 周勃 and his son Zhou Yafu 周亚夫, based on the descriptions of their tombs in *Shuijingzhu*, but this hypothesis is by no means a certainty. Ten pits to the south of the graves contain a large number of pottery figurines. Altogether there are more than 1,800 figurines of foot soldiers and more than 580 figurines of mounted soldiers. The soldiers are holding weapons in their hands and wearing armor and are arranged in neat formations.[8] It is recorded that in the Han dynasty when important military officials died the imperial court would give them elaborate funerals and used military formations in the funerary processions. The large group of pottery figurines at Yangjiawan could be a model of such a funeral formation (fig. 297).

Although most of the models of carriages, people, and horses were wooden or ceramic in Han dynasty tombs, there are exceptions. A remarkale example of bronze models of carriages, horses, soldiers, and servants has been found in the Han tombs at Leitai in Wuwei, Gansu[6] (figs. 298–300). As I described in a previous chapter, processions of carriages and horses constituted an important motif in Eastern Han murals found in brick chamber tombs. The Han tomb of Leitai does not have such murals, but instead used bronze models. In the front of the procession were soldiers mounted on horses and holding spears and *ji*-halberds. The rear of the procession was made up of various carriages and attendants who were either handling the carriages and the horses or were simply in attendance. Altogether in the procession were seventeen soldiers, twenty-eight servants and attendants, thirty-nine horses, and fourteen carriages, forming a remarkable and unique sight. To acquire such furnishings obviously required vast sums of manpower and money. In late Eastern Han, officials and generals in border regions very often were wealthy and powerful and were capable of indulging in anything they wanted. The Han tomb of Leitai is a true indication of this fact.

Perhaps because money was becoming increasingly important in the Han dynasty, the use of coins in graves became quite fashionable. Even in the large graves of nobility and bureaucrats, where there were already many valuable goods, some coins would be included to symbolize their weatlth. In Western Han, although coins were used in tombs, the number used was often small. It increased in Eastern Han. In the Han tomb of Leitai, mentioned earlier, which dates from late Eastern Han, there were more than 28,000 coins.[10] In some regions, such as Changsha of Hunan, clay (mortuary) coins were used in addition to bronze coins. These are not a reflection of the frugality of the tomb master but of prevailing custom. In the Han tomb of Mawangdui, for example, with its quantities of valuable grave goods, clay coins were still used instead of bronze coins[11] (fig. 301).

The nobles, bureaucrats, and landowners of the Han dynasty were fond of burying books as grave goods. Books at the time were often on silk or on slips of bamboo or wood. Such written materials have been unearthed in large quanitities from Han tombs since Liberation. At the Western Han tomb at Mawangdui were found silk books of *Laozi* 老子, *Yi jing* 易经, *Zhan guo ce* 战国策 and in the Western Han tomb at Shuanggudui were found bamboo books of *Shi jing* 诗经 and *Cang Jie pian* 苍颉篇[12] (figs. 302, 303). From a Western Han tomb at Yinqueshan in Linyi, Shandong, came *Sunzi bing fa* 孙子兵法, *Sun Bin bing fa* 孙膑兵法, *Yanzi chun qiu* 晏子春秋 and other bamboo books[13] (fig. 304). A wooden slip book of *Yi li* 仪礼 was found in an early Eastern Han tomb at Mozuizi, Wuwei, in Gansu (fig. 305), and wooden slips of medicinal texts were found from an early Eastern Han tomb at Hantanpo 旱滩坡 in Wuwei.[14] These books have been preserved because either special, effective preservation measures were taken, or the tombs were submerged in water, or they were preserved by extremely dry conditions. Presumably books were a common grave furnishing in Han dynasty tombs, but in most cases they have not survived.

Seals were another object that was used by landowners and bureaucrats of the Han dynasty for burial. Some of the seals were private seals, others official seals. Almost a hundred have been found in the Han tombs in the Changsha area alone in the last two decades or so.[15] From tomb number 2 at Mawangdui came three seals, the inscriptions being "Seal of Marquis Dai," "The Chengxiang 丞相 [Chancellar] of Changsha," and "Li Cang 利苍." The first two are of gilded bronze, and the third is of jade. They helped determine the name and identity of the master of the tomb[16] (fig. 306). Most of the seals of the Han belonged to men, but there were exceptions. Tomb number 2 of Mancheng was the tomb of Dou Wan, the wife of Liu Sheng, Prince Jing of Zhongshan. From her tomb came seals inscribed with the characters "Dou Wan" 窦绾 and "Dou Jun Xu" 窦君须[17] (fig. 307).

In Eastern Han tombs were sometimes found sales contracts for the purchase of the tomb plot, in the form of elongated lead plates called *mai di juan*.[18] They were probably symbolic contracts, placed in the tomb for the security of the deceased, testifying to his right of possession. Sometimes the inscription included the admonition that all persons who were buried within the plot area should become his servants. Although such sales contracts were for the use in the afterlife, they also reflect the fierceness of the struggles for land in real life and some of the situations which led peasants to become bond servants.

Tombs of the middle and, especially, the late Eastern Han period often contained what are called "tomb security jars." These bottles were inscribed in red on the outside; the inscriptions often began with a notation on the year, month, and date, and always end with the phrase *ru lü ling* 如律令 ("as ordered by the spell")[19] (fig. 308). As suggested by the red inscriptions, the function of these jars was to assure the tranquility of the remaining members of the family, to assure the security of the tomb of the dead, and in the name of "the angels of the god" to eliminate the guilt of the living and seek blessing for the dead. In late Eastern Han Taoism became quite popular, and these bottles were probably indicative of Taoist concepts. Their use was by this time quite common and they even found their way into the tombs of famous upper-class people among the bureaucrats and landowners, such as those of the Yang 杨 lineage at Hongnong 弘农 in Huayin, Shaanxi.[20]

FAMILY AND LINEAGE GRAVES

There were literary records pertaining to the burial of husband and wife in the same tomb before the Han, but such burials have not yet been found in the archaeological record at such an early date. Excavations have shown that the husband-and-wife burials of the Warring States period were in fact two separate burials in two grave pits next to each other. The same custom was followed even in early and middle Western Han. After middle Western Han, however, husband-and-wife burials in the same pit became popular; in late Western Han and throughout Eastern Han such burials were the rule (figs. 309, 310).

The manorial economy of the Han dynasty caused the family members among the landowning class to be very close, especially in Eastern Han. This intimacy was reflected in mortuary practices in long-continuing family tombs. Members of the same family of several generations were often buried together. Persons who died away from home, no matter how far away, had to be brought back home to be interred in the family tomb, the so-called "return to the old cemetery." An example is the Yang lineage cemetery at Hongnong in Huayin, Shaanxi. The Hongnong Yang lineage was a famous lineage during the Han, and their cemetery in Huayin was the center of much attention. The monuments erected at the cemetery have often been mentioned in books since the Tang and Song dynasties. Archaeological excavations in 1959 disclosed seven tombs in orderly arrangement;

namely, the bodies were buried from east to west according to generation. Those who were buried here were Yang Zhen 杨震, Yang Mu 杨牧, Yang Rang 杨让, Yang Tong 杨统, Yang Zhuo 杨著, Yang Fu 杨馥, and Yang Biao 杨彪. They belonged to four generations and succeeded each other over a period of a whole century.[21]

IMPERIAL MAUSOLEUMS

The tombs of the highest rank among all noble burials were, of course, those of the emperors. The scale of the imperial mausoleums was not to be compared to the tombs of mere nobles and officials. Aside from Ba Ling 霸陵, the tomb of Wen Di, and Du Ling 杜陵, the tomb of Xuan Di, which are located in the southeastern suburbs of Changan, all the other imperial tombs of Western Han, nine mausoleums in all, were constructed on the high ground northwest of Changan and north of the Weishui River.[22] The imperial tombs of Eastern Han, other than the Yuan Ling of Guang Wu Di, which is at Mengjin north of Luoyang, are all thought to be situated on Mang Shan north and west of Luoyang.[23] In general, Western Han imperial tombs were modeled on the Qin Shi Huang tomb, and Eastern Han imperial tombs followed the Western Han tradition. No archaeological excavations have yet taken place at any of the Han imperial mausoleums, and our understanding of them is confined to the structures above ground. The Ba Ling of the Western Han emperor Wen Di was built on a natural hill, but all the others had large mounds of rammed earth built over them; the mounds were mostly rectangular, similar to the Egyptian pyramids. Each of the mounds was then surrounded by a large, square enclosure, with a door on each of the four sides. Sleeping and working halls were built inside the enclosure for ritual purposes, and residential quarters were built for attendants. Mao Ling 茂陵, Emperor Wu Di's tomb, is the largest example. According to investigations in 1962, the enclosure was 480 m east to west and 414 m north to south, about one li square according to the Han system. The walls of the enclosure were about 6 m thick. The earthen mound at the center of the enclosure was 360 m square and 46 m tall, truly a majestic sight[24] (fig. 311). In the neighborhood of imperial mausoleums, there were often satellite graves in which were buried meritorious officials and imperial relatives. Near Mao Ling are the graves of Wei Qing 卫青 and Huo Qubing 霍去病 nearby, and of Huo Guang 霍光, a little farther away.[25] To the northeast of Chang Ling, the tomb of Han Gao Zu, more than seventy satellite tombs have been located. The two tombs at Yangjiawan mentioned earlier are among them and are the only ones that have been excavated.[26] In the Han dynasty, as soon as an emperor was enthroned he began to build his own grave, calling it his Shou Ling 寿陵, or "longevity grave." It is said that probably a third of all national income in taxes and tributes was spent on the construction of this longevity grave and its furnishings. In addition, under the Internal Revenue Department there was an office called the Dong Yuan Jiang 东园匠; it along with the Kao Gong Shi 考工室 and the You Gong Shi 右工室 were known as the Three Construction Offices. The Dong Yuan Jiang specialized in the preparation of imperial funerary articles such as caskets, jade shrouds with gold threads, and various mortuary objects. These treasures, collectively called the Dong Yuan Mi Qi 东园秘器, cost in the tens of millions annually.

GRAVES OF PRISONER-LABORERS AND OF THE POOR

Exploited by the ruling class, Han dynasty peasants often became bankrupt and turned into bond servants, or they were found guilty of crimes and turned into prisoner-laborers. Prisoner-laborers engaged in heavy work in handicraft shops managed by the state. They were also sent into the labor force for construction projects, such as road and bridge construction, opening of mountain passes, irrigation and canal work, building of city walls, and construction of palaces and imperial mausoleums. The imperial mausoleums, like the Qin Shi Huang tomb, were often built using prisoner-laborers in the tens of thousands brought in from all over the country. In 1972, in an area about 1.5 km northwest of Yang Ling (the imperial tomb of the Han emperor Jing Di) in Xianyang of Shaanxi, a satellite cemetery was excavated, in which, in an area of about eighty thousand square meters, were buried an estimated ten thousand plus prisoner-laborers.[29] The tomb pits were irregularly arranged, some rectangular, some amorphous. In each pit was buried either a single person or many persons. Some of the skeletons had iron shackles on their necks and some on their feet, indicating that these mausoleum builders were the category of prisoner-laborers called *tu qian* 髡钳, those who labored with their shackles on. *Shiji* ("Jing Di ben ji") states that "those prisoner-laborers who participated in the construction of Yang Ling were given an amnesty." *Hanshu* ("Jing Di ji") also states that "prisoner-laborers who constructed the Yang Ling were pardoned from the death penalty." These passages suggest that the construction of the Yang Ling was mainly done by prisoner-laborers, a hypothesis that has been confirmed by archaeological excavations. The magnificent imperial mausoleums were built on top of the bodies of thousands of slaves!

Another cemetery of prisoner-laborers was found in Xidajiaocun, in Yanshixian, Henan, at a spot about 2.5 km from the Eastern Han capital city of Luoyang. For a long time farmers in that area have turned up skeletons during farm work, and they call that area the "Ditch of the Skeletons." In the early years of the twentieth century, many inscribed bricks were found here. Referred to as "prisoner-laborer bricks," they have been noted in scholarly works, bringing this area to the attention of archaeologists. The whole area of the cemetery was over 50,000 square m. In 1964, about 2,000 square m of this cemetery were excavated, bringing to light in excess of five hundred graves of prisoner-laborers[28] (fig. 312).

The graves were rectangular pits, about 2 m long and half a meter wide, less than 1 m deep. The pits were placed one alongside another, with little room in between (figs. 313, 314). Among the skeletons that were found, 96 percent were men and 4 percent were women. Most of them were in their youth and early adulthood and many showed signs of wear on their bones. A few graves contained one or two coins, but the overwhelming majority of the graves were empty of any furnishings. One or two broken bricks were found in each grave, with incised inscriptions on them recording the name of the supervising unit, the skill if any of the prisoner, the presence of shackles, the original prison, the organizational unit to which the prisoner belonged, and the date of death and the name of the penalty. On the last point, there are such terms as "Tu qian" 髡钳, "Wan cheng dan" 完城旦, "Gui xin" 鬼薪, "Si kou" 司寇, and so forth, with the first two the most common (figs. 315–18). From studies of these inscriptions it is clear that the overwhelming majority of the prisoners were laboring people; very few of them were nobles or officials. They came to Luoyang from prisons all over the country to engage in forced labor. The 500-plus graves date from A.D. 107 to 121, namely, a brief interval of less than fourteen years. Obviously the prisoner-laborers died continually, probably from heavy labor and extremely poor living conditions, and when they died they were buried in shallow, small graves. Sometimes, after only a few years their graves would be turned over to make room for new dead prisoners.

Other aspects of Han tombs also illustrate the opposition between rich and poor during the Han dynasty. In 1955 a group of poor people's graves were excavated in Luoyang, Henan; they date from late Eastern Han. The cemetery was quite far from the Henanxian seat of the time and was located in a low, depressed area. The caskets were extremely simple: some bodies were buried in pottery, some pits were lined with brick fragments, some pits were covered with tiles, and other pits were bare. The grave furnishings were also extremely simple, usually consisting of a few coarse pottery vessels or a few coins[29] (figs. 319, 320). These stand in sharp contrast to the large graves described earlier of the emperors, nobility, bureaucrats, and landowners.

285. Various foods furnished in Han tomb number 1 at
Mawangdui, Changsha

286. Bamboo basket containing food in Han tomb number 1 at Mawangdui, Changsha

287. Large wine urns from Han tomb in Mancheng

288. Silk robe buried in Han tomb number 1 at Mawangdui in Changsha

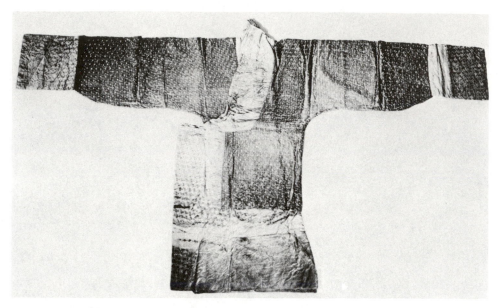

289. Another silk robe found in same tomb as fig. 288

290. Silk gauze with printed patterns and painted colors, buried in
Han tomb number 1 at Mawangdui in Changsha

291. Silk brocade with attached feathers and embroidery, buried in Han tomb number 1 at Mawangdui in Changsha

292. Pottery model of stove, unearthed from Han tomb in Luoyang

293. Pottery model of multistoried granary, unearthed from Han tomb in Yingyang, Henan

294. Pottery model of farm field, unearthed from Han tomb in Lianxian, Guangdong

295. Horse-and-chariot pit burial in the Han tomb at Dabaotai, Beijing

296. Wooden human figures buried in Han tomb number 1 at Mawangdui, Changsha

297. Pottery figures of warriors on horseback, unearthed from Han tomb at Yangjiawan in Xianyang, Shaanxi

298. Bronze carriage and horse buried in Han tomb at Leitai in Wuwei, Gansu

299. Bronze carriage and horse buried in the Han tomb at Leitai in Wuwei, Gansu

300. Bronze horses buried in Han tomb at Leitai in Wuwei, Gansu

301. Clay coins unearthed from Han tomb number
1 at Mawangdui, Changsha

302. Silk book unearthed from Han tomb
number 1 at Mawangdui, Changsha (*Laozi*,
version A, in part)

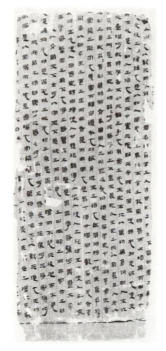

303. Silk book unearthed
from Han tomb number 1
at Mawangdui, Changsha
(*Laozi*, version B, in part)

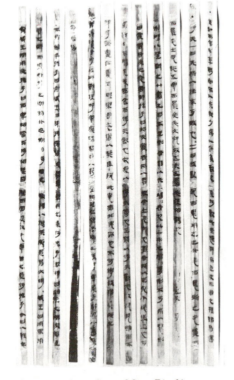

304. Bamboo slips of *Sun Bin bing
fa* (in part), unearthed from Han
tomb at Yinqueshan, Linyi,
Shandong

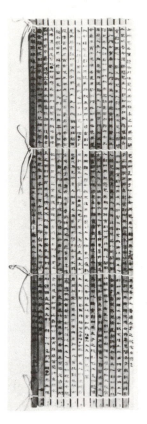

305. Wooden slips of *Yi li*, unearthed from Han tomb at Mozuizi, Wuwei, Gansu (reproductions)

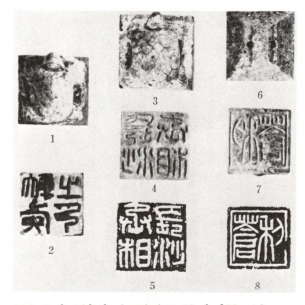

306. Seals with the inscriptions "Seal of Marquis Dai," "Chengxiang of Changsha," and "Li Cang," unearthed from Han tomb number 2 at Mawangdui, Changsha

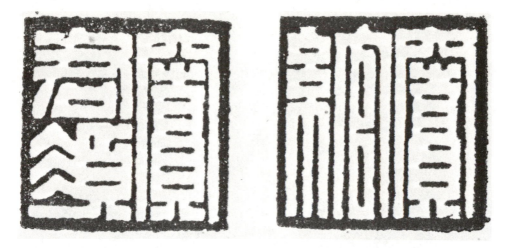

307. Bronze seals with the inscriptions "Dou Wan" and "Dou Jun Xu," unearthed from Han tomb number 2 in Mancheng

308. "Tomb security jar" (dated second year of Chu Ping), unearthed from Han tomb in Luoyang

309. Husband-and-wife burial in Western Han tomb in Luoyang

310. Husband-and-wife burial in Eastern Han tomb in Luoyang

311. Earthen mound of the mausoleum of Emperor Wu Di ("Mao Ling") in Xingpingxian, Shaanxi

312. Cemetery of prisoner-laborers of Eastern Han, excavated at Xidajiaocun, Yanshixian, Henan

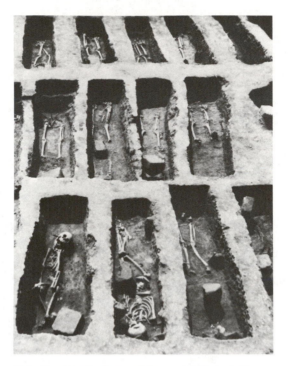

313. Tombs of prisoner-laborers of Eastern Han,
excavated at Xidajiaocun, Yanshixian, Henan

314. Skeletons and inscribed bricks in the
tombs of prisoner-laborers of Eastern Han,
excavated at Xidajiaocun, Yanshixian, Henan

315. Prisoner-laborer brick inscribed with the designation "Kun qian," unearthed from a prisoner-laborer tomb at Xidajiaocun, Yanshixian, Henan

316. Prisoner-laborer brick inscribed with "Wan cheng dan," unearthed from prisoner-laborer grave at Xidajiaocun, Yanshixian, Henan

317. Prisoner-laborer brick inscribed with "Gui xin," unearthed from prisoner-laborer grave at Xidajiaocun, Yanshixian, Henan

318. Prisoner-laborer brick inscribed with "Si kou," unearthed from prisoner-laborer grave at Xidajiaocun, Yanshixian, Henan

319. Commoner's grave of Han dynasty,
unearthed in Luoyang

320. Commoner's grave of Han dynasty,
unearthed in Luoyang

Appendix: A Supplementary Bibliography of Western Sources

The following is a highly selective list of major works in the Western languages on Han archaeology, prepared by the editor, which is meant to supplement the original sources in Chinese and Japanese given in the footnotes. It includes only works wherein important archaeological material is reported or studied.

Ayscough, Florence. 1939. "An Uncommon Aspect of Han Sculpture: Figures from Nan-yang." *Monumenta Serica* 4:334–44.

Bergman, Folke. 1939. *Archaeological Researches in Sinkiang, Especially the Lop-nor Region.* Stockholm: Bokförlags Aktiebolaget Thule.

Bielenstein, Hans. 1976. "Lo-yang in Later Han Times." *Bulletin of the Museum of Far Eastern Antiquities* 48:1–142.

Buck, David D. 1975. "Three Han Dynasty Tombs at Ma-wang-tui." *World Archaeology* 7:30–44.

Bulling, A. 1960. *The Decoration of Mirrors of the Han Period: A Chronology.* Ascona: Artibus Asiae Supplementum 20.

Cammann, S. 1948. "The 'TLV' Pattern on Cosmic Mirrors of the Han Dynasty." *Journal of America Oriental Society* 66, no. 4:159–67.

Chang, K. C. 1981. "Archaeology," in *Report of the Han Studies Delegation.* Y. S. Yu, ed. Washington: Committee for Scholarly Communication with the People's Republic of China.

Chavannes, Édouard. 1893. *La Sculpture sur pierre en Chine au temps des deux dynasties Han.* Paris: E. Leroux.

———. 1909. "La Sculpture à l'époque des Hans." *Mission archéologique dans la Chine septentrionale.* Vol. 1, part 1. Paris: E. Leroux.

Chaves, Jonathan. 1968. "A Han Painted Tomb at Loyang." *Artibus Asiae* 30:5–27.

Cheng, Te-k'un. 1978. "Ch'in-Han Architectural Remains." *Journal of the Insitute of Chinese Studies, The Chinese University of Hong Kong* 9, no. 2:503–83.

Croissant, Doris. 1964. "Funktion und Wanddekor der opferschreine von Wu-Liang-Tz'u: Typologische und Iconographische Untersuchungen." *Monumenta Serica* 23:88–152.

Drake, F. S. 1943. "Sculptured Stones of the Han Dynasty." *Monumenta Serica* 8:286–93.

Dubs, H. H. 1964. "Han 'Hill Censers,'" in *Studia Serica B. Karlgren Dedicata.* Copenhagen: Munksgaard.

Fairbank, Wilma. 1941. "The Offering Shrines of Wu Liang Tz'u." *Harvard Journal of Asiatic Studies* 6:1–36.

————. 1942. "A Structural Key to Han Mural Art." *Harvard Journal of Asiatic Studies* 7.

————, and M. Kitano. 1954. "Han Mural Paintings in the Pei-yuan Tomb at Liao-yang, South Manchuria." *Artibus Asiae* 17, nos. 3–4.

Finsterbusch, K. 1966, 1970. *Verzeichnis und Motivindex der Handarstellungen*. 2 vols. Weisbaden.

Fischer, Otto. 1931. *Die Chinesische Malerei der Han-Dynastie*. Berlin: Neff Verlag.

Franke, Wolfgang. 1948. "Die Han-Zeitlichen Felsengraeber bei Chia-ting." *Studia Serica* 7:19–39.

Hotaling, Stephen James. 1978. "The City Walls of Han Ch'ang-an." *T'oung Pao* 64:1–46.

Janse, O. R. T. 1947. *Archaeological Research in Indochina*. 3 vols. Cambridge: Harvard University Press.

Karlgren, B. 1941. "Huai and Han." *Bulletin of the Museum of Far Eastern Antiquities* 13.

Laufer, B. 1909. *Chinese Pottery of the Han Dynasty*. Leiden: E. J. Brill.

————. 1911. *Chinese Grave Sculptures of the Han Period*. London: E. L. Morice.

Loewe, Michael. 1961. "The Measurement of Grain during the Han Period." *T'oung Pao* 49:64–95.

————. 1965. "The Wooden and Bamboo Strips Found at Mon-chü-tzu." *Journal of the Royal Asiatic Society* 1965:13–26.

————. 1978. "Manuscripts Found Recently in China: A Preliminary Survey." *T'oung Pao* 63, no. 2/3:99–136.

————. 1979. *Ways to Paradise—The Chinese Quest for Immortality*. London: Allen & Unwin.

Rawson, Jessica. 1973. "A Group of Han Dynasty Bronzes with Chased Decoration and Some Related Ceramics." *Oriental Art* 19, no. 4:1–16.

Riboud, Krishna. 1973. "Some Remarks on Strikingly Similar Han Figured Silks Found in Recent Years in Diverse Sites." *Archives of Asian Art* 26:12–25.

Rostortzeff, M. 1927. *Inlaid Bronzes of the Han Dynasty in the Collection of C. T. Loo*. Paris/Brussels.

Rudolph, Richard C. 1965. "Notes on the Han Dynasty Reliefs at Nanyang." *Symposium in Honor of Dr. Li Chi on His Seventieth Birthday*. Part 1, pp. 97–104, The Tsing Hua Journal.

————. 1965. "Newly Discovered Chinese Painted Tombs." *Archaeology* 18:171–80.

————. 1973. "Two Recently Discovered Han Tombs." *Archaeology* 26, no. 2:106–15.

————, and Wen Yu. 1951. *Han Tomb Art of West China*. Berkeley and Los Angeles: University of California Press.

Schloss, Ezekiel. 1979. *Art of the Han*. New York: China Institute of America.

Segalen, V. G. de Voisins, and J. Lartique. 1935. *L'art funéraire à l'époque des Han*. Paris: P. Genthner.

Shih, Hsioyen. 1959. "I-nan and Related Tombs." *Artibus Asiae* 22:277–312.

————. 1968. "Review of *Chinese Pottery of the Han Dynasty* by Berthold Laufer." *Artibus Asiae* 30:347–51.

Tomita, Kojito. 1933. *Portfolio of Chinese Paintings in the Museum (Han to Sung Periods)*. Boston: Museum of Fine Arts.

Trubner, H. 1961. *Arts of the Han Dynasty*. New York: Chinese Art Society of America, Asia House.

Tsiang, K. R. 1978. "Glazed Stonewares of the Han Dynasty. Part One: The Eastern Group." *Artibus Asiae* 60, nos. 2/3:143–76.

Watt, J. C. Y. 1970. *A Han Tomb in Lei Cheng Uk*. Hong Kong: City Museum and Art Gallery.

White, W. C. 1939. *Tomb Tile Pictures of Ancient China*. Toronto: University of Toronto Press.

Yang, Lien-sheng. 1947. "A Note on the So-called TLV Mirrors and the Game Liu-po." *Harvard Journal of Asiatic Studies* 9: 202–06.

Notes

CHAPTER 1

1. Wang Zhongshu 王仲殊, "Han Changan cheng kaogu gongzuo di chubu shouhuo" 汉长安城考古工作的初步收获 [Preliminary results of the archaeological investigation of the Han dynasty city of Changan], *Kaogu Tongxun* 考古通讯, 1957, no. 5, pp. 102–04.

2. Institute of Archaeology, Chinese Academy of Social Sciences, *Han Changan cheng yizhi fajue baogao* 汉长安城遗址发掘报告 [Report of the excavation of the ruins of the Han dynasty city of Changan]. In preparation.

3. The Han text *Sanfu juelu* 三辅决录 is said to contain the phrase, "san tu dong kai" 三途洞开, or "the three roads [or the three-laned road] opened wide." The *Xi jing fu* 西京赋 contains the line, "san tu yi ting, fang gui shier" 三途夷庭，方轨十二, or "the three roads are level and straight, and they have twelve parallel tracks." *Xue Zong* 薛综's commentary explains this line thus: "Each side has three gates, and each gate has three lanes; therefore, it refers to the three roads. Each road contains four wheel tracks; therefore, it refers to having twelve tracks."

4. Wang Zhongshu (see n. 1 above), pp. 104, 105.

5. See n. 2 above.

6. Wang Zhongshu (n. 1 above), pp. 106–08.

7. See n. 2 above.

8. See n. 2 above.

9. See n. 2 above.

10. Han City Work Team, Institute of Archaeology, Chinese Academy of Social Sciences, "Han Changan cheng wuku yizhi fajue di chubu shouhuo" 汉长安城武库遗址发掘的初步收获 [Preliminary results of the excavation of the site of the armory in the Han dynasty city of Changan], *Kaogu* 考古, 1978, no. 4, pp. 261–69, pls. 9–11.

11. See n. 2 above.

12. Hei Guang 黑光, "Xi'an Han Taiyechi chutu yijian juxing shi yu" 西安汉太液池出土一件巨形石鱼 [A gigantic stone fish unearthed near Han dynasty Taiyechi in Xi'an], *Wenwu* 文物, 1975, no. 6, pp. 91, 92.

13. Yu Weichao 俞伟超, "Han Changan cheng xibeibu kancha ji" 汉长安城西北部勘查记 [Notes on the investigations in the northwestern part of the Han dynasty city of Changan], *Kaogu Tongxun*, 1966, no. 5, pp. 20–26, pl. 7.

14. Wang Zhongshu, "Han Changan cheng kaogu gongzuo xuji" 汉长安城考古工作续记 [Further notes on the results of archaeological work on the Han city of Changan], *Kaogu Tongxun*, 1958, no. 4, p. 25, pl. 4.

15. In *Hou Hanshu* ("Annals of Emperor Xian Di"), it is recorded that in the third moon of 191, "houses outside Xuanpingmen Gate were destroyed without cause." In the biographies of Dong Zhuo both *Weizhi* and *Hou Hanshu* refer to an event in which Wang Yun took Emperor Xian Di up to the gatetower atop Xuanpingmen Gate.

16. See n. 14 above; pp. 25–27, pls. 1–4.

17. Both *Jinshu* 晋书 and *Shiliuguo Chunqiu* 十六国春秋 record that in 345 B.C. Shi Hu 石虎,

leading 160,000 troops, stationed himself at the Weiyanggong palace in Changan. See pp. 27–29 of my article cited in n. 14 above.

18. See pp. 31, 32, pl. 4 of my article cited in n. 14 above.

19. Xi'an City Cultural Relics Commission, ''Xi'an Sanqiao zhen Gaoyao cun chutu di Xi Han tongqi qun'' 西安三桥镇高窑村出土的西汉铜器群 [A Western Han assemblage of bronze vessels unearthed at Gaoyaocun, Sanqiaozhen, Xi'an], *Kaogu*, 1963, no. 2, pp. 62–70, pls. 3, 4.

20. Chen Zhi 陈直, ''Gu qiwu wenzi congkao'' 古器物文字丛考 [Miscellaneous notes on ancient vessel inscriptions], *Kaogu*, 1963, no. 2, pp. 80–82.

21. Gu Tiefu 顾铁符, ''Xi'an fujin suojian di Xi Han shidiao yishu'' 西安附近所见的西汉石雕艺术 [Stone sculptures seen near Xi'an], *Wenwu Cankao Ziliao* 文物参考资料, 1955, no. 11, pp. 3–5.

22. Yu Weichao 俞伟超, ''Yingdang shenzhong yinyong gudai wenxian'' 应当慎重引用古代文献 [Ancient texts should be quoted with care], *Kaogu Tongxun*, 1957, no. 2, p. 76.

23. Hu Qianying 胡谦盈, ''Feng Gao diqu zhu shuidao di tacha'' 丰镐地区诸水道的踏察 [A walking survey of the various water courses in the Feng Gao area], *Kaogu*, 1963, no. 4, pp. 189, 190, 194.

24. Huang Zhanyue 黄展岳, ''Han Changan cheng nanjiao lizhi jianzhu di weizhi jiqi youguan wenti'' 汉长安城南郊礼制建筑的位置及其有关问题 [The location of the ritual structures to the south of the Han city of Changan and related problems], *Kaogu*, 1960, no. 9, pp. 53–58.

25. Tang Jinyu 唐金裕, ''Xi'an xijiao Han dai jian zhu yizhi fajue baogao'' 西安西郊汉代建筑遗址发掘报告 [Report on the excavations of Han dynasty architectural sites in the western suburbs of Xi'an], *Kaogu Xuebao* 考古学报, 1959, no. 2, pp. 45–54, pls. 1–9.

26. Han City Excavation Team, Institute of Archaeology, ''Han Changan cheng nanjiao lizhi jianzhu qun fajue jianbao'' 汉长安城南郊礼制建筑群发掘简报 [Brief report on the group of ritual structures to the south of the Han city of Changan], *Kaogu*, 1960, no. 7, p. 38; Luo Zhongru 雒忠如, ''Xi'an xijiao faxian Han dai jianzhu yizhi'' 西安西郊发现汉代建筑遗址 [Han dynasty architectural remains found in the western suburbs of Xi'an], *Kaogu Tongxun*, 1957, no. 6, pp. 26–30, pl. 8.

CHAPTER 2

1. Umehara Sueji 梅原末治, (*Zōtei*) *Rakuyō Kinson kobo shūei* （增订）洛阳金村古墓聚英 [Treasures from the ancient tomb of Jincun, Luoyang] (Kyoto: Kobayashi, 1944), pp. 1–2.

2. Luoyang Archaeology Team, Institute of Archaeology, ''Han Wei Luoyang cheng chubu kancha'' 汉魏洛阳城初步勘查 [Preliminary surveys of the Han and Wei cities of Luoyang], *Kaogu* 考古, 1973, no. 4, pp. 198–99, pl. 2.

3. Ibid., pp. 198–201.

4. Ibid., p. 200.

5. Ibid., pp. 199, 202, 203.

6. Wang Zhongshu 王仲殊, ''Han Changan cheng kaogu gongzuo shouhuo xuji'' 汉长安城考古工作收获续记 [Further notes on the results of archaeological work at the Han city of Changan], *Kaogu Tongxun* 考古通讯, 1958, no. 4, p. 24.

7. Xi'an City Cultural Relics Commission, ''Xi'an Sanqiao zhen Gaoyao cun chutu di Xi Han tongqi qun'' 西安三桥镇高窑村出土的西汉铜器群 [Assemblage of Western Han bronzes unearthed at Gaoyao village in Sanqiaozhen, Xi'an], *Kaogu*, 1963, no. 2, p. 68, pl. 4.

8. Huang Zhanyue 黄展岳, ''Xi'an Sanqiao Gaoyao cun Xi Han tongqi mingwen bushi'' 西安三桥高窑村西汉铜器铭文补释 [A supplementary explanation of the inscriptions on Western Han bronzes from Gaoyao village, Sanqiao, Xi'an], *Kaogu*, 1963, no. 4, pp. 199, 200.

9. Pp. 199, 209, 203 of article cited in n. 2 above.

10. Zuo Ming 作铭, ''Yongledadian juan 9561 yin Yuan Henanzhi di gudai Luoyang tu shisi fu'' 永乐大典卷 9561 引元河南志的古代洛阳图十四幅 [Fourteen ancient maps of Luoyang in the

Henanzhi of the Yuan dynasty quoted in volume 9561 of *Yongledadian*]," *Kaogu Xuebao* 考古学报,
1956, no. 2, p. 39, fig. 2.

11. Pp. 207, 208 of article cited in n. 2 above.

12. Ibid., pp. 202, 208, pl. 2.

13. Ibid., pp. 203, 204.

14. Ibid., p. 200, pl. 3.

15. Ibid., pp. 199, 202, 203.

16. Luoyang Archaeology Team, Institute of Archaeology, Chinese Academy of Sciences, "Han
Wei Luoyang cheng yihao fangzhi he chutu di wa wen" 汉魏洛阳城一号房址和出土的瓦文
[House floor no. 1 and unearthed tile inscriptions in the city of Luoyang of the Han and Wei
dynasties], *Kaogu*, 1973, no. 4, pp. 209–14, pl. 1.

17. Pp. 204–06, pl. 3 of article cited in n. 2 above.

18. Su Bai 宿白, "Bei Wei Luoyang cheng he Bei Mang lingmu" 北魏洛阳城和北邙陵墓 [The
city of Luoyang of the Northern Wei and the imperial tombs of the Northern Mang], *Wenwu* 文物,
1978, no. 7, pp. 42–46, pl. 4.

19. P. 198 of article cited in n. 2 above.

20. Institute of Archaeology, Chinese Academy of Social Sciences, *Han Wei Luoyang cheng yizhi
fajue baogao* 汉魏洛阳城遗址发掘报告 [Report on the excavations of the Luoyang city of Han and
Wei dynasties]. In preparation.

21. Yan Wenru 阎文儒, "Luoyang Han Wei Sui Tang chengzhi kancha ji" 洛阳汉魏隋唐
城址勘查记 [Notes on the investigation of Luoyang city sites of the Han, Wei, Sui, and Tang
dynasties], *Kaogu Xuebao*, 1955, no. 9, p. 121, pl. 4.

22. See n. 20 above.

23. Luoyang Archaeology Team, Institute of Archaeology, Chinese Academy of Social Sciences,
"Han Wei Luoyang cheng nanjiao di Lingtai yizhi" 汉魏洛阳城南郊的灵台遗址 [The site of
Lingtai in the southern suburb of Luoyang city of the Han and Wei dynasties], *Kaogu*, 1978, no. 1,
pp. 54–57, pls. 1–3.

24. See n. 2 above.

CHAPTER 3

1. Archaeological Excavation Team of Luoyang District, *Luoyang Shaogou Han mu* 洛阳烧沟
汉墓 [Han tombs at Shaogou, Luoyang] (Beijing: Kexue Press, 1959), pp. 112, 113, 156–58, pl. 20.
Yangtze Valley Archaeological Workers' Training Institute, Second Class, "Hubei Jiangling Fenghuangshan Xi Han mu fajue jian bao" 湖北江陵凤凰山西汉墓发掘简报 [Brief report on the
excavation of Western Han tombs at Fenghuangshan, Jiangling, Hubei], *Wenwu* 文物, 1974, no. 6,
p. 51. Hubei Provincial Museum, "Guanghua Wuzuofen Xi Han mu" 光化五座坟西汉墓 [Western
Han tombs at Wuzuofen, Guanghua], *Kaogu Xuebao* 考古学报, 1976, no. 2, p. 168, pl. 6. Hunan
Provincial Museum et al., *Changsha Mawangdui yi hao Han mu* 长沙马王堆一号汉墓 [Han tomb
number 1 at Mawangdui, Changsha] (Beijing: Wenwu Press, 1973), pp. 35–37, pls. 257–64. Xuzhou
Museum, "Jiangsu Xuzhou Kuishan Xi Han mu" 江苏徐州奎山西汉墓 [Western Han tombs at
Kuishan, Xuzhou], *Kaogu* 考古, 1974, no. 2, p. 120. Nanjing Museum et al., "Haizhou Xi Han Huo He
mu qingli jianbao" 海州西汉霍贺墓清理简报 [Brief report on the clearance of the tomb of Huo He
of the Western Han in Haizhou], *Kaogu*, 1974, no. 3, pp. 185, 186; Liu Liang 刘亮, "Guanyu Xi Han
Huo He mu chutu ji di jianding" 关于西汉霍贺墓出土稷的鉴定 [On the identification of the millet
unearthed from the Huo He tomb of the Western Han], *Kaogu*, 1978, no. 2, p. 90; Nan Po 南波,
"Jiangsu Lianyungangshi Haizhou Xi Han Shi Chi Yao mu" 江苏连云港市海州西汉侍其繇墓
[The tomb of Shi Chi Yao of the Western Han in Haizhou, Lianyungang city, Jiangsu], *Kaogu*, 1975,
no. 3, p. 176. Archaeological Team of Guangxi Autonomous Region, "Guangxi Guixian Luobowan
yihao mu fajue jianbao" 广西贵县罗泊湾一号墓发掘简报 [Brief report on tomb number 1 at

Luobowan, Guixian, Guangxi], *Wenwu*, 1978, no. 9, p. 32. Guangzhou City Cultural Relics Commission, "Guangzhou Xicun Huangdigang 42-hao Dong Han mukuomu fajue jianbao" 广州西村皇帝冈 42 号东汉木椁墓发掘简报 [Brief report on the excavation of Eastern Han wooden-chambered tomb number 42 at Huangdigang in Xicun, Guangzhou], *Kaogu Tongxun* 考古通讯, 1958, no. 8, pp. 42, 43.

2. Shaanxi Provincial Museum Writing Team, "Mizhi Dong Han huaxianshi mu fajue jianbao" 米脂东汉画象石墓发掘简报 [Brief report on the Eastern Han tomb with painted stones in Mizhi], *Wenwu*, 1972, no. 3, pp. 71–73.

Nakao Susuke 中尾佐助, "Henan sheng Luoyang Han mu chutu di daomi" 河南省洛阳汉墓出土的稻米 [Rice unearthed from Han tomb in Luoyang, Henan], *Kaogu Xuebao*, 1957, no. 4, 79–82.

4. Institute of Archaeology, Chinese Academy of Sciences, *Xin Zhongguo di kaogu shouhu* 新中国的考古收获 [Archaeological results in the new China] (Beijing: Wenwu Press, 1961), p. 77.

5. Yang Shiting 杨式挺, "Tantan Shixia faxian di zaipeidao yiji" 谈谈石峡发现的栽培稻遗迹 [On the remains of cultivated rice found in Shixia], *Wenwu*, 1978, no. 7, p. 28. Hunan Provincial College of Agronomy et al., *Changsha Mawangdui yihao Han mu chutu dong zhi wu biaoben di yanjiu* 长沙马王堆一号汉墓出土动植物标本的研究 [Studies of animal and plant remains unearthed from Han tomb number 1 at Mawangdui in Changsha] (Beijing: Wenwu Press, 1978), pp. 1–3.

6. Excavation and Study Team for Han Tomb Number 167 at Fenghuangshan, "Jiangling Fenghuangshan yiliuqihao Han mu fajue jianbao" 江陵凤凰山一六七号汉墓发掘简报 [Brief report on the excavation of Han tomb number 167 at Fenghuangshan in Jiangling], *Wenwu*, 1976, no. 10, p. 34, pl. 2.

7. He Guanbao 贺官保, "Luoyang Laocheng xibeijiao 81-hao Han mu" 洛阳老城西北郊 81 号汉墓 [Han tomb number 81 in the northwest suburb of the old city of Luoyang], *Kaogu*, 1964, no. 8, p. 406. Yang Shiting 杨式挺, "Guanyu Guangdong zaoqi tieqi di ruogan wenti" 关于广东早期铁器的若干问题 [Some problems relating to early iron implements in Guangdong], *Kaogu*, 1977, no. 2, p. 104. Dongbei Museum, "Liaoyang Sandaohao Xi Han cunluo yizhi" 辽阳三道壕西汉村落遗址 [Village remains of the Western Han at Sandaohao in Liaoyang], *Kaogu Xuebao*, 1957, no. 1, p. 121, pl. 5.

8. Zhang Zengqi 张增祺, "Cong chutu wenwu kan Zhanguo zhi Xi Han shiqi Yunnan he Zhongyuan diqu di miqie quanxi" 从出土文物看战国至西汉时期云南和中原地区的密切关系 [The close interrelationship of Yunnan and the Central Plains area during the Warring States period and the Western Han dynasty as seen from archaeological relics], *Wenwu*, 1978, no. 10, pp. 32, 33. The Archaeological Section, Institute of Dunhuang Relics, "Dunhuang Tianshuijing Han dai yizhi di diaocha 敦煌甜水井汉代遗址的调查 [The investigation of the Han dynasty site at Tianshuijing in Dunhuang], *Kaogu*, 1975, no. 2, pp. 112–14.

9. Tang Yunming 唐云明, "Baoding dong Biyangcheng diaocha" 保定东壁阳城调查 [The investigation of Biyangcheng east of Baoding], *Wenwu*, 1959, no. 9, p. 82. Nanjing Museum, "Liguoyi gudai liantielu di diaocha ji qingli" 利国驿古代炼铁炉的调查及清理 [Investigation and clearance of ancient iron-smelting furnaces at Liguoyi], *Wenwu*, 1960, no. 4, pp. 46, 47.

10. Zhang Zhenxin 张振新, "Han dai di niu geng" 汉代的牛耕 [The use of cattle in plowing in the Han dynasty], *Wenwu*, 1977, no. 8, p. 60; Zhuang Dongming 庄冬明 "Tengxian Changchengcun faxian Han dai tie nong ju shiyu jian" 滕县长城村发现汉代铁农具十余件 [More than ten iron agricultural implements of the Han dynasty discovered at Changchengcun in Tengxian], *Wenwu Cankao Ziliao* 文物参考资料, 1958, no. 3, p. 82.

11. Institute of Archaeology, Chinese Academy of Social Sciences, et al., *Mancheng Han mu* 满城汉墓 [Han tombs in Mancheng] (Beijing: Wenwu Press, 1978), pp. 59, 60.

12. Shaanxi Provincial Museum, "Shaanxi sheng faxian di Han dai tie hua he pi tu" 陕西省发现的汉代铁铧和䥱土 [Han dynasty iron plowshares and moldboards discovered in Shaanxi province], *Wenwu*, 1966, no. 1, p. 23, pls. 3, 4.

13. Zhang Zhenxin 张振新, "Han dai di niu geng," p. 60.

14. P. 23, pl. 3 of article cited in n. 12 above.

15. Gansu Provincial Museum, "Wuwei Mozuizi san zuo Han mu fajue jianbao" 武威磨咀子三座汉墓发掘简报 [Brief report on the excavations of three Han dynasty tombs at Mozuizi, Wuwei], *Wenwu*, 1972, no. 12, pp. 13, 14, fig. 23. Shanxi Provincial Cultural Relics Commission, "Shanxi Pinglu Zaoyuancun Han mu bihua" 山西平陆枣园村汉墓壁画 [The murals in the Han dynasty tomb at Zaoyuancun in Pinglu, Shanxi], *Kaogu*, 1959, no. 9, p. 463. Jiangsu Provincial Cultural Relics Commission, *Jiangsu Xuzhou Han huaxiang shi* 江苏徐州汉画象石 [Pictorial stones of the Han dynasty in Xuzhou, Jiangsu] (Beijing: Kexue Press, 1959), p. 12, pl. 61. Fu Xihua 傅惜华, *Han dai huaxiang quan ju (chubian)* 汉代画象全集（初编）[A complete collection of the pictorial art of the Han dynasty (preliminary volume)] (Shanghai: Commercial Press, 1950), pl. 96. Pp. 70, 71, 73 of reference cited in n. 2 above. Inner Mongolia Autonomous Region Museum, Archaeological Team, *Holingor Han mu bihua* 和林格尔汉墓壁画 [Mural paintings from the Han dynasty tomb at Holingor] (Beijing: Wenwu Press, 1978), pp. 20, 123, 145, 146.

16. Gansu Provincial Museum et al., "Jiayuguan Wei Jin mu bihua di ticai he yishu jiazhi" 嘉峪关魏晋墓壁画的题材和艺术价值 [Subject matter and artistic value of the mural paintings in the Wei and Jin dynasty tombs at Jiayuguan], *Wenwu*, 1974, no. 9, p. 76, pl. 1.

17. P. 463, pl. 1 of "Shanxi Pinglu Zaoyuancun Han mu bihua," n. 15 above.

18. P. 23, fig. 11 of reference cited in n. 12 above.

19. P. 67, pls. 1 and 3 of reference cited in n. 16 above.

20. Xu Hengbin 徐恒彬, "Jiantan Guangdong Lianxian chutu di Xi Jin litian batian moxing" 简谈广东连县出土的西晋犁田耙田模型 [A brief discussion of clay models showing soil turning and soil raking of Western Jin unearthed in Lianxian, Guangdong], *Wenwu*, 1976, no. 3, pp. 75, 76.

21. Qin Zhongxing 秦中行, "Zhengguoqu qushou yizhi diaocha ji" 郑国渠渠首遗址调查记 [On the investigation of the canal head of the Zhengguoqu canal], *Wenwu*, 1974, no. 7, p. 35.

22. Sichuan Guanxian Cultural and Educational Bureau, "Dujiangyan chutu Dong Han Li Bing shixiang" 都江堰出土东汉李冰石像 [Stone statue of Li Bing of Eastern Han unearthed in Dujiangyan], *Wenwu*, 1974, no. 7, pp. 27, 28, pl. 18. Wang Wencai 王文才, "Dong Han Li Bing shixiang yu Dujiangyan shui ze" 东汉李冰石像与都江堰水则 [Stone statue of Li Bing of Eastern Han and the water gauge for the Dujiang weir], *Wenwu*, 1974, no. 7, pp. 29, 30.

23. Fu Xihua, *Han dai huaxiang quan ju (Chubian)*, pls. 1 and 3.

24. Pp. 125–27, pls. 29 and 30 of *Luoyang Shaogou Han mu* (n. 1 above). Qin Zhongxing 秦中行, "Ji Hanzhong chutu di Han dai pichi moxing" 记汉中出土的汉代陂池模型 [Models of water ponds of the Han dynasty unearthed in Hanzhong], *Wenwu*, 1976, no. 3, pp. 77, 78. Liu Zhiyuan 刘志远, "Chengdu Tianhuishan yai mu qingli ji" 成都天回山崖墓清理记 [Note on the clearance of a cliff-burial at Tianhuishan in Chengdu], *Kaogu Xuebao*, 1958, no. 1, p. 97, pl. 4. Pp. 33, 34 of article cited in n. 8 above.

25. Yin Difei 殷涤非, "Anhui sheng Shouxian Anfengtang faxian Han dai zhaba gongcheng yizhi" 安徽省寿县安丰塘发现汉代闸坝工程遗址 [Site of a Han dynasty sluice-gate and dam construction found in the Anfeng pond in Shouxian, Anhui], *Wenwu*, 1960, no. 1, pp. 61–62.

26. Liu Zhiyuan 刘志远, "Sichuan Han dai huaxiang zhuan fanying di shehui shenghuo" 四川汉代画象砖反映的社会生活 [Social life reflected in pictorial bricks of the Han dynasty in Sichuan], *Wenwu*, 1975, no. 4, p. 46, pl. 1.

27. Yu Fuwei 余扶危, et al., "Luoyang Dongguan Dong Han xunren mu" 洛阳东关东汉殉人墓 [Eastern Han tomb with human sacrificial victims at Dongguan, Luoyang], *Wenwu*, 1973, p. 2, p. 57; Henan Provincial Museum, "Jiyuan Sijiangou sanzuo Han mu di fajue" 济源泗涧沟三座汉墓的发掘 [Excavation of three Han dynasty tombs at Sijiangou in Jiyuan], *Wenwu*, 1973, no. 2, pp. 50–52.

28. Mancheng Excavation Team, Institute of Archaeology, Chinese Academy of Sciences, "Mancheng Han mu fajue jiyao" 满城汉墓发掘纪要 [Major results of the excavation of the Han tombs in Mancheng], *Kaogu*, 1972, no. 1, p. 9.

29. Shandong Provincial Museum et al., "Linyi Yinqueshan si zuo Xi Han muzang" 临沂银雀山四座西汉墓葬 [Four Western Han tombs at Yinqueshan, Linyi], *Kaogu*, 1975, no. 6, p. 367, pl. 9.

30. Dingxian Museum, "Hebei Dingxian 43-hao Han mu fajue jianbao" 河北定县43号汉墓发掘简报 [Brief report on the excavation of Han tomb number 43 in Dingxian, Hebei], *Wenwu*, 1973, no. 11, p. 12, fig. 26. Sichuan Provincial Museum, "Sichuan Xinduxian faxian yipi huaxiang zhuan" 四川新都县发现一批画象砖 [A group of pictorial bricks found in Xinduxian, Sichuan], *Wenwu*, 1980, no. 2, p. 56, pl. 7.

31. Pp. 47, 48, 52–55, 68–73 of *Changsha Mawangdui yihao Han mu chutu dong zhi wu biaoben di yanjiu* (see n. 5 above).

32. P. 46, pl. 1 of article cited in n. 26 above.

33. Pp. 77, 78 of "Ji Hanzhong chutu di Han dai pichi moxing" (n. 24 above).

34. Xia Nai 夏鼐, "Wuoguo gudai can sang si chou di lishi" 我国古代蚕桑丝绸的历史 [History of silkworm raising and silk in ancient China], *Kaogu*, 1972, no. 2, pp. 14, 15.

35. Pp. 20, 21 of *Holingor Han mu bihua* (n. 15 above).

36. Pp. 44, 45, pls. 7, 8 of "Hubei Jiangling Fenghuangshan jian bao" (n. 1 above).

37. Qiu Xigui 裘锡圭, "Hubei Jiangling Fenghuangshan shihao mu chutu jiandu kaoshi" 湖北江陵凤凰山十号墓出土简牍考释 [An interpretation of some written slips unearthed from tomb number 10 at Fenghuangshan in Jiangling, Hubei], *Wenwu*, 1974, no. 7, pp. 56, 57.

38. Pp. 20, 21, 101, 102, 146, 147 of *Holingor Han mu bihua* (n. 15 above).

39. Ibid., pp. 79, 121–27.

40. P. 99, pl. 8 of "Chengdu Tianhuishan yai mu qingli ji" (n. 24 above).

41. Cultural Relics Rescue Team, Jiayuguan City, "Jiayuguan Han huaxiang zhuan mu" 嘉峪关汉画象砖墓 [Han tomb with pictorial bricks in Jiayuguan], *Wenwu*, 1972, no. 12, p. 27, pl. 6.

CHAPTER 4

1. Hemudu Site Excavation Team, "Zhejiang Hemudu yizhi dierqi fajue di zhuyao shouhu" 浙江河姆渡遗址第二期发掘的主要收获 [Major results of the second season of excavations of the Hemudu site in Zhejiang], *Wenwu* 文物, 1980, no. 5, pl. 3.

2. Hebei Provincial Museum et al., "Hebei Gaochengxian Taixicun Shang dai yizhi 1973 nian di zhongyao faxian" 河北藁城县台西村商代遗址1973年的重要发现 [Important discoveries at the Shang site at Taixicun, Gaochengxian, Hebei, in 1973], *Wenwu* 文物, 1974, no. 8, pp. 47, 48, pl. 1; Taixi Archaeology Team, Hebei Provincial Cultural Relics Department, "Hebei Gaocheng Taixicun Shang dai yizhi fajue jianbao" 河北藁城台西村商代遗址发掘简报 [Brief report on the excavation of the Shang dynasty site at Taixicun, Gaocheng, Hebei], *Wenwu*, 1979, no. 6, pp. 37, 43. Anyang Excavation Team, Institute of Archaeology, Chinese Academy of Sciences, "1958–1959 nian Yinxu fajue jianbao" 1958–1959年殷墟发掘简报 [Brief report on the excavations at Yinxu in 1958–1959], *Kaogu* 考古, 1961, no. 2, p. 70.

3. Wang Shixiang 王世襄, "Zhongguo gudai qigong zashu" 中国古代漆工杂述 [Miscellaneous notes on the lacquer craft of ancient China], *Wenwu*, 1979, no. 3, p. 49.

4. Luoyang Museum, "Luoyang Pangjiagou wuzuo Xi Zhou mu di qingli" 洛阳庞家沟五座西周墓的清理 [Clearance of five Western Zhou tombs at Pangjiagou, Luoyang], *Wenwu*, 1972, no. 10, p. 22. Institute of Archaeology, Chinese Academy of Sciences, *Shangcunling Guoguo mudi* 上村岭虢国墓地 [Cemetery of the state of Guo at Shangcunling], (Beijing: Kexue Press, 1959), p. 19, pl. 41. Shi Xingbang 石兴邦, "Changan Puducun Xi Zhou muzang fajue ji" 长安普渡村西周墓葬发掘记 [A note on the excavation of Western Zhou burials at Puducun in Changan], *Kaogu Xuebao* 考古学报, 1954, no. 8, p. 124, pl. 4.

5. Shang Chengzuo 商承祚, *Changsha chutu qiqi tulu* 长沙出土漆器图录 [Illustrated cata-

logue of lacquer wares unearthed in Changsha], (Shanghai: Shanghai Press, 1955). Umehara Sueji 梅原末治, (Zotei) Rakuyō Kinson kobo shūei (増订) 洛阳金村古墓聚英 [Treasures from the ancient tomb at Jincun, Luoyang] (Kyoto: Kobayashi, 1944), pp. 25–27, pls. 30–35. Hunan Provincial Cultural Relics Commission, "Changsha chutu di sanzuo daxing mukuomu 长沙出土的三座大型 木椁墓 [Three large wooden-chambered graves unearthed in Changsha], Kaogu Xuebao, 1957, no. 1, pp. 93–101, pls. 1–2. Hubei Provincial Bureau of Culture, Archaeology Team, "Hubei Jiangling sanzuo Chu mu chutu dapi zhongyao wenwu" 湖北江陵三座楚墓出土大批重要文物 [A large quantity of important cultural relics unearthed from the three Chu tombs in Jiangling, Hubei], Wenwu, 1966, no. 5, pp. 33–39, 54, 55; Jingzhou District Museum, "Hubei Jiangling Tengdian yihao mu fajue jianbao" 湖北江陵藤店一号墓发掘简报 [Brief report on tomb number 1 at Tengdian in Jiangling, Hubei], Wenwu, 1973, no. 9, p. 11. Suixian Leigudun Tomb Number 1 Archaeological Excavation Team, "Hubei Suixian Zenghouyi mu fajue jianbao" 湖北随县曾侯乙墓发掘简报 [Brief report on the excavation of the tomb of Zeng Hou Yi in Suixian, Hubei], Wenwu, 1979, no. 7, pp. 10, 11. Henan Provincial Bureau of Culture, Archaeology Team Number 1, "Xinyang Changtaiguan fajue yizuo Zhanguo damu" 信阳长台关发掘一座战国大墓 [A large grave of the Warring States period excavated at Changtaiguan, Xinyang], Wenwu Cankao Ziliao 文物参考资料, 1957, no. 9, pp. 21, 22; Henan Provincial Bureau of Culture, Archaeology Team, "Xinyang Changtaiguan dierhao Chu mu di fajue" 信阳长台关第二号楚墓的发掘 [The excavation of Chu tomb number 2 at Changtaiguan, Xinyang], Kaogu Tongxun 考古通讯, 1958, no. 11, pp. 79, 80; idem, Henan Xinyang Chu mu chutu wenwu tulu 河南信阳楚墓出土文物图录 [An illustrated catalogue of the cultural relics unearthed from the Chu tombs in Xinyang, Henan] (Henan Renmin Press, 1959). Sichuan Provincial Cultural Relics Commission, "Chengdu Yangzishan di 172-hao mu fajue baogao" 成都羊子山第 172 号墓发掘报告 [Report on the excavation of tomb number 172 at Yangzishan in Chengdu], Kaogu Xuebao, 1956, no. 4, pp. 14–16, pls. 7, 8.

6. Harada Yoshito 原田淑人 et al., Rakurō 楽浪 [Lolang] (Tokyo: Tōkō Shoin, 1930), pp. 36–49, pls. 43–81; Oba Tsuneyoshi 小場恒吉 et al., Rakurō Kanbo 楽浪漢墓 [Han Tombs in Lolang] (Tokyo: Rakurō Kanbo Kankōkai, 1974). Umehara Sueji 梅原末治, "Mōko Noin-Ula hakken no ibutsu" 蒙古ノインウラ発現の遺物 [Remains found in Noin-Ula, Mongolia], Tōyō Bunko Ronsō 27 (1960): 28–34, pls. 59–65.

7. Luoyang District Archaeology Team, Luoyang Shaogou Han mu (Beijing: Kexue Press, 1959), pp. 203–05, pls. 60–61. Shandong Provincial Department of Cultural Relics, "Shandong Wendeng di Han mukuomu ji qiqi" 山东文登的汉木椁墓及漆器 [Han dynasty wooden-chambered tomb and lacquer wares in Wendeng, Shandong], Kaogu Xuebao, 1957, no. 1, pp. 129, 130, pls. 1, 2. Jiangsu Provincial Cultural Relics Commission et al., "Jiangsu Yancheng Sanyangdun Han mu qingli baogao" 江苏盐城三羊墩汉墓清理报告 [Report on the clearance of Han tombs at Sanyangdun in Yancheng, Jiangsu], Kaogu, 1964, no. 8, pp. 397, 398, pl. 5. Nanjing Museum, "Jiangsu Lianyungangshi Haizhou Wangtongzhuang Han mukuomu" 江苏连云港市海州网疃庄 汉木椁墓 [Han wooden-chambered tomb at Wangtongzhuang, Haizhou, Lianyungang city, Jiangsu], Kaogu, 1963, no. 6, pp. 287, 288, color plate 1. Zhao Renjun 赵人俊, "Ningbo diqu fajue di gu muzang he guwenhua yizhi" 宁波地区发掘的古墓葬和古文化遗址 [Ancient graves and ancient cultural sites excavated in the Ningpo district], Wenwu Cankao Ziliao, 1956, no. 4, pp. 81, 82. Institute of Archaeology, Chinese Academy of Sciences, Changsha fajue baogao 长沙发掘报告 [Report on the excavations in Changsha] (Beijing: Kexue Press, 1957), pp. 120–23, pls. 74–82. Guangzhou City Cultural Relics Commission, "Guangzhoushi Longshenggang 43-hao Tong Han mukuomu" 广州市龙生冈 43 号东汉木椁墓 [Wooden-chambered tomb number 43 of Eastern Han at Longshenggang in Guangzhou], Kaogu Xuebao, 1957, no. 1, pp. 150–52, pls. 4–6; idem, "Guangzhou Huanghuagang 003-hao Xi Han mukuomu fajue jianbao" 广州黄花冈 003 号西汉木椁墓 发掘简报 [Brief report on the excavation of wooden-chambered tomb number 003 of Western Han at Huanghuagang in Guangzhou], Kaogu Tongxun, 1958, no. 4, pp. 39, 40, pls. 7, 8. Guizhou Provincial Museum, "Guizhou Qingzhen Pingba Han mu fajue baogao" 贵州清镇平坝汉墓发掘 报告 [Report on the excavation of a Han tomb at Pingba, Qingzhen, Guizhou], Kaogu Xuebao, 1959,

no. 1, pp. 99, 100, pl. 6; Guizhou Provincial Cultural Relics Commission, "Guizhou Qingzhen Pingba Han zhi Song mu fajue jianbao" 贵州清镇平埧汉至宋墓发掘简报 (Brief report on the excavations of Han- to Song-period tombs at Pingba, Qingzhen, Guizhou], Kaogu, 1961, no. 4, p. 209, pl. 1. Gansu Provincial Museum, "Wuwei Mozuizi san zuo Han mu fajue jianbao" 武威磨咀子三座汉墓发掘简报 [Brief report on three Han tombs at Mozuizi, Wuwei], Wenwu, 1972, no. 12, pp. 14, 15, pl. 4.

8. Archaeological Reporting Team, Guangxi Zhuang Autonomous Region, "Guangxi Hepu Xi Han mukuomu" 广西合浦西汉木椁墓 [Wooden-chambered tomb of Western Han in Hepu, Guangxi], Kaogu, 1972, no. 5, pp. 27, 28. Archaeology Team, Guangxi Zhuang Autonomous Region, "Guangxi Luobowan yihao mu fajue jianbao" 广西罗泊湾一号墓发掘简报 [Brief report on tomb number 1 at Luobowan, Guangxi], Wenwu, 1978, no. 9, pp. 31, 32. Nanjing Museum et al., "Haizhou Xi Han Huo He mu" 海州西汉霍贺墓 [Tomb of Huo He of Western Han in Haizhou], Kaogu, 1974, no. 3, pp. 181–83, pls. 4, 5. Shandong Provincial Museum et al., "Linyi Yinqueshan sizuo Xi Han muzang" 临沂银雀山四座西汉墓葬 [Four Western Han tombs at Yinqueshan in Linyi], Kaogu, 1975, no. 6, p. 369, pls. 7, 8. Mancheng Excavation Team, Institute of Archaeology, Chinese Academy of Sciences, "Mancheng Han mu fajue jiyao" 满城汉墓发掘纪要 [Major results of the excavations of the Han tombs in Mancheng], Kaogu, 1972, no. 1, p. 14. Anhui Provincial Archaeology Team, "Fuyang Shuanggudui Xi Han Ruyinhou mu fajue jianbao" 阜阳双古堆西汉汝阴侯墓发掘简报 [Brief report on the excavation of the tomb of Ruyinhou of Western Han at Shuanggudi in Fuyang], Wenwu, 1978, no. 8, pp. 15–17, 20, 21.

9. Hunan Provincial Museum et al., Changsha Mawangdui yihao Han mu 长沙马王堆一号汉墓 (Beijing: Wenwu Press, 1973), pp. 76–96, pls. 154–77. Yangtze Valley Archaeology Training Institute, Second Class, "Hubei Jiangling Fenghuangshan Xi Han mu fajue jianbao" 湖北江陵凤凰山西汉墓发掘简报 [Brief report on the excavation of a Western Han tomb at Fenghuangshan in Jiangling, Hubei], Wenwu, 1974, no. 6, pp. 46–48, 59, 60, pls. 1, 9; Jinancheng Fenghuangshan Han Tomb Number 168 Excavation and Reporting Team, "Hubei Jiangling Fenghuangshan 168-hao Han mu fajue jianbao" 湖北江陵凤凰山一六八号汉墓发掘简报 [Brief report on the excavation of Han tomb number 168 at Fenghuangshan, Jiangling, Hubei], Wenwu, 1975, no. 9, pp. 4, 5, pls. 5–8; Fenghuangshan Han Tomb Number 167 Excavation and Reporting Team, "Jiangling Fenghuangshan 167-hao Han mu fajue jianbao" 江陵凤凰山一六七号汉墓发掘简报 [Brief report on the excavation of Han tomb number 167 at Fenghuangshan in Jiangling], Wenwu, 1976, no. 10, pp. 32, 33. Hubei Provincial Museum et al., "Hubei Yunmeng Xi Han mu fajue jianbao" 湖北云梦西汉墓发掘简报 [Brief report on Western Han tombs in Yunmeng, Hubei], Wenwu, 1973, no. 9, pp. 24, 25, pl. 1.

10. Hunan Provincial Museum, Changsha Mawangdui yihao Han mu, p. 76.

11. Ibid., pp. 76, 77.

12. Institute of Archaeology, Chinese Academy of Sciences, "Mawangdui er san hao Han mu fajue di zhuyao shouhu" 马王堆二、三号汉墓发掘的主要收获 [Major results of the excavation of Han tombs number 2 and 3 at Mawangdui], Kaogu, 1975, no. 1, p. 57.

13. P. 53 of article cited in n. 3 above.

14. Pp. 122, 123, pl. 83 of Chansha fajue baogao (n. 7 above).

15. Harada Yoshito et al., Rakurō, pp. 42, 43, pls. 56–58; Koizumi Akio 小泉顕夫 et al., Saikyōzuka 彩篋冢 [Mound with painted baskets] (Tokyo: Chosen Kosoki Kenkyukai, 1934), pp. 41–43, pls. 41–50.

16. Nan Po 南波, "Jiangsu Lianyungangshi Haizhou Xi Han Shi Qi Yao mu" 江苏连云港市海州西汉侍其繇墓 [Tomb of Shi Qi Yao of the Western Han in Haizhou, Lianyungang city, Jiangsu], Kaogu, 1975, no. 3, pp. 172–74, pl. 6.

17. P. 228, color plate, pl. 1, in Nanjing Museum, "Jiangsu Lianyungangshi Haizhou Wangtongzhuang Han mukuomu" (see n. 7 above).

18. P. 203, pl. 60 of Luoyang Shaogou Han mu (n. 7 above); p. 47, pl. 60 of Koizumi (n. 15 above).

19. Oba Tsuneyoshi 小場恒吉 et al., Rakurō Kanbo 楽浪漢墓 [Han tombs in Lolang], vol. 1 (Tokyo: Rakuro Kanbo Kankokai, 1974), pp. 35–38.

20. Himoto Kamejiro 榧本亀次郎 et al., *Rakurō Ōko bo* 楽浪王光墓 [Tomb of Wang Guang in Lolang] (Tokyo: Chosen Koseki Kenkyukai, 1935), p. 36, pl. 50.

21. Mizuno Seiichi 水野清一 et al., *Mōkyō Yokōken Kanbo josa rakuhō* 蒙疆阳高县汉墓调查略报 [Preliminary report of the investigation of Han tombs in Yanggaoxian in Inner Mongolia] (Tokyo: Yamato Shoin, 1943), p. 23.

22. Pp. 120, 121, pl. 78 of *Changsha fajue baogao* (n. 7 above).

23. Hunan Provincial Museum, *Hunan Han dai qiqi tulu* 湖南汉代漆器图录 [Illustrated catalog of Han dynasty lacquer wares in Hunan] (Hunan Renmin Press, 1965), p. 27.

24. Pp. 77, 78, pl. 167 of *Changsha Mawangdui yihao Han mu* (n. 9 above).

25. Pp. 28–30, pl. 59 of Umehara, ''Mōko Noin-Ula hakken no ibutsu'' (n. 6 above).

26. P. 397 of ''Jiangsu Yancheng Sanyangdun Han mu qingli baogao'' (n. 7 above).

27. Umehara Sueji 梅原末治, *Shina Kandai kinen mei shikki zusetsu* 支那汉代纪年铭漆器图说 [Illustrated catalogue of lacquer wares with dated inscriptions from the Han dynasty in China] (Kyoto: Bunseido, 1943), pp. 40, 41, pl. 35.

28. Himoto Tojin 榧本杜人 et al., ''Kandai kinen mei shikki shusei'' 汉代纪年铭漆器集成 [Collection of Han dynasty lacquer wares with dated inscriptions], in *Rakurō Kanbo*, vol. 1 (Tokyo: Rakurō Kanbo Kankōkai, 1974), p. 96.

29. Mai Yinghao 麦英豪, ''Qin Shi Huang tongyi Lingnan diqu di lishi zuoyung'' 秦始皇统一岺南地区的历史作用 [Historical role of the unification of the Lingnan area under Qin Shi Huang], *Kaogu*, 1975, no. 4, p. 208.

30. Pp. 31, 40 of ''Guangxi Luobowan yihao mu fajue jianbao'' (n. 8 above).

31. Jiang Yingju 蒋英炬, ''Linyi Yinqueshan Xi Han mu qiqi mingwen kaoshi'' 临沂银雀山西汉墓漆器铭文考释 [Interpretation of the inscriptions on lacquer ware in the Western Han tomb at Yinqueshan, Linyi],'' *Kaogu*, 1975, no. 6, pp. 349–51.

32. Yu Weichao 俞伟超, ''Mawangdui yihao Han mu chutu qiqi zhidi zhu wenti'' 马王堆一号汉墓出土漆器制地诸问题 [Problems relating to the place of manufacture of the lacquer wares unearthed in Han tomb number 1 at Mawangdui], *Kaogu*, 1975, no. 6, pp. 344–48.

33. Pp. 20, 21 of ''Fuyang Shuanggudui Xi Han Ruyinhou mu fajue jianbao'' (n. 8 above).

34. Pp. 41–44, pls. 36–38, 47 of article cited in n. 27 above).

35. Pp. 24–26, 35, 36 of ''Hubei Yunmeng Xi Han mu fajue jian bao'' (n. 9 above).

36. Pp. 110–11 of article cited in n. 28 above.

37. Song Zhimin 宋治民, ''Han dai mingke suojian zhiguan xiaoji'' 汉代铭刻所见职官小记 [Notes on offices seen in Han dynasty inscriptions], *Kaogu*, 1979, no. 5.

CHAPTER 5

1. Mancheng Excavation Team, Institute of Archaeology, Chinese Academy of Sciences, ''Mancheng Han mu fajue jiyao'' 满城汉墓发掘纪要 [Major results of the excavation of the Han tombs in Mancheng], *Kaogu*, 1972, no. 1, pp. 10, 11, pls. 4–6; Institute of Archaeology, Chinese Academy of Sciences, et al., *Mancheng Han mu* 满城汉墓 (Beijing: Wenwu Press, 1978), pp. 36–38, 45–50, pls. 8–10, 16.

2. Xiao Yun 肖蕴, ''Mancheng Han mu chutu di cuo jin yin niao chong shu tong hu'' 满城汉墓出土的错金银鸟虫书铜壶 [Bronze *hu*-vessel with gold- and silver-inlaid bird-and-worm inscription unearthed in the Han tomb in Mancheng], *Kaogu* 考古, 1972, no. 5, pp. 49–52, pl. 7; Zhang Zhenlin 张振林 et al., ''Guanyu Mancheng Han mu tong hu niao zhuan wen shiwen di taolun'' 关于满城汉墓铜壶鸟篆文释文的讨论 [Discussion of the transcription of the bird-seal-inscription on the bronze *hu*-vessel from the Han tomb in Mancheng], *Kaogu*, 1979, no. 4, pp. 356–59; Zhang Zhenglang 张政烺, ''Mancheng Han mu chutu cuo jin yin niao chong shu tong hu (jia) shiwen'' 满城汉墓出土错金银鸟虫书铜壶〈甲〉释文 [Transcription of the bronze *hu*-vessel A with gold- and silver-inlaid bird-and-worm inscription unearthed from the Han tomb in Mancheng], *Zhonghua Wenshi Luncong* 中华文史论丛, 1979, no. 3, pp. 1–6.

3. Mancheng Excavation Team, "Mancheng Han mu fajue jiyao" (see n. 1 above), p. 11.

4. Umehara Sueji 梅原末治, (Zōtei) Rakuyō Kinson kobo shūei（增订）洛阳金村古墓聚英 [Treasures from the ancient tomb of Jincun, Luoyang], (Kyoto: Kobayashi, 1944), pp. 21, 22, pl. 18.

5. Xi'an City Cultural Relics Commission, "Xi'an Sanqiaozhen Gaoyao cun chutu di Xi Han dongqi qun" 西安三桥镇高窑村出土的西汉铜器群 [A group of Western Han bronzes unearthed in Gaoyaocun, Sangiaozhen, Xi'an], Kaogu, 1963, no. 2, pp. 62–70, pls. 3, 4.

6. Chen Zhi 陈直, "Guqiwu wenzi congkao" 古器物文字丛考 [Miscellaneous notes on inscriptions on ancient vessels], Kaogu, 1963, no. 2, pp. 80–82; Huang Zhanyue 黄展岳, "Xi'an Sanqiao Gaoyaocun Xi Han tongqi qun mingwen bushi" 西安三桥高窑村西汉铜器群铭文补释 [Supplementary explanations of the inscriptions on the group of Western Han bronzes from Gaoyaocun, Sanqiao, Xi'an], Kaogu, 1963, no. 2, pp. 198–200.

7. Chen Zhi, "Guqiwu wen zi congkao" (n. 6 above).

8. Mancheng Excavation Team, "Mancheng Han mu fajue jiyao," pp. 11–12, pl. 6. Archaeology Reporting Team, Guangxi Zhuang Autonomous Region, "Guangxi Hepu Xi Han mukuomu" 广西合浦西汉木椁墓 [Wooden-chambered tomb of the Western Han period in Hepu, Guangxi], Kaogu, 1972, no. 5, p. 20, pl. 7. Gansu Provincial Museum, "Wuwei Leitai Han mu" 武威雷台汉墓 [Han tomb at Leitai in Wuwei], Kaogu Xuebao 考古学报, 1974, no. 2, pp. 100–01, pl. 13.

9. Institute of Archaeology, Chinese Academy of Sciences, Changsha fajue baogao 长沙发掘报告 [Report on excavations in Changsha] (Beijing: Kexue Press, 1957), p. 112.

10. Pp. 23–25 of "Guangxi Hepu Xi Han mukuomu" (n. 8 above).

11. Wuzhou City Museum, "Guangxi Wuzhoushi jin nian lai chutu di yipi Han dai wenwu" 广西梧州市近年来出土的一批汉代文物 [Han dynasty relics unearthed recently in Wuzhou city, Guangxi], Wenwu 文物, 1977, no. 2, pp. 70–71.

12. Guo Yong 郭勇, "Shanxi sheng Youyuxian chutu di Xi Han tongqi" 山西省右玉县出土的西汉铜器 [Bronze vessels unearthed in Youyu county, Shanxi], Wenwu, 1963, no. 11, pp. 4–12.

13. Xia Nai 夏鼐, "Wuchanjieji wenhua dageming zhong di kaogu xin faxian" 无产阶级文化大革命中的考古新发现 [New archaeological discoveries made during the Great Proletarian Cultural Revolution], Kaogu, 1972, no. 1, p. 33.

14. Pp. 98–100, pl. 11 of "Wuwei Leitai Han mu" (n. 8 above).

15. Ibid., pp. 90–103, pls. 3–12.

16. Hunan Provincial Museum et al., Changsha Mawangdui yihao Han mu 长沙马王堆一号汉墓 (Beijing: Wenwu Press, 1973), p. 128, pl. 178.

17. Mancheng Excavation Team, "Mancheng Han mu fajue jiyao" (n. 1 above), p. 17.

18. Wang Shilun 王士伦, Zhejian sheng chutu tongjing xuan ji 浙江省出土铜镜选集 [Selected bronze mirrors in Zhejiang] (Zhongguo Gudian Yishu Press,1957).

19. Northeast Museum, "Liaoyang Sandaohao liangzuo bihua mu di qingli gongzuo jianbao" 辽阳三道壕两座壁画墓的清理工作简报 [Brief report on the clearance of two tombs with murals at Sandaohao, Liaoyang], Wenwu Cankao Ziliao 文物参考资料, 1955, no. 12, pp. 51, 52.

20. Luo Ping 罗平, "Hebei Chengde zhuangqu Han dai kuangyie yizhi di diaocha" 河北承德专区汉代矿冶遗址的调查 [The investigation of a Han dynasty mining and smelting site in Chengde district, Hebei], Kaogu Tongxun 考古通讯, 1957, no. 1, pp. 22–27.

21. He Zicheng 贺梓城, "Xi'an Han cheng yizhi fujin faxian Han dai tongding shi kuai" 西安汉城遗址附近发现汉代铜锭十块 [Ten copper ingots of the Han dynasty discovered in the Han city ruins in Xi'an], Wenwu Cankao Ziliao, 1956, no. 3, p. 82.

22. Fang Guojin 方国锦, "Liu jin tong hu" 鎏金铜斛 [The gilded bronze hu], Wenwu Cankao Ziliao, 1958, no. 9, pp. 69, 70.

23. Haroda Yoshito 原田淑人 et al., Rakurō 楽浪 [Lolang] (Tokyo: Tōkō Shoin, 1930), p. 39, pls. 44, 45.

24. Mancheng Excavation Team, "Mancheng Han mu fajue jiyao" (see n. 1 above), p. 77.

CHAPTER 6

1. Fan Wenlan 范文澜, *Zhongguo Tongshi* 中国通史 [General history of China], 5th ed. (Beijing: Renmin Press, 1978), vol. 2, p. 59.

2. Guangzhou City Cultural Relics Department et al., "Guangzhou Qin Han zaochuan gong-chang yizhi shi jue" 广州秦汉造船工场遗址试掘 [Test excavation of a shipyard site of the Qin-Han period in Guangzhou], *Wenwu* 文物, 1977, no. 4, pp. 1–16, pls. 2–5.

3. Xia Nai 夏鼐, "Kaoguxue yu Kejishi" 考古学与科技史 [Archaeology and the history of science and technology], *Kaogu* 考古, 1977, no. 2, p. 84; Shanghai Jiaotong University Shipbuilding History Team, "Qin Han shiqi di chuanbo" 秦汉时期的船舶 [Ships of the Qin-Han period], *Wenwu*, 1977, no. 4, p. 21.

4. Zhejiang Province Cultural Relics Commission, "Hangzhou Gudang Han dai Zhu Lechang mu qingli jianbao" 杭州古荡汉代朱乐昌墓清理简报 [Brief report on the clearance of the tomb of Zhu Lechang of the Han dynasty at Gudang, Hangzhou], *Kaogu*, 1959, no. 3, pp. 150–52.

5. Inner Mongolia Autonomous Region Archaeology Team, "Huhehaote Ershijiazi gucheng chutu di Xi Han tiejia" 呼和浩特二十家子古城出土的西汉铁甲 [Iron armor of Western Han unearthed at an ancient town site at Ershijiazi in Huhehaute], *Kaogu*, 1975, no. 4, pp. 249–53, pl. 9. Institute of Archaeology, Chinese Academy of Social Sciences, et al., *Mancheng Han mu* 满城汉墓 (Beijing: Wenwu Press, 1978), pp. 66–68.

6. Institute of Archaeology, Chinese Academy of Social Sciences, *Han Changan cheng yizhi fajue baogao* 汉长安城遗址发掘报告 [Report on the excavations of the Han city of Changan]. In preparation.

7. Henan Provincial Museum et al., "Henan Han dai yetie jishu chu tan" 河南汉代冶铁技术初探 [Preliminary discussion of iron technology of the Han dynasty in Henan], *Kaogu Xuebao* 考古学报, 1978, no. 1, p. 13.

8. Fenghuangshan Han Tomb Number 167 Excavation and Reporting Team, "Jiangling Fenghuangshan 167-hao Han mu fajue jianbao" 江陵凤凰山167号汉墓发掘简报 [Brief report on the excavation of Han tomb number 167 at Fenghuangshan in Jiangling), *Wenwu*, 1976, no. 10, p. 34.

9. Institute of Archaeology, Chinese Academy of Social Sciences, *Mancheng Han mu fajue baogao* 满城汉墓发掘报告 [Report on the excavation of the Han dynasty tombs in Mancheng]. In press.

10. Luoyang District Archaeology Team, *Luoyang Shaogou Han mu* 洛阳烧沟汉墓 [Han tombs in Shaogou, Luoyang] (Beijing: Kexue Press, 1959), pp. 196, 197, pl. 58.

11. Gansu Provincial Museum, "Wuiwei Leitai Han mu" 武威雷台汉墓 [Han tomb at Leitai, Wuwei], *Kaogu Xuebao*, 1974, no. 2, p. 103, pls. 16, 17.

12. Luo Zhenyu 罗振玉, *Qi Lu fengni ji cun* 齐鲁封泥集存 [Catalogue of seal clays from Qi and Lu] (1912), pp. 10, 11, 45.

13. Li Jinghua 李京华, "Han dai tie nongqi mingwen shishi" 汉代铁农器铭文试释 [A tentative interpretation of some inscriptions on iron agricultural implements of the Han dynasty], *Kaogu*, 1974, no. 1, pp. 61–66.

14. Su Tianjun 苏天钧, "Shi nian lai Beijing shi suo faxian di zhongyao yizhi" 十年来北京市所发现的重要遗址 [Important sites found in Beijing in the last decade], *Kaogu*, 1959, no. 3, p. 136. Li Buqing 李步青, "Shandong Tengxian faxian tie fan" 山东滕县发现铁范 [Iron molds discovered in Tengxian, Shandong], *Kaogu*, 1960, no. 7, p. 72. Nanjing Museum, "Liguoyi gudai lian tie lu di diaocha ji qingli" 利国驿古代炼铁炉的调查及清理 [Investigation and clearance of ancient iron-smelting funaces at Liguoyi], *Wenwu*, 1960, no. 4, pp. 46, 47.

15. Pp. 1–4 of article cited in n. 7 above.

16. Henan Bureau of Culture, Archaeology Team, *Gongxian Tieshenggou* 巩县铁生沟 (Beijing: Wenwu Press, 1962), pp. 5–26, pls. 9–13.

17. P. 4 of article cited in n. 7 above.

18. Henan Provincial Bureau of Culture, Archaeology Team, "Nanyang Han dai tie gongchang

fajue jianbao" 南阳汉代铁工厂发掘简报 [Brief report on the Han dynasty iron foundry in Nan-yang], *Wenwu*, 1960, no. 1, pp. 58–60.

19. Pp. 11–13, pl. 1 of article cited in n. 7 above.

20. Li Zhong 李众, "Zhongguo fengjian shehui qianqi gangtie yelian jishu fazhan di tantao" 中国封建社会前期钢铁冶炼技术发展的探讨 [An exploration of the development of steel and iron manufacturing techniques in the early period of Chinese feudal society], *Kaogu Xuebao* 考古学报, 1975, no. 2, pp. 1–20; Beijing Steel and Iron College et al., *Zhongguo yejin jianshi* 中国冶金简史 [A short history of metallurgy in China] (Beijing: Kexue Press, 1978), pp. 40–136.

21. Nanjing Museum, "Jiangsu Liuhe Chengqiao erhao Dong Zhou mu" 江苏六合程桥二号东周墓 [Eastern Zhou tomb number 2 at Chengqiao in Liuhe, Jiangsu], *Kaogu*, 1974, no. 2, p. 120, pl. 6.

22. Hebei Provincial Cultural Relics Department, "Hebei Yixian Yanxiadu 44-hao mu fajue baogao" 河北易县燕下都44号墓发掘报告 [Report on the excavation of tomb number 44 at Yanxiadu in Yixian, Hebei), *Kaogu*, 1974, no. 4, pp. 231, 232; Beijing Steel and Iron College, Pressure Processing Program, "Yixian Yanxiadu 44-hao mu tieqi jinxiang kaocha chubu baogao" 易县燕下都44号墓铁器金相考察初步报告 [Preliminary report on the metallographical examination of the iron implements from tomb number 44 at Yanxiadu in Yixian], *Kaogu*, 1975, no. 4, pp. 241, 242.

23. Li Zhong, (see n. 20 above), pp. 11–13; pp. 54–57 of *Mancheng Han mu* (n. 5 above).

24. Li Zhong, ibid., p. 5, pl. 1.

25. Ibid., pp. 6, 7.

26. P. 57 of *Mancheng Han mu* (n. 5 above).

27. Pp. 20, 21 of article cited in n. 7 above.

28. See n. 9 above.

29. Liu Xinjian 刘心健 et al., "Shandong Cangshan faxian Dong Han Yongchu ji nian tie dao" 山东苍山发现东汉永初纪年铁刀 [An Eastern Han iron knife with a Yongchu date discovered in Cangshan, Shandong], *Wenwu*, 1974, no. 12, p. 61, pl. 5.

30. Li Zhong (see n. 20 above), p. 14, pl. 6.

31. Shandong Provincial Museum, "Han huaxiang yetie tu shuoming" 汉画象冶铁图说明 [Explanation of the Han iron foundry picture], *Wenwu*, 1959, no. 1, p. 2.

32. Fu Xihua 傅惜华, *Han dai huaxiang quan ji chu bian* 汉代画象全集初编 [A complete collection of the pictorial art of the Han dynasty (preliminary volume)]. (Shanghai: Commercial Press, 1950), pl. 73.

CHAPTER 7

1. Luoyang District Archaeology Team, *Luoyang Shaogou Han mu* 洛阳烧沟汉墓 [Han tombs in Shaogou, Luoyang] (Beijing: Kexue Press, 1959), pp. 109–12, pls. 1, 22. Institute of Archaeology, Chinese Academy of Social Sciences, et al., *Mancheng Han mu* 满城汉墓 [Han tombs in Mancheng] (Beijing: Wenwu Press, 1978), p. 40, pl. 5.

2. Hebei Provincial Cultural Relics Commission, "Hebei Wuanxian Wuji gucheng zhong di yao zhi" 河北武安县午汲古城中的窑址 [Kiln remains in the city of Wuji in Wuanxian, Hebei], *Kaogu* 考古, 1959, no. 7, pp. 339–42, pl. 8.

3. Yellow River Reservoir Archaeology Team, "1957 nian Henan Shanxian fajue jianbao" 1957年河南陕县发掘简报 [Brief report on the excavations in Shanxian, Henan, in 1957], *Kaogu Tongxun* 考古通讯, 1958, no. 11, p. 76; Henan Provincial Bureau of Culture, Archaeology Team, "Henan Tongbo Wangang Han mu di fajue" 河南桐柏万冈汉墓的发掘 [Excavation of Han tombs in Wangang, Tongbo, Henan], *Kaogu*, 1964, no. 8, pp. 386–88.

4. *Luoyang Shaogou Han mu* (see n. 1 above), pp. 103–06, color plates 1–3. Mancheng Excavation Team, Institute of Archaeology, Chinese Academy of Sciences, "Mancheng Han mu fajue jiyao" 满城汉墓发掘纪要 [Major results of the excavation of the Han tombs in Mancheng], *Kaogu*, 1972, no. 1, pp. 13–14.

5. Shandong Provincial Museum et al., "Linyi Yinqueshan sizuo Xi Han muzang" 临沂银雀山四座西汉墓葬 [Four Western Han tombs at Yinqueshan in Linyi], *Kaogu*, 1975, no. 6, p. 364, pl. 6. Anhui Provincial Archaeology Team et al., "Fuyang Shuanggudui Xi Han Ruyinhou mu fajue jianbao" 阜阳双古堆西汉汝阴侯墓发掘简报 [Brief report on the tomb of Marquis Ruyin of Western Han at Shuanggudui, Fuyang], *Wenwu* 文物, 1978, no. 8, pp. 17, 23. Hubei Provincial Museum et al., "Yunmeng Xi Han mu fajue jianbao" 云梦西汉墓发掘简报 [Brief report on Western Han tombs in Yunmeng], *Wenwu*, 1973, no. 9, pp. 24, 27.

6. Henan Provincial Bureau of Culture, Archaeology Team, "Henan Tongbo Wangang Han mu di fajue" (see n. 3 above), pp. 386, 387.

7. Institute of Archaeology, Chinese Academy of Sciences, *Changsha fajue baogao* 长沙发掘报告 [Report on the excavations in Changsha] (Beijing: Kexue Press, 1957), pp. 104–06, pls. 57–61; Mai Yinghao 麦英豪, "Guangzhou Huaqiaoxincun di Xi Han mu" 广州华侨新村的西汉墓 [Western Han Tombs at Huaqiaoxincun in Guangzhou], *Kaogu Xuebao* 考古学报, 1958, no. 2, pp. 52–64, pls. 4–9.

8. Su Bingqi 苏秉琦, *Doujitai Goudongqu muzang* 斗鸡台沟东区墓葬 [Burials in Goudongqu, Doujitai] (Beijing: Beijing University Press, 1948), pp. 143–46, 170–89; Luoyang District Archaeology Team, *Luoyang Shaogou Han mu* (n. 1 above), pp. 100–05, pl. 21.

9. Mizuno Seiichi 水野清一, "Ryoku yūto ni tsuite" 緑釉陶について [On green-glazed porcelain], in *Sekai Toji Zenshū* 世界陶磁全集 (Tokyo: Kowaide Shobō, 1955) 8:236–38.

10. Institute of Archaeology, *Changsha fajue baogao* (see n. 7 above), pp. 107–09, pl. 61. Nanjing Museum et al., "Haizhou Xi Han Huo He mu qingli jianbao" 海州西汉霍贺墓清理简报 [Brief report on the clearance of the tombs of Huo He of Western Han in Haizhou], *Kaogu*, 1974, no. 3, p. 185, pl. 5.

11. Pp. 107, 108, pl. 21 of *Luoyang Shaogou Han mu* (n. 1 above).

12. A.D. 227: Wuhan City Cultural Relics Commission, "Wuchang Renjiawan Liuchao chuqi muzang qingli jianbao" 武昌任家湾六朝初期墓葬清理简报 [Brief report on the clearance of tombs of early Six Dynasties period at Renjiawan, Wuchang] *Wenwu cankao ziliao* 文物参考资料, 1955, no. 12, pp. 68–70; Cheng Xinren 程欣人, "Wuhan chutu di liangkuai Dong Wu qianjuan shiwen" 武汉出土的两块东吴铅券释文 [Annotated transcription of two lead documents of the Eastern Wu dynasty unearthed in Wuhan], *Kaogu*, 1965, no. 10, p. 529. A.D. 251: Ni Zhenkui 倪振逵 et al., "Nanjing Zhaoshigang faxian Sanguo shidai Sun Wu you ming ciqi" 南京赵士冈发现三国时代孙吴有铭瓷器 [Inscribed porcelain of Sun Wu of the Three Kingdoms period discovered at Zhaoshigang, Nanjing], *Wenwu Cankao Ziliao*, 1955, no. 8, pp. 156–57. A.D. 265: Nanjing Museum, *Jiangsu sheng chutu wenwu xuanji* 江苏省出土文物选集 [Selected cultural relics unearthed in Jiangsu province] (Beijing: Wenwu Press, 1963), figs. 127, 128.

13. Ye Hongming 叶宏明 et al., "Guanyu wuoguo ciqi qiyuan di kanfa" 关于我国瓷器起源的看法 [A view of the origin of porcelain in China], *Wenwu*, 1978, no. 10, pp. 86, 87.

14. Institute of Archaeology, Chinese Academy of Sciences, *Luoyang Zhongzhoulu* 洛阳中州路 (Beijing: Kexue Press, 1959), p. 134, pl. 85. Boxian Museum, "Boxian Fenghuangtai yihao Han mu qingli jianbao" 亳县凤凰台一号汉墓清理简报 [Brief report on the clearance of Han tomb number 1 at Fenghuangtai in Boxian], *Kaogu*, 1974, no. 3, pp. 187, 188, pl. 6.

15. Anhui Province, Boxian Museum, "Boxian Cao Cao zongzu muzang" 亳县曹操宗族墓葬 [Tombs of lineage members of Cao Cao in Boxian], *Wenwu*, 1978, no. 8, pp. 33, 34, 39.

16. Shaanxi Province Cultural Relics Commission et al., "Xianyang Yangjiawan Han mu fajue jianbao" 咸阳杨家湾汉墓发掘简报 [Brief report on the Han dynasty tomb at Yangjiawan in Xianyang], *Wenwu*, 1977, no. 10, pp. 10–16, pls. 1, 3.

17. Institute of Archaeology, Chinese Academy of Sciences, *Huixian fajue baogao* 辉县发掘报告 [Report on Excavations in Huixian] (Beijing: Kexue Press, 1956), p. 141, pl. 101.

18. Yu Weichao 俞伟超, "Han dai di ting shi tao wen" 汉代的'亭''市'陶文 [Han dynasty pottery inscriptions with the characters "ting" and "shi"], *Wenwu*, 1963, no. 2, pp. 34–38.

19. P. 37 of *Luoyang Zhongzhoulu* (n. 14 above).

20. See n. 18 above.

21. Luo Zhenyu 罗振玉, *Qi Lu fengni jicun* 齐鲁封泥集存 [Collection of seal clays from Qi and Lu] (1912), p. 48.

22. Chen Zhi 陈直, *Liang Han jingji shi liao luncong* 两汉经济史料论丛 [Discussion of data on the economic history of the two Han dynasties] (Xi'an: Shaanxi Renmin Press, 1958), pp. 169, 170.

23. Henan Provincial Bureau of Culture, Archaeology Team, "Henan Yuxian Baisha Han mu fajue baogao" 河南禹县白沙汉墓发掘报告 [Report on the excavations of Han tombs at Baisha in Yuxian, Henan], *Kaogu Xuebao*, 1959, no. 1, pp. 62–70, pl. 1. Pp. 8–22, pls. 1–3, 6 of *Luoyang Shaogou Han mu* (n. 1 above).

24. Henan Provincial Bureau of Culture, Archaeology Teams Number 1 and 2, *Henan chutu kongxinzhuan tuopian ji* 河南出土空心砖拓片集 [Catalogue of rubbings of hollow bricks unearthed in Henan] (Beijing: Renmin Art Press, 1963).

25. Guo Baojun 郭宝钧, "Luoyang xijiao Han dai juzhu yizhi" 洛阳西郊汉代居住遗址 [Han dynasty dwelling site in the Western suburb of Luoyang], *Kaogu Tongxun*, 1956, no. 1, pp. 19–23, pls. 1–4.

26. Institute of Archaeology, Chinese Academy of Social Sciences, *Han Changan cheng yizhi fajue baogao* 汉长安城遗址发掘报告 [Report of the excavations of the city site of Changan of the Han dynasty]. In preparation.

27. Pp. 91, 92, pl. 13 of *Luoyang Shaogou Han mu* (n. 1 above).

28. Liu Zhiyuan 刘志远, *Sichuan Han dai huaxiangzhuan yishu* 四川汉代画象砖艺术 [The pictorial brick art of the Han dynasty in Sichuan] (Chinese Classic Art Press, 1958).

29. Institute of Archaeology, Chinese Academy of Sciences, *Fengxi fajue baogao* 沣西发掘报告 [Report on archaeological excavations on the west bank of the Feng river] (Beijing: Wenwu Press, 1962), pp. 26, 27, pl. 11.

30. Pp. 46–49, pls. 30–34 of *Luoyang Zhongzhoulu* (n. 14 above).

31. Inner Mongolia Autonomous Region Archaeology Team, *Neimenggu chutu wenwu xuan ji* 内蒙古出土文物选集 [Selected cultural relics unearthed in Inner Mongolia] (Beijing: Wenwu Press, 1963), p. 7, figs. 71, 72.

32. An Zhimin 安志敏, "Qinghai di gudai wenhua" 青海的古代文化 [Ancient cultures in Qinghai], *Kaogu*, 1959, no. 7, p. 381; An Zhimin 安志敏, "Yuanxing yuan nian wadang buzheng" 元兴元年瓦当补正 [Supplement and correction concerning the "Yuanxing First Year" eaves tile), *Kaogu*, 1959, no. 11, pp. 626–28.

33. Institute of Archaeology, Han City Excavation Team, "Han Changan cheng nanjiao lizhi jianzhu yizhiqun fajue jianbao" 汉长安城南郊礼制建筑遗址群发掘简报 [Brief report on the group of ritual structure sites in the southern suburb of Changan city of the Han dynasty], *Kaogu*, 1960, no. 7, p. 38; Luo Zhongru 雒忠如, "Xi'an nanjiao faxian Handai jianzhu yizhi" 西安南郊发现汉代建筑遗址 [Han dynasty architectural sites discovered in the southern suburb of Xi'an], *Kaogu Tongxun*, 1957, no. 6, pp. 26–30, pl. 8.

34. Chen Zhi 陈直, "Qin Han wadang gaishu" 秦汉瓦当概述 [A general description of the eaves tiles of Qin and Han], *Wenwu*, 1963, no. 11, pp. 20–24.

35. Pp. 170–71 of reference cited in n. 22 above.

CHAPTER 8

1. Shei Wei 史为, "Changsha Mawangdui yihao Han mu di guan kuo zhidu" 长沙马王堆一号汉墓的棺椁制度 [The coffin and wooden chamber in the Han tomb number 1 at Mawangdui in Changsha], *Kaogu* 考古, 1972, no. 6, pp. 49–52. Jinancheng Fenghuangshan Han Tomb Number 168 Excavation and Reporting Team, "Hubei Jiangling Fenghuangshan yiliubahao Han mu fajue jianbao" 湖北江陵凤凰山一六八号汉墓发掘简报 [Brief report on the excavation of Han tomb number 168 at Fenghuangshan in Jiangling, Hubei], *Wenwu* 文物, 1975, no. 9, p. 2, pl. 1. Beijing

Municipality Ancient Tombs Excavation Office, "Dabaotai Xi Han mukuomu fajue jianbao" 大葆台西汉木椁墓发掘简报 [Brief report on the excavation of the wooden chamber grave of Western Han at Dabaotai], *Wenwu*, 1977, no. 6, pp. 23–29, pl. 4. Institute of Archaeology, Chinese Academy of Sciences, et al., "Mawangdui er san hao Han mu fajue di zhuyao shouhu" 马王堆二、三号汉墓发掘的主要收获 [Major results of the excavation of Han tombs number 2 and 3 at Mawangdui], *Kaogu*, 1975, no. 1, p. 48.

2. Shandong Provincial Museum, "Qufu Jiulongshan Han mu fajue jianbao" 曲阜九龙山汉墓发掘简报 [Brief report on the excavation of the Han tomb at Jiulongshan in Qufu], *Wenwu*, 1972, no. 5, pp. 39–41.

3. Institute of Archaeology, Chinese Academy of Social Sciences, et al., *Mancheng Han mu* 满城汉墓 (Beijing: Wenwu Press, 1978), pp. 14–17, pl. 3.

4. Luoyang District Archaeology Team, *Luoyang Shaogou Han mu* 洛阳烧沟汉墓 [Han tombs in Shaogou, Luoyang] (Beijing: Kexue Press, 1959), p. 30, pl. 6.

5. Luoyang Museum, "Luoyang Xi Han Pu Qianqiu bihua mu fajue jianbao" 洛阳西汉卜千秋壁画墓发掘简报 [Brief report on the excavation of the frescoed tomb of Pu Qianqiu of Western Han in Luoyang], *Wenwu*, 1977, no. 6, pp. 8–12, pls. 1–3.

6. Guo Moruo 郭沫若, "Luoyang Han mu bihua shitan" 洛阳汉墓壁画试探 [An exploratory study of the murals in the Han tomb in Luoyang], *Kaogu Xuebao* 考古学报, 1964, no. 2, pp. 1–5.

7. Xia Nai 夏鼐, "Wuchanjieji wenhua da geming zhong di kaogu xin faxian" 无产阶级文化大革命中的考古新发现 [New archaeological discoveries during the Great Proletarian Cultural Revolution], *Kaogu*, 1972, no. 1, p. 33. Hebei Provincial Bureau of Culture, Archeology Team, "Hebei Dingxian Beizhuang Han mu fajue baogao" 河北定县北庄汉墓发掘报告 (Report on the excavation of the Han tomb at Beizhuang in Dingxian, Hebei], *Kaogu Xuebao*, 1964, no. 2, pp. 127–33.

8. Beijing History Museum et al., *Wangdu Han mu bihua* 望都汉墓壁画 [Han tomb wall pictures in Wangdu] (Beijing: Chinese Classic Art Press, 1955), pp. 3–14, pls. 8, 9.

9. An Jinhuai 安金槐, et al., "Mixian Dahuting Han dai huaxiangshi mu he bihua mu" 密县打虎亭汉代画象石墓和壁画墓 [Han dynasty tombs with pictorial stones and murals at Dahuting, Mixian], *Wenwu*, 1972, no. 10, p. 52, pl. 1.

10. Inner Mongolia Autonomous Region Museum Archaeology Team, *Holingor Han mu bihua* 和林格尔汉墓壁画 [Murals in the Han dynasty tomb at Holingor] (Beijing: Wenwu Press, 1978).

11. Zhou Dao 周到, et al., "Tanghe Zhenzhichang Han huaxiangshi mu di fajue" 唐河针织厂汉画象石墓的发掘 [Excavation of the Han tomb with pictorial stones at the needlework factory at Tanghe], *Wenwu*, 1973, no. 6, pp. 26, 27, 33–36. Yin Ruzhang 殷汝章, "Shandong Anqiu Moushan Shuiku faxian daxing shike Han mu" 山东安邱牟山水库发现大型石刻汉墓 [Large Han tomb with engraved stones discovered at the Moushan reservoir in Anqiu in Shandong], *Wenwu*, 1960, no. 5, pp. 55–59. Shandong Provincial Museum, "Shandong Cangshan Yuanjia yuan nian huaxiangshi mu" 山东苍山元嘉元年画象石墓 [Tomb with pictorial stone dated to the first year of Yuanjia in Cangshan, Shandong], *Kaogu*, 1975, no. 2, pp. 124, 125. Zeng Zhaoyue 曾昭燏 et al., *Yinan gu huaxiangshi mu fajue baogao* 沂南古画象石墓发掘报告 [Report on the excavation of the ancient tomb with pictorial stones in Yinan] (Beijing: Bureau of Cultural Relics, Ministry of Culture, 1956), pp. 3–11, pls. 5–7, 9–16.

12. Ibid., pp. 12, 21, pls. 24, 49.

13. Liu Zhiyuan 刘志远, *Sichuan Han dai huaxiangzhuan yishu* 四川汉代画象砖艺术 [Pictorial brick art of the Han dynasty in Sichuan] (Beijing: Chinese Classical Art Press, 1958).

14. Liu Zhiyuan 刘志远, "Chengdu Tianhuishan yaimu qingli ji" 成都天迴山崖墓清理记 [Clearance of cliff burials at Tianhuishan in Chengdu], *Kaogu Xuebao*, 1958, no. 1, pp. 88–93, pls. 1–2.

15. Hubei Bureau of Culture, Archaeology Team, "Hubei Jiangling sanzuo Chu mu chutu dapi zhongyao wenwu" 湖北江陵三座楚墓出土大批重要文物 [Large amount of important relics unearthed from three Chu tombs in Jiangling, Hubei], *Wenwu*, 1966, no. 5, p. 33.

16. Fu Xinian 傅熹年, "Zhanguo Zhongshan wang Xi mu chutu di zhaoyu tu jiqi lingyuan guizhi di yanjiu" 战国中山王𰿕墓出土的兆域图及其陵园规制的研究 [The mausoleum plan unearthed in the tomb of Xi, the king of Zhongshan of the Warring States period, and the study of the tomb plan], *Kaogu Xuebao*, 1980, no. 1, pp. 113–15, pl. 1; Yang Hongxun 杨鸿勋, "Zhanguo Zhongshan wang ling ji zhaoyutu yanjiu" 战国中山王陵及兆域图研究 [Study of the mausoleum of the king of Zhongshan in the Warring States period and the mausoleum plan], *Kaogu Xuebao*, 1980, no. 1, pp. 127–32.

17. Chen Mingda 陈明达, "Han dai di shi que" 汉代的石阙 [Stone monumental towers of the Han dynasty], *Wenwu*, 1961, no. 12, pp. 9–23.

18. Kong Ciqing 孔次青, "Shandong Qufu Konglin faxian Han dai shi shou" 山东曲阜孔林发现汉代石兽 [Han dynasty stone animals discovered in the Konglin in Qufu, Shandong], *Kaogu*, 1964, no. 4, p. 209; Tao Mingkuan 陶鸣宽 et al., "Lushanxian di Dong Han shike" 芦山县的东汉石刻 [Eastern Han stone sculptures in Lushanxian], *Wenwu Cankao Ziliao* 文物参考资料, 1957, no. 10, pp. 41, 42.

19. Tianjin Municipality Cultural Relics Department et al., "Wuqingxian faxian Dong Han Shanyu Huang mu bei" 武清县发现东汉鲜于璜墓碑 [Tomb stele of Shanyu Huang of Eastern Han discovered in Wuqingxian], *Wenwu*, 1974, no. 8, pp. 68–70.

20. Henan Provincial Bureau of Culture, Archaeology Team Number 2, "Luoyang Jin mu di fajue" 洛阳晋墓的发掘 [Excavation of Jin tombs in Luoyang], *Kaogu Xuebao*, 1957, no. 1, pp. 181–84.

21. Hunan Provincial Museum et al., *Changsha Mawangdui yihao Han mu* 长沙马王堆一号汉墓 [Han tomb number 1 at Mawangdui, Changsha], (Beijing: Wenwu Press, 1973), pp. 13–27, pl. 26.

22. Ibid., pp. 39–43, Pl. LXXI. Same as 4, p. 57, Pl. VI. Linyi Jinqueshan Han Tomb Excavation Team, "Shandong Linyi Jinqueshan jiuhao mu fajue jianbao" 山东临沂金雀山九号墓发掘简报 [Brief report on the excavation of tomb number 9 at Jinqueshan in Linyi, Shandong], *Wenwu*, 1977, no. 11, pp. 25, 26, pl. 1.

23. Gansu Provincial Museum et al., *Wuwei Han jian* 武威汉简 [Han tablets in Wuwei] (Beijing: Wenwu Press, 1964), pp. 148–49, pl. 23.

24. Shi Wei 史为, "Guanyu jinlü yuyi di ziliao jianjie" 关于金缕玉衣的资料简介 [A short introduction to the materials on the gold-threaded jade shroud], *Kaogu*, 1972, no. 2, pp. 48–50.

25. Technical Laboratory, Institute of Archaeology, Chinese Academy of Sciences, "Mancheng Han mu jinlü yuyi di qingli he fuyuan" 满城汉墓金缕玉衣的清理和复原 [Study and restoration of the gold-threaded jade shroud in the Han tomb in Mancheng], *Kaogu*, 1972, no. 2, pp. 39–47. Hebei Provincial Museum et al., "Dingxian 40-hao Han mu chutu di jinlü yuyi" 定县40号汉墓出土的金缕玉衣 [Gold-threaded jade shroud unearthed from Han tomb number 40 in Dingxian], *Wenwu*, 1976, no. 7, pp. 57–59, pl. 4. Fujita Kunio 藤田国雄 et al., *Chūka Jinmin Kyōwakoku shutsudo bumbutsuten zushū* 中华人民共和国出土文物展图录 [A catalogue of the exhibition of archaeological finds in the People's Republic of China], (Tokyo: Asahi Shinbunshya, 1973), pl. 95. Boxian Museum, Anhui Province, "Boxian Cao Cao zongzu muzang" 亳县曹操宗族墓葬 [Tombs of lineage members of Cao Cao in Boxian], *Wenwu*, 1978, no. 8, p. 36, fig. 19.

26. Pp. 149–51 of "Hebei Dingxian Beizhuang Han mu fajue baogao" (see n. 7 above).

27. Shaanxi Province Cultural Relics Commission et al., "Xianyang Yangjiawan Han mu fajue jianbao" 咸阳杨家湾汉墓发掘简报 [Brief report on the excavation of Han tomb at Yangjiawan, Xianyang], *Wenwu*, 1977, no. 10, p. 16.

28. Institute of Archaeology, Chinese Academy of Sciences, *Changsha fajue baogao* 长沙发掘报告 [Report on archaeological excavations in Changsha] (Beijing: Kexue Press, 1957), p. 55.

29. Hubei Provincial Museum et al., "Hubei Yunmeng Xi Han mu fajue jianbao" 湖北云梦西汉墓发掘简报 [Brief report on the excavation of Western Han tombs in Yunmeng, Hubei], *Wenwu*, 1973, no. 9, p. 24, fig. 44, 45. Nanjing Museum et al., "Haizhou Xi Han Huo He mu qingli jianbao" 海州西汉霍贺墓清理简报 [Brief report on the clearance of the tomb of Huo He of

Western Han in Haizhou], *Kaogu*, 1974, no. 3, pp. 183, 184, fig. 5. Nan Po 南波, "Jiangsu sheng Lianyungangshi Haizhou Xi Han Shi Qi Yao mu" 江苏省连云港市海州西汉侍其縣墓 [Tomb of Shi Qi Yao of Western Han at Haizhou in Lianyungang city in Jiangsu province], *Kaogu*, 1975, no. 3, p. 175, fig. 6.

CHAPTER 9

1. Hunan Provincial College of Agronomy et al., *Changsha Mawangdui yihao Han mu chutu dong zhi wu biaoben di yanjiu* 长沙马王堆一号汉墓出土动植物标本的研究 [Studies of animal and plant remains from Han tomb number 1 at Mawangdui, Changsha] (Beijing: Wenwu Press, 1978).

2. Hunan Provincial Museum et al., *Changsha Mawangdui yi hao Han mu* 长沙马王堆一号汉墓 [Han tomb number 1 at Mawangdui, Changsha] (Beijing: Wenwu Press), pp. 130–42, 154, 155, pls. 11, 219–22.

3. Institute of Archaeology, Chinese Academy of Sciences, et al., *Mancheng Han mu* 满城汉墓 (Beijing: Wenwu Press, 1978), pp. 40, 41, pl. 5.

4. Pp. 46–75, pls. 78–152 of work cited in n. 1 above.

5. Fenghuangshan Han Tomb Number 167 Excavation and Reporting Team, "Jiangling Fenghuangshan 167-hao Han mu fajue jianbao" 江陵凤凰山一六七号汉墓发掘简报 [Brief report on the excavation of Han tomb number 167 at Fenghuangshan, Jiangling], *Wenwu* 文物, 1976, no. 10, p. 35.

6. Shandong Provincial Museum, "Qufu Jiulongshan Han mu fajue jianbao" 曲阜九龙山汉墓发掘简报 [Brief report on the excavation of Han tombs at Jiulongshan, Qufu], *Wenwu*, 1972, no. 5, pp. 41, 42.

7. Beijing Municipality Ancient Graves Excavation Office, "Dabaotai Xi Han mukuomu fajue jianbao" 大葆台西汉木槨墓发掘简报 [Brief report on wooden-chambered tomb of Western Han at Dabaotai], *Wenwu*, 1977, no. 6, p. 23, pl. 4.

8. Zhan Li 展力 et al., "Shi tan Yangjiawan Han mu qibing yong" 试谈杨家湾汉墓骑兵俑 [A tentative discussion of the figurines of mounted soldiers from the Han tomb of Yangjiawan], *Wenwu*, 1977, no. 10, pp. 22–46.

9. Gansu Provincial Museum, "Wuwei Leitai Han mu" 武威雷台汉墓 [Han tomb at Leitai in Wuwei], *Kaogu Xuebao* 考古学报, 1974, no. 2, pp. 90–97, pls. 3–9.

10. Ibid., pp. 104, 105.

11. P. 126, pls. 226, 227 of work cited in n. 2 above.

12. Institute of Archaeology, Chinese Academy of Sciences, et al., "Mawangdui er san hao Han mu fajue di zhuyao shouhu" 马王堆二、三号汉墓发掘的主要收获 [Major results of the excavation of Han tombs number 2 and 3 at Mawangdui], *Kaogu* 考古, 1975, no. 1, pp. 48–55; Mawangdui Han Silk Books Study Group, *Mawangdui han mu boshu* 马王堆汉墓帛书 [Silk books from Han tombs at Mawangdui], vols. 1–3 (Beijing: Wenwu Press, 1974). Anhui Province Archaeology Team et al., "Fuyang Shuanggudui Xi Han Ruyinhou mu fajue jianbao" 阜阳双古堆西汉汝阴侯墓发掘简报 [Brief report on the excavation of the tomb of the marquis of Ruyin of Western Han at Shuanggudui in Fuyang], *Wenwu*, 1978 (8), p. 15, Pl. II.

13. Shandong Provincial Museum et al., "Shandong Linyi Xi Han mu faxian *Sunzi bing fa* he *Sun Bin bing fa* deng zhujian di jianbao" 山东临沂西汉墓发现孙子兵法和孙膑兵法等竹简的简报 [Brief report on the discovery of *Sunzi bing fa*, *Sun Bin bing fa*, and other bamboo slips from a Western Han tomb in Linyi, Shandong], *Wenwu*, 1974, no. 2, pp. 16–18, pls. 1–8; Yinqueshan Han Tomb Bamboo Slips Study Group, *Yinqueshan Han mu zhujian* 银雀山汉墓竹简 [Bamboo slips from the Han tomb at Yinqueshan], vol. 1 (Beijing: Wenwu Press, 1975).

14. Gansu Provincial Museum et al., *Wuwei Han jian* 武威汉简 [Han Slips from Wuwei] (Beijing: Wenwu Press, 1964). Gansu Provincial Museum et al., "Wuwei Hantanbo Han mu fajue

jianbao'' 武威旱滩坡汉墓发掘简报 [Brief report on the excavation of Han tomb at Hantanbo in Wuwei], *Wenwu*, 1973, no. 12, pp. 18–21, pls. 1–4; idem, *Wuwei Han dai yi jian* 武威汉代医简 [Medical Tablets of the Han dynasty in Wuwei] (Beijing: Wenwu Press, 1975).

15. Zhou Shirong 周世荣, ''Changsha chutu Xi Han yinzhang ji qi youguan wenti yanjiu'' 长沙出土西汉印章及其有关问题研究 [Western Han seals from Changsha and related problems], *Kaogu*, 1978, no. 4, pp. 271–79.

16. Hunan Provincial Museum et al., ''Changsha Mawangdui er san hao mu fajue jianbao'' 长沙马王堆二、三号墓发掘简报 [Brief report on tombs number 2 and 3 at Mawangdui, Changsha], *Wenwu*, 1974, no. 7, p. 40, pl. 15.

17. Mancheng Excavation Team, Institue of Archaeology, Chinese Academy of Sciences, ''Mancheng Han mu fajue jiyao'' 满城汉墓发掘纪要 [Major results of the excavation of Han tomb in Mancheng], *Kaogu*, 1972, no. 1, p. 17.

18. Lu Po 鲁波, ''Han dai Xu Sheng mai di qian juan jian jie'' 汉代徐胜买地铅券简介 [A short introduction to the lead document concerning a sale of land by Xu Sheng of the Han dynasty], *Wenwu*, 1972, no. 5, pp. 60–62.

19. Institute of Archaeology, Chinese Academy of Sciences, *Luoyang Zhongzhoulu* 洛阳中州路 (Beijing: Kexue Press, 1959), p. 134, pl. 88.

20. Shaanxi Provincial Cultural Relics Commission, ''Tongguan Diaoqiao Han dai Yang shi mu qun fajue jianji'' 潼关吊桥汉代杨氏墓群发掘简记 [A brief note on the excavation of the Yang lineage graves of Han dynasty at Diaoqiao, Tongguan], *Wenwu*, 1961, no. 1, p. 59.

21. Wang Zhongshu 王仲殊, ''Han Tongting Hongnong Yangshi zhongying kaolüe'' 汉潼亭弘农杨氏冢茔考略 [A short examination of the Yang lineage graves at Hongnong in Han era Tongting], *Kaogu*, 1963, no. 1, pp. 33–38.

22. Du Baoren 杜葆仁, ''Xi Han zhu ling weizhi kao'' [A study of the locations of the imperial mausoleums of Western Han], 西汉诸陵位置考 *Kaogu yu Wenwu* 考古与文物, 1980, no. 1, pp. 29–33; Adachi Kiroku 足立喜六, *Chōan shiseki kō* 长安史迹考 [A study of historical monuments in Changan] (Chinese translation: Shanghai: Commercial Press, 1935), pp. 63–86.

23. Li Jianren 李健人, *Luoyang gu jin tan* 洛阳古今谈 [Talks on Luoyang's past and present] (Heluo Press, 1936), pp. 309–10.

24. Shaanxi Provincial Cultural Relics Commission, ''Shaanxi Xingpingxian Mao Ling kancha'' 陕西兴平县茂陵勘查 [Investigation of Mao Ling in Xingpingxian, Shaanxi], *Kaogu*, 1964, no. 2, pp. 86–89.

25. Mao Ling Relics Preservation Office et al., ''Mao Ling he Huo Qubing mu'' 茂陵和霍去病墓 [Mao Ling and the tomb of Huo Qubing], *Wenwu*, 1976, no. 7, pp. 87–89, pl. 3.

26. Shaanxi Provincial Cultural Relics Commission et al., ''Xianyang Yangjiawan Han mu fajue jianbao'' 咸阳杨家湾汉墓发掘简报 [Brief report of the excavation of a Han tomb at Yangjiawan in Xianyang], *Wenwu*, 1977, no. 10, p. 10.

27. Qin Zhongxing 秦中行, ''Han Yang Ling fujin qiantu mu di faxian'' 汉阳陵附近钳徒墓的发现 [Discovery of tombs of shackled convict-laborers near Yang Ling of Han], *Wenwu*, 1972, no. 7, pp. 51–53.

28. Luoyang Archaeology Team, Institute of Archaeology, Chinese Academy of Sciences, ''Dong Han Luoyang cheng nanjiao di xingtu mudi'' 东汉洛阳城南郊的邢徒墓地 [Cemetery of prisoner-laborers in the southern suburb of Luoyang city of Eastern Han], *Kaogu*, 1972, no. 4, pp. 2–17, pls. 4, 5.

29. Henan Provincial Bureau of Culture, Archaelogy Team, ''1955 nian Luoyang Jianxiqu xiaoxing Han mu fajue baogao'' 1955年洛阳涧西区小型汉墓发掘报告 [Report of the excavations of small tombs of Han Dynasty in the area west of the Jian river in Luoyang in 1955], *Kaogu Xuebao* 考古学报, 1959, no. 2, pp. 75–89, pls. 1, 2.

Index